THE *IPSO FACTO* EFFECTED DISMISSAL OF RELIGIOUS

THE CATHOLIC UNIVERSITY OF AMERICA
CANON LAW STUDIES
No. 259

THE *IPSO FACTO* EFFECTED DISMISSAL OF RELIGIOUS

A HISTORICAL CONSPECTUS AND A COMMENTARY

BY

BENEDICT ANTHONY PFALLER, O.S.B., J.C.L.
MONK OF ASSUMPTION ABBEY, RICHARDTON, NORTH DAKOTA

A DISSERTATION

SUBMITTED TO THE FACULTY OF THE SCHOOL OF CANON LAW OF THE CATHOLIC UNIVERSITY OF AMERICA IN PARTIAL FULFILLMENT OF THE REQUIREMENTS FOR THE DEGREE OF DOCTOR OF CANON LAW

THE CATHOLIC UNIVERSITY OF AMERICA PRESS
WASHINGTON, D. C.
1948

Nihil Obstat:
HIERONYMUS D. HANNAN, A.M., LL.B., S.T.D., J.C.D.,
Censor Deputatus

Imprimi Potest:
✠ CUTHBERTUS GOEB, O.S.B., A.M.,
Abbas Monasterii B. M. V. Assumptae

Imprimatur:
✠ VINCENTIUS J. RYAN, D.D.,
Episcopus Bismarckiensis
Bismarck, N. Dak., June 16, 1947.

PRINTED IN THE UNITED STATES OF AMERICA
MURRAY & HEISTER—WASHINGTON, D. C.

BEATAE MARIAE VIRGINI
IN COELUM ASSUMPTAE

TABLE OF CONTENTS

FOREWORD

Until the human will is confirmed in eternity, the possibility of change remains. Even when a choice good and permanent in its nature is made, the fickleness of frail humanity can be diverted from a pristine high purpose. It is lamentable but true that even in the religious life the ideals of former years are at times abandoned, with consequent injury not only to the individual who thus abandons his high purpose, but also to the Church and the religious institute which share the disgrace and shame of the wayward member. With her timeless wisdom the Church provides a defense for the innocent institute whereby a delinquent religious is juridically separated from the institute or from communal life. However, there are cases which by reason of their very enormity cannot brook the delay that always accompanies the regular course of dismissal, without very grave scandal to the faithful and very grave harm to the religious institute and even to religion itself. In these the Church anticipates the power ordinarily delegated to religious superiors, and in canon 646 directly decrees the dismissal of such a member by the very operation of law.

The amount of space devoted in this work to the "Historical Conspectus" should not mislead the reader to believe that this institute has a long history. As a matter of fact, this specific form of dismissal appeared as new legislation only in 1911. Consequently its direct antecedents date only from that year. However, in order both to gain a proper understanding of this new institute and to give the reader a similar insight, it was deemed advisable to delve into the history of dismissal as a whole, and to present in this work the results of that investigation.

In tracing the course of dismissal during the centuries, both in its contributing and contrasting factors, the writer made an effort to indicate the circumstances that gradually brought about changes in the law, and finally produced the evolution of the institute as found in the present legislation. The history of the consequences for religious of the three crimes specified in the canon as *ipso facto* effecting a dismissal will necessarily also be touched upon in the present work, but only insofar as they have immediate bearing on the development of this specific form of dismissal.

The purpose of the canonical commentary is to present as clearly as possible the meaning of canon 646 and of the other canons in their relation to it; to evaluate and arrive, when possible, at a conclusion on disputed points; and, finally, to furnish some ideas or conclusions hitherto not considered, and to elaborate and clarify the conclusions which have already been drawn by authors on the subject. In particular, this form of dismissal will not be treated as a canonical penalty, but as the peculiar sanction for specified violations of the profession-contract. This is deemed the logical explanation to be drawn from the notion of contract implicitly contained in the act of profession. In the consideration of the three crimes an attempt will be made to find the solution most conformable to law and reason for the many controversies that abound. Finally, since canon 646 concisely indicates that the juridic effects of this dismissal are, for the most part, the same as those which are enacted in canons 648, 669, and 670, and since these canons have already been the subject matter of two dissertations written in recent years, the last chapter will be devoted to a brief résumé only of the principal points and conclusions in the matter of those effects and of the return of the religious thus dismissed.

The writer takes this occasion to express his sincere gratitude to his Abbot, Rt. Rev. Cuthbert Goeb, O.S.B., for the opportunity of advanced study in canon law. He also expresses his indebtedness to all the members of the Faculty of the School of Canon Law of the Catholic University of America.

UT IN OMNIBUS GLORIFICETUR DEUS

CHAPTER I

PRELIMINARY NOTIONS

ARTICLE 1. THE TERM "RELIGIOUS"

The preliminary canons of Book Two, Part Two, of the Code state and establish the nomenclature of the law on religious.[1] There the Church defines the religious state as "the firmly established manner of living in community, by which the faithful undertake to observe, not only the ordinary precepts, but also the evangelical counsels, by means of the vows of obedience, chastity, and poverty."[2] A Religious Institute (termed *religio* in the Code) is described as "a society, approved by legitimate ecclesiastical authority, whose members tend to evangelical perfection according to the laws proper to their Society, by the profession of public vows, either perpetual or temporary, the latter renewable after the lapse of a fixed time."[3]

The present juridical discipline recognizes and concerns itself only with the organized pursuit of Christian perfection, and legislates only for authoritatively approved societies and the members of such societies. Hence, it does not take cognizance of groups of ascetics who do not acknowledge the authority of the Church,[4]

[1] Larraona, "Commentarium Codicis in partem secundam libri II codicis, quae est: De Religiosis"—*Commentarium pro Religiosis* (later [1935], *Commentarium Pro Religiosis et Missionariis*) (Romae 1920—), I (1920), 19; II (1921), 134 (the article henceforth will be cited as "Commentarium Codicis" and the periodical as *CpR* up to 1934 inclusive, and as *CpRM* from 1935 onward); Wernz-Vidal, *Ius Canonicum* (7 tomes in 8 vols., Tom. III, *De Religiosis,* Romae: Apud Aedes Universitatis Gregorianae, 1933), III, n. 39; Creusen-Garesché-Ellis, *Religious Men and Women in the Code* (4. English ed., Milwaukee: Bruce, 1942), p. 8; Beste, *Introductio in Codicem* (editio altera, Collegeville, Minn.: St. John's Abbey Press, 1944), p. 308.

[2] Canon 487.

[3] Canon 488, 1°.

[4] Cf. canons 87 and 538.

or belong to its fold. Though the heterodox,[5] non-Catholics,[6] or pagans[7] should join together, form a group in the pursuit of religious perfection and lead a common life, they are not religious in the sense of canon law; at most, they can bind themselves to God only by private vows.

Secondly, within the fold of the Church, the common law does not consider as religious those who live in groups that do not have proper authorization.[8] Thus members of a voluntary pious group of the faithful, even when living together with the knowledge and consent of ecclesiastical authority, are not religious; for such action does not constitute the *approval* required for a religious community.[9]

Thirdly, even in approved institutes the common law considers as religious only those who have made profession of the three public vows of poverty, chastity, and obedience, and who are bound to the observance of a certain rule and the community life. Consequently, novices and postulants, though the former are included under the name of religious as to favors,[10] do not come under the term "religious."[11] Similarly hermits who have not made profession in a religious community are not religious.[12]

---

[5] Oesterle, *Praelectiones Iuris Canonici* (Vol. I, Romae: in Collegio S. Anselmi, 1931), I, 223; Beste, *Introductio in Codicem,* p. 305.

[6] Augustine, *A Commentary on the New Code of Canon Law* (8 vols., Vol. III, *Religious and Laymen,* 5. ed., St. Louis: Herder, 1938), III, 43, 198 (hereafter cited *A Commentary*); Beste, *Introductio in Codicem,* p. 356.

[7] Augustine, *A Commentary,* III, 43.

[8] Canon 492, § 1. Cf. S. C. de Relig., *Normae secundum quas Sacra Congregatio de Religiosis in Novis Religiosis Congregationibus Approbandis procedere solet,* 6 mart. 1921—*Acta Apostolicae Sedis, Commentarium Officiale* (Romae, 1909–1929; Civitate Vaticana, 1929—), XIII (1921), 312–319 (hereafter cited *AAS*).

[9] Creusen-Garesché-Ellis, *Religious Men and Women in the Code,* p. 22.

[10] Canon 567, § 1.

[11] Sipos, *Enchiridion Iuris Canonici* (3. ed., Pécs: Ex Typographia "Haladas R. T.," 1936), p. 334 (hereafter cited *Enchiridion*).

[12] It should be noted that the common life is not intrinsically required for the religious state; for in times past even anchorites could be true religious. But the Church, in virtue of its power to control the religious state and to determine the manner of entering it by the profession of vows, is fully authorized to predicate the existence of the religious upon the observance of the common life. In fact, long standing discipline has required the

Secular Tertiaries and Oblates are not religious, since they live in the world under the direction of an Order, and endeavor to attain Christian perfection according to the spirit of the Order, in a manner compatible with secular life.[13] As such, though they are a specified association of the faithful, they cannot be properly styled religious.[14]

Religious, then, are all those who have made public profession of vows in any authoritatively approved institute.[15] As just intimated, the term "religious," in the proper sense, applies only to those who have made a *public* profession of vows. However, in this sense it is applicable to a wide range of subjects. Thus it extends to both the Latin and the Oriental Disciplines;[16] it makes no distinction between men and women;[17] it includes all who publicly profess the vows of religion, whether by temporary[18] or perpetual, simple or solemn vows, and thus adopt the

---

observance of the cenobitic life for the religious state. Hence, if one would now insist on entering the *religious state* as a solitary, he would be in a state of rebellion, not of perfection; on the other hand, although the strictly eremitical life no longer belongs to the religious state, it is not prohibited by the Church—Wernz, *Ius Decretalium* (2. ed., 6 vols., Romae et Prati, 1905–1914), III, n. 590, III; Wernz-Vidal, *Ius Canonicum,* III, n. 8, III. As regards the Oriental Disciplines, the eremitical life is not only not prohibited, but is compatible with the juridically recognized religious state—Coussa, *Epitome Praelectionum de Iure Ecclesiastico Orientali* (2 vols., Vol. II, Venetiis: Typis Polyglottis Insulae S. Lazari, 1941), II, 11–13 (hereafter cited *Epitome*).

[13] Canon 702, § 1. Cf. Reinmann, *The Third Order Secular of Saint Francis,* The Catholic University of America Canon Law Studies, n. 50 (Washington, D. C.: The Catholic University of America, 1928); Deutsch, *Manual for Oblates of St. Benedict* (Collegeville, Minnesota: St. John's Abbey Press, 1937), for full details.

[14] Augustine, *A Commentary,* III, 444.

[15] Canon 488, 7°.

[16] Canon 1. Cf. Coussa, *Epitome,* I, 10.

[17] Canon 490.

[18] By an authentic interpretation conditional vows, i.e., those taken to last "as long as I live in the Congregation" or in words to this effect, are to be considered as temporary vows—Pontificia Commissio ad Codicis Canones authentice interpretandos (hereafter cited P.C.I.), 1 mart. 1921—*AAS,* XIII (1921), 177; cf. Maroto, "Annotationes"—*CpR,* II (1921), 129–133. As Vermeersch ("Annotationes"—*Periodica de Re Canonica et Morali utili praesertim Religiosis et Missionariis* [*Periodica de Religiosis et Missionariis,*

religious life, i.e., the complete and juridic state of acquiring perfection;[19] and it embraces those who are enrolled in the various types of the religious life: in exempt or non-exempt institutes,[20] in institutes of pontifical or diocesan approval,[21] and in clerical or lay institutes.[22]

Moreover, just as one becomes a religious in the act of profession, so only then does he cease to be a religious when that bond is broken. This may occur variously: at expiration of vows,[23] through a dispensation, an indult of secularization,[24] and in some forms of dismissal.[25] For that reason, the following remain religious:[26] the exclaustrated,[27] those dismissed in perpetual vows,[28] apostates and fugitives,[29] those promoted to dignities,[30] and all who legitimately dwell outside community life.[31]

The members of societies which are not properly religious institutes, but in which the members imitate the manner of life of religious by living in community under the government of superiors according to approved constitutions, without the bond of the usual three vows, cannot properly be designated by the name

---

8 vols., Brugis, 1905–1919; from 1920: *Periodica de Re Canonica et Morali utili praesertim Religiosis et Missionariis,* 7 vols., Brugis, 1920–1927; from 1927: *Periodica de Re Morali, Canonica, Liturgica,* Brugis (1927–1936) et Romae (1937—)], X (1922), 326 [hereafter cited *Periodica*]) correctly notes, such vows are improperly called "conditional." The profession is not conditional, but is made for a period of time the duration of which is uncertain.

19 Canon 574; cf. Larraona, "Commentarium Codicis," *CpR,* I (1920), 19.

20 Canon 488, 2o.

21 Canon 488, 3o.

22 Canons 488, 4o, and 107.

23 Canon 637.

24 Canon 640.

25 Canons 648 and 669, § 1.

26 Goyeneche, *Iuris Canonici Summa Principia, De Religiosis* (Romae: Commentarium Pro Religiosis, 1938), p. 10, note 5 (hereafter cited *De Religiosis*); Coussa, *Epitome,* II, 13.

27 Canon 639.

28 Canon 669, § 1.

29 Canon 645.

30 Canon 627.

31 E.g., pastors. Cf. canon 630.

of religious.[32] Yet, by special provision of the Code, many of the laws for religious are also made applicable to these societies, due allowance being made for the changes required by the nature of the bond binding them to the society, viz., an oath, a promise or a pledge.[33]

In short, then, under the term "religious" come all who have made public profession of vows in a community recognized by the Church, and they remain such as long as the bond exists. In this sense it includes: Latins and Orientals; men and women, professed of solemn and simple, perpetual and temporary vows; clerical and lay institutes; exclaustrated and dismissed religious; apostates and fugitives; those legitimately outside the cloister; and those promoted to dignities.

Article 2. The Bond of Profession

When by reason of profession a person becomes a religious, there arises a social element, or bond, by which he is joined to a specific institute, and incorporated into it as a member.[34] The precise nature of this bond was the object of a disagreement among pre-Code authors. Some held that it was a bilateral contract, and necessarily required the consent of both parties just as other reciprocal contracts.[35] Other authors ruled out the notion

---

[32] Canon 673.

[33] Maroto, "Annotationes," *CpR*, II (1921), 133; Vermeersch, "Annotationes," *Periodica*, X (1922), 326.

[34] Cervia, *De Professione Religiosa* (Dissertatio ad Lauream in Iuris Canonici Facultate Pontificiae Universitatis Gregorianae: Bologna, 1938), p. 4.

[35] Panormitanus, *Commentaria in Quinque Libros Decretalium* (5 vols. in 7, Venetiis: 1588), Lib. III, *de regularibus et trans.*, c. 13, n. 10 and c. 17, n. 3 (hereafter cited *Commentaria*); Suarez, *Opera Omnia* (ed. C. Berton, 26 vols., Parisiis, 1856–1866), *De religione,* tract. VII, lib. VI, c. II, nn. 14, 28 and tract. VIII, lib. III, c. IV, n. 1 (hereafter cited *De religione*); Reiffenstuel, *Jus Canonicum Universum* (5 vols. in 7, Parisiis, 1864–1870), lib. III, tit. XXXI, n. 167; Schmalzgrueber, *Ius Ecclesiasticum Universum* (5 vols. in 12, Romae, 1843–1845), lib. III, tit. XXXI, n. 149; Ferraris, *Prompta Bibliotheca Canonica, Juridica, Moralis, Theologica, necnon Ascetica, Polemica,. Rubricistica, Historica* (8 vols., ed. noviss., mendis expurgata, Parisiis, 1852–1857), s.v. "Regularis Professio," n. 40 (hereafter cited *Prompta Bibliotheca*); Wernz, *Ius Decretalium,* III, n. 640.

of contract in religious profession, but did not deny that a bond existed between a member and his institute.[36]

Since the promulgation of the Code of Canon Law, the great majority of authors favor the opinion that religious profession is a contract.[37] Thus there is recognized a twofold element, religious and social, in the act of profession.[38] The first is the profession of vows (*nuncupatio votorum*) to God, whereby one enters into a quasi-contract juridically recognized by the Church.[39] This is spiritual in character, unilateral, and gives rise to obligations. The resulting bond transcends every human right, for God is its terminus.[40]

In this profession of vows there is implicitly contained another contract: namely, that between the religious and the institute, as

---

[36] Billuart, *Summa Sancti Thomae* (9 vols. in 8, ed. nova, Letouzey et Ané, Parisiis, n.d.), Tom. V, *Tractatus de Statu Religioso,* Dissert. IV, art. III, § 1; Molitor, *Religiosi Juris Capita Selecta* (Ratisbonae, 1909), cap. I, n. 42.

[37] Wernz-Vidal, *Ius Canonicum,* III, n. 300; Papi, *Religious Profession* (New York: Kenedy, 1918), p. 5; Schaefer, *De Religiosis* (3. ed., Roma: S. A. L. E. R., 1940), n. 263; Fanfani, *De Iure Religiosorum ad Normam Codicis Iuris Canonici* (2. ed., Taurini-Romae: Marietti, 1925), n. 240 (hereafter cited *De Iure Religiosorum*); Frey, *The Act of Religious Profession,* The Catholic University of America Canon Law Studies, n. 63 (Washington, D. C.: The Catholic University of America, 1931), p. 4; Coronata, *Institutiones Iuris Canonici* (5 vols., Vol. I, 2. ed., Taurini: Marietti, 1939), I, n. 589 (hereafter cited *Institutiones*); Vermeersch-Creusen, *Epitome Iuris Canonici* (3 vols., 6. ed., Mechliniae-Romae: Dessain, 1937–1946), I, n. 722 (hereafter cited *Epitome*); O'Neill, *The Dismissal of Religious in Temporary Vows,* The Catholic University of American Canon Law Studies, n. 166 (Washington, D. C.: The Catholic University of America Press, 1942), pp. 72–73; Tabera, "De Dimissione Religiosorum"—*CpR,* XI (1930), 277. Cervia (*De Professione Religiosa,* p. 69), on the other hand, rejects the idea of contract, for the reason that it would demand relations of commutative justice. He prefers to consider the social element as consisting in *incorporation* in an approved institute, with resulting relations of legal and distributive justice.

[38] Diaz, "Studia Varia—Congressus Iuridicus Internationalis"—*CpR,* XV (1934), 426; Cervia, *op. cit.,* p. 4; cf. Zeiger, "Professio in manus"—*Acta Congressus Iuridici Internationalis* (5 vols., Romae: Libraria Pont. Instituti Utriusque Iuris, 1935–1937), III (1936), 187–202.

[39] Coronata, *Institutiones,* I, n. 589; Schaefer, *loc. cit.*

[40] Schaefer, *loc. cit.*

evidenced in the surrendering of self (*traditio sui*) and in the acceptance of the competent superior.[41] This is a human bond, bilateral in character, which creates a whole group of reciprocal rights and duties between the institute and the religious.[42] The firmness and perpetuity of this bond depends upon the type of vows taken, but as such binds in justice.[43]

Since the religious family in which profession is made is an ecclesiastical institute, this surrender (*traditio*) is also made to the Church. Moreover, the subject of this latter right is not God, but the Institute or the Church, which therefore are entitled completely to govern it.[44] Finally, though there is a real distinction between the professing of vows and the surrendering of self, by ecclesiastical law both must concur simultaneously, and one cannot exist without the other.[45]

On the basis of this bilateral contract, the obligations of the institute correspond to the rights of the professed member and vice versa.[46] The institute is obliged to direct the religious in things spiritual, aiming at spiritual perfection through the manner of life proper to the respective institute, under the guidance of competent superiors. The community is further obligated to provide its members with support, clothing, food and lodging; to admit the individual member to living in common with its other members; to grant him participation in all goods of the community; to retain him as a member for the duration of his vows; to treat him after the manner of a son.[47]

---

[41] Frey, *The Act of Religious Profession,* p. 6; Papi, *Religious Profession,* p. 4; Schaefer, *loc. cit.*

[42] Creusen-Garesché-Ellis, *Religious Men and Women in the Code,* n. 222; Schaefer, *loc. cit.;* Goyenesche, *De Religiosis,* n. 62; Vermeersch-Creusen, *loc. cit.*

[43] Vermeersch-Creusen, *loc. cit.;* Coronata, *loc. cit.*

[44] Wernz-Vidal, *op. cit.,* p. 10, nota 14.

[45] Cervia, *De Professione Religiosa,* p. 4; Papi, *Religious Profession,* p. 4; Sipos, *Enchiridion,* p. 374; Schaefer, *loc. cit.*

[46] ". . . contractus ultro citroque obligatorius . . ."—Schmalzgrueber, *loc. cit.;* Wernz-Vidal, *Ius Canonicum,* III, n. 300; Coronata, *loc. cit.;* Schaefer, *loc. cit.;* Beste, *Introductio in Codicem,* p. 382; Chelodi, *Ius Canonicum de Personis* (3. ed. curavit Pius Ciprotti, Trento: Libreria Moderna Editrice, 1942), n. 271 (hereafter cited *Ius de Personis*).

[47] Schmalzgrueber, *loc. cit.;* Wernz-Vidal, *loc. cit.;* Coronata, *loc. cit.;* Goyeneche, *De Religiosis,* n. 62.

The professed religious, on his part, transfers to the institute the right to utilize his faculties of soul and body. He foregoes his liberty of action and of the use of goods. He agrees to live in accordance with the obedience, poverty and chastity that he has vowed to observe, and in conformity with the rules and regulations of his respective institute, with regard to both spiritual and temporal matters.[48]

All the above-mentioned obligations, pertaining respectively to the institute and to its members, are to be fulfilled according to the approved rules and constitutions of the community, and according to the will of its superior within the powers granted the latter by common and particular law.[49]

Implicit in the profession-contract, as executed between an institute and its subjects through the act and acceptance of profession, is the condition that the religious shall strive earnestly to conform to the respective Rules and Constitutions. Hence an institute may justly discharge a member whose perverse conduct occasions grave detriment to the common good. The society is then exercising its natural right to use means morally necessary for its welfare, which in certain instances requires that a delinquent religious be dismissed from the institute.[50]

The force of such action on the part of the community need not be a complete severance of contractual relation with the party, for the continuance or cessation of the contract is dependent upon the continuance or cessation of the vows. It is rather a withholding of the rights that would have been due to the religious had he fulfilled his part of the contract. In this action the religious institute, as a subordinate society, must proceed according to the norms established by the perfect society, the Catholic Church.

---

[48] Wernz-Vidal, *loc. cit.;* Coronata, *loc. cit.;* O'Neill, *op. cit.*, p. 73.

[49] Frey, *op. cit.*, pp. 6–7.

[50] Suarez, *De Religione*, tract. VIII, lib. III, c. IV, n. 4; Tabera, "art. cit."—*CpR*, XI (1930), 278; Michalicka, *Judicial Procedure in Dismissal of Clerical Exempt Religious*, The Catholic University of America Canon Law Studies, n. 19 (Washington, D. C.: The Catholic University of America, 1923), p. 5.

Article 3. Notion of Dismissal

The bond arising from religious profession is, by its very nature, meant to endure. Nevertheless, the law recognizes that it is subject to the vicissitudes of human frailty. Hence, the legislator at the end of the tract on religious has inserted canons to govern the withdrawal from the state chosen in profession.[51] Not only can a religious *by his own free choice*, licitly or illicitly, depart from this state; but he can also be forced to do so at the demand of another.[52]

Departure from a religious community, then, is of three kinds: (1) the licit egress; (2) the illicit egress; (3) the dismissal by legitimate superiors. Egress is licit: (a) at the expiration of vows,[53] (b) with proper dispensation; (c) after obtaining an indult of exclaustration or secularization;[54] (d) through lawful transfer to another institute.[55] Egress is illicit when it is undertaken on the sole authority of the religious bound by vows, i.e., by apostasy and flight.[56] Finally, egress imposed by legitimate authority constitutes dismissal. It is the latter that requires further consideration here.

Before the Code, various terms, such as "expulsion" (*eiectio seu expulsio*) and "dismissal" ("*dimissio*"), were used to designate the forced egress of a religious. Each term usually had its own restricted meaning.[57] Post-Code authors[58] are in substantial agreement as to what these terms indicated, though some lay stress on the type of vows involved and others on the form of procedure.

---

[51] Hippolytus a S. Familia, "De Dimissione Religiosorum"—*Analecta Ordinis Carmelitarum Discalceatorum* (Romae, 1926—), IV (1929–1930), 98 (hereafter cited *Analecta O. C. D.*).

[52] Palombo, *De Dimissione Religiosorum* (Taurini-Romae: Marietti, 1931), n. 1.

[53] Canon 637.

[54] Canons 638–643.

[55] Canons 632–636.

[56] Canons 644–645.

[57] Palombo, *op. cit.*, n. 2.

[58] Wernz-Vidal, *Ius Canonicum*, III, n. 434; Palombo, *loc. cit.;* Tabera, *ibid.*, p. 279, nota 17; Hippolytus a S. Familia, "art. cit."—*Analecta O. C. D.*, IV (1930), 156; Goyeneche, *De Religiosis*, n. 103.

The terms indicated different procedures based on the greater or lesser intensity of the bond involved.[59] Thus, expulsion related only to a delinquent and incorrigible religious in solemn vows who was expelled through a judicial process. Dismissal, on the other hand, signified the act whereby a competent superior, without judicial process, separated a simply professed member from the institute upon ascertaining the fact that there existed certain grave and just causes, not necessarily reflecting upon the religious' guilt or incorrigibility.[60] In addition, expulsion left upon the religious the obligations of his vows; dismissal included, by its very nature, a dispensation from the vows.[61]

However, it must be noted that the use of these terms was not always consistent, and that sometimes they were used interchangeably.[62] These distinctions have not been preserved by the Code, principally in view of the elimination of the former distinction between regulars and religious of simple vows. Now one and the same term is applied to all to indicate the forced egress of both classes. This is the word "dismissal," which has, consequently, acquired a new and wider meaning.[63]

Post-Code authors generally agree in defining dismissal as "the forced or unwilled separation of a religious from the religious institute, imposed by legitimate authority for canonical reasons." [64] While adhering substantially to this definition, some authors use

---

[59] Michalicka, *Judicial Procedure in Dismissal of Clerical Exempt Religious,* p. 10.

[60] Wernz-Vidal, *loc. cit.;* and others.

[61] Creusen-Garesché-Ellis, *Religious Men and Women in the Code,* n. 343.

[62] Wernz-Vidal, *loc. cit.*

[63] Hippolytus a S. Familia, *loc. cit.;* Tabera, *ibid.,* p. 278, nota 11.

[64] Pejška, *Ius Canonicum Religiosorum* (3. ed., Friburgi Brisgoviae: Herder, 1927), p. 189; Sipos, *Enchiridion,* p. 408; Oesterle, *Praelectiones Iuris Canonici,* I, 367; Michalicka, *op. cit.,* p. 10; Hippolytus a S. Familia, "art. cit."—*Analecta O. C. D.,* IV (1930), 157; Goyeneche, *De Religiosis,* n. 103; Blat, *Commentarium Textus Codicis Iuris Canonici* (5 vols. in 6, lib. II, pars II–III, *Ius de Religiosis et Laicis iuxta Codicis Ordinem,* 3. ed., Romae: Apud "Angelicum," 1938), II, pars II–III, n. 657 (hereafter cited *Ius de Religiosis*) ; Toso, *Ad Codicem Iuris Canonici Commentaria Minora,* Lib. II, pars II (Romae: Jus Pontificium, 1927), p. 242 (hereafter cited *Commentaria Minora*) ; and others.

the term "egress"[65] instead of "separation." The use of the word "separation" is more in conformity with the divisions of the Code, which treats egress and dismissal under two separate titles.[66]

The authors who speak of dismissal as an egress maintain that the distinction between the two titles is only that between voluntary and involuntary egress. Nevertheless, the separate treatment of the Code seems to indicate that there are real differences between egress and dismissal. Toso[67] states that Title XV deals with the unilateral action of the religious, while Title XVI treats of the unilateral action of the institute. Hence, though an egress of religious occurs also in their dismissal, the emphasis is not on their departure, but on the action of the institute. Accordingly, many authors, either in express words or by the tenor of their definition, stress that dismissal is a "forced" separation, i.e., imposed by legitimate authority. Further, in terming it "an involuntary separation" they mean to imply that no choice is left to the religious, though generally the religious is willing, in the sense that he has placed the causes.[68]

As O'Leary[69] notes, the word "dismissal" itself gives rise to further misunderstandings. In common parlance it ordinarily signifies a thorough and complete discharge or expulsion of a member from an organization. In this ordinary conception of dismissal there is no further bond between the organization and the dismissed member; and such a one ceases in every way to belong to the organization. No doubt, much of this misunderstanding is traceable to the pre-Code meaning of dismissal, and

---

[65] Fanfani, *De Iure Religiosorum,* p. 493; Coronata, *Institutiones,* I, n. 645; Wernz-Vidal, *loc. cit.;* Palombo, *loc. cit.;* Schaefer, *De Religiosis,* n. 574; Chelodi, *Ius de Personis,* n. 289; O'Leary, *Religious Dismissed after Perpetual Profession,* The Catholic University of America Canon Law Studies, n. 184 (Washington, D. C.: The Catholic University of America Press, 1943), p. 1; O'Neill, *The Dismissal of Religious in Temporary Vows,* p. 74.

[66] Lib. II, pars II, tit. XV De egressu e religione; tit. XVI De dimissione religiosorum.

[67] *Loc. cit.*

[68] Coronata, *loc. cit;* Chelodi, *loc. cit.*

[69] *Op. cit.,* pp. 1–2.

even to the definition cited as giving its post-Code meaning. The use of the phrase "from a religious institute" does not allow sufficiently for the difference of effects that follow according as the vows of the dismissed are temporary or perpetual. The definition is valid for those in temporary vows, since dismissal in such cases breaks the bond.[70] However, this effect cannot be predicated of the dismissal of religious in perpetual vows, for these remain true religious, bound to their vows and to the institute.[71]

Besides being a member of the religious state in general, a religious dismissed after perpetual vows is also a member of the particular institute in which he made his profession of vows.[72] Though he is a separated member he must still be reckoned among the members of his organization until he is dispensed from his vows, or until he transfers to another religious institute. Only by such means can a religious sever the juridical bond that binds him to a particular institute.[73] Hence O'Leary rightly inserts the words *from the communal life* in place of the words *from the religious institute* in his definition of dismissal after perpetual profession.[74]

In order to include both types of vows under a single definition, it seems necessary to term dismissal as "the forced or unwilled separation of a religious from the religious institute or from the communal life, imposed by legitimate authority according to the norms of law." Thus, dismissal in relation to those in temporary vows destroys the bond,[75] and so is termed a *separation from the religious institute;* whereas dismissal as applied to those in perpetual vows leaves the bond intact, but removes the religious from intercourse with the community and his confrères, and so is termed *separation from the communal life.*

[70] Canon 648.

[71] Canon 669, § 1.

[72] Wernz-Vidal, *op. cit.*, III, n. 451.

[73] O'Leary, *op. cit.*, pp. 2–4.

[74] O'Leary, *op. cit.*, pp. 1 and 5.

[75] The same is true of those in perpetual vows, the automatic dispensation of which by the Constitutions or by Apostolic Indults accompanies dismissal—cf. canon 669, § 1.

Finally, it should be noted that the term "dismissal" has sometimes been inaccurately applied.[76] It should not be used in reference to those religious who follow the suggestion of their superiors, when for the purpose of preserving their good name the superiors urge them to petition for a dispensation of their own accord under circumstances in which their conduct actually merits dismissal. These religious cannot be called canonically dismissed.

Hence, from the definition of dismissal which has been given, it is evident that dismissal is distinct from (1) the transfer to another institute or monastery of the same institute;[77] (2) the voluntary egress from a religious institute, whether licitly by an indult of exclaustration or an indult of secularization,[78] or illicitly by means of apostasy or flight;[79] (3) the dispensation of the vows;[80] (4) the exclusion of the religious from the making of perpetual vows or from the renewal of temporary vows;[81] (5) the provisory sending of the religious away from the religious house.[82]

In closing this chapter, one should finally note that dismissal is divided into various legal modes according as it affects the causes of dismissal and the status of the subjects dismissed. Thus the authors distinguish between dismissal *a iure* and dismissal *ab homine*,[83] and in the latter note further subdivisions based on the type of the institute and the kind of vows.[84] However, since

---

[76] Cf. O'Leary, *op. cit.*, pp. 4–5.

[77] Canons 632–636.

[78] Canons 638–640.

[79] Canons 644–645.

[80] Oesterle, *op. cit.*, p. 368.

[81] Canon 637.

[82] Canons 653 and 668. In these two canons the Code uses the expression *"ad saeculum remitti,"* and refers to the action that can be taken against a guilty religious in cases of great scandal and when there would be danger to the good name of the community in a delayed act of dismissal. It is not a dismissal in the strict sense, but rather a precautionary measure. This action is to be followed by regular dismissal proceedings. Cf. Schaefer, *De Religiosis*, nn. 586 and 595.

[83] N. B. The admission of the form known as dismissal *ab homine* is not to be understood as implying that there is a form of dismissal not contained in the law of the Code; but rather as designating the forms of dismissal in which the law requires the intervention of an agent.

[84] E.g., Blat, *op. cit.*, n. 657; Goyeneche, *De Religiosis*, n. 103.

these distinctions imply simply another mode in the stating of the Code's divisions, it will suffice to enumerate the latter. The Code in title XVI of Book II, part II, has (1) a single canon that sets forth the circumstances of the *a iure* or *ipso facto* effected dismissal;[85] and (2) three chapters providing for the *ab homine* effected dismissals; namely, (a) the authoritative dismissal of religious in temporary vows;[86] (b) the authoritative dismissal of clerical non-exempt and lay religious in perpetual vows;[87] and (c) the judicial process for the dismissal of clerical exempt religious in perpetual vows.[88] The last chapter (IV) of this title presents the effects of the dismissal of those in perpetual vows.[89]

The present dissertation deals with the first species of dismissal; namely, the *ipso facto* effected dismissal. In the treatment of this dismissal, the following observation of Woywod (1880–1941) finds full application:

> "Ecclesiastical legislation is usually conservative. Laws introducing sudden and far-reaching changes in the discipline of the Church are rare. A careful perusal of the Code will convince the reader that this monumental work contains a systematic summary of former laws rather than new laws. The changes, which in the course of time become necessary, are made slowly and with much deliberation." [90]

The fact that this kind of dismissal appears in ecclesiastical law for the first time in the decree *Quum singulae,* May 16, 1911,[91]

---

[85] Canon 646.

[86] Canons 647, 648. Cf. O'Neill, *The Dismissal of Religious in Temporary Vows.*

[87] Canons 649–653.

[88] Canons 654–668. Cf. Michalicka, *Judicial Procedure in Dismissal of Clerical Exempt Religious.* Goyeneche (*De Religiosis,* n. 119) states that even this dismissal is *administrative* in substance.

[89] Canon 669–672. Cf. O'Leary, *Religious Dismissed After Perpetual Profession.*

[90] Woywod, *A Practical Commentary on the Code of Canon Law* (8. ed., revised by Callistus Smith, 2 vols., New York: Wagner, 1944), I, n. 4.

[91] S. C. de Rel., decr. *Quum singulae,* 16 maii 1911, n. 18—*AAS,* III (1911), 237; *Codicis Iuris Canonici Fontes,* cura Emi Petri Card. Gasparri editi (9 vols., Romae [postea Civitate Vaticana]: Typis Polyglottis

would seem to deny the general rule; but it is especially here that one must seek canonical foreshadowings in order to understand the present legislation. This can perhaps best be done through a tracing of the historical development, from the juridical viewpoint, of dismissal as an institute in general. One can in this manner at length more intelligently review the immediate circumstances that prompted the enactment of the legislation which provides for this specific form of dismissal.

Vaticanis, 1923–1939; Vols. VII, VIII, IX ed. cura et studio Emi Iustiniani Serédi), n. 4409 (hereafter cited *Fontes*). Cf. Tabera, "De Dimissione Religiosorum"—*CpR.*, XI (1930), 411–412.

PART I

HISTORICAL CONSPECTUS

CHAPTER II

BEFORE THE DECRETALS OF GREGORY IX

Article 1. Monastic Rules

From the very beginning of organized religious life, provision was made for the expulsion or dismissal of monks whose conduct was persistently incorrigible. This is evidenced by an examination of the old monastic rules. Thus in the Rule of St. Macarius (d. 395), Abbot of the Monastery of Nitria (Egypt), and disciple of St. Anthony (d. 356), the Founder of the Cenobitic Life,[1] the norm of dismissal is mentioned briefly: "*Qui vero saepius corripitur et non se emendaverit, novissimus in ordine stare iubeatur. Qui, si nec sic quidem se emendaverit, extraneus habeatur . . .*"[2]

Nevertheless, the holy Founders,[3] before they came to this ex-

[1] Migne, *Patrologiae Cursus Completus, Series Graeca* (161 vols., Parisiis: 1856–1866), XXVI, 835 (hereafter cited *MPG*); Thomassinus, *Vetus et Nova Ecclesiae Disciplina circa Beneficia et Beneficiarios* (Editio postrema, cum Parisiensi accuratissime collata, 10 vols., Magontiaci, 1787), tom. I, lib. III, cap. XII, *De Origine Monasteriorum et Abbatiarum,* par III, p. 93.

[2] Cap. XVII—Migne, *Patrologiae Cursus Completus, Series Latina* (221 vols., Parisiis: 1844–1864), CIII, 449 (hereafter cited *MPL*).

[3] S. Benedictus Abbas Anianensis, "Concordia Regularum"—*MPL,* CIII, 1029 sqq. In the East special mention must be made of: St. Pachomius (d. 346), Abbot of Tabennisi,—*MPL,* XXIII, 81–82; C. 84, *MPL,* L, 293; *St. Basil* (d. 379), *Regulae Fusius Tractatae,* Inter. 28,—*MPG,* XXXI, 987–990; Regulae XLIV, LVII, LXI, *Regulae Brevius Tractatae,—MPG,* XXXI, 1110, 1120, 1123; *Regula Orientalis, MPL,* CIII, 1034; N. 35; "*Vigilii Diaconi Regula Monachorum,*"—*MPL,* L, 379–380. In the West: St. Cyprian (d. 258), *De Habitu Virginum,* 17,—*MPL,* IV, 456; *Corpus Scriptorum Ecclesiasticorum Latinorum* (Vindobonae, 1866—), III, pt. I, 200; St. Augustine (d. 430), *Ep. CCXI,* 11,—*MPL,* XXXIII, 962 sq.; Jordanus de Saxonia, *Liber Vitasfratrum* (Ad fidem Codicum recensuerunt, prolegomenis, apparatu critico, notis instruxerunt Rudolphus Arbesmann et Winfridus Hümpfner: Cosmopolitan Science and Art Service Co., Inc., 1943), Appendix C, VII, n. 110, p. 499; St. Benedict (480–543),

treme, enjoined that every possible means be used to convert the recalcitrant monk to obedience and regular observance. In the ancient literature of monks no better document attests to this solicitude of abbot or superior towards a failing brother than the Rule of St. Benedict.[4] The norm found in chapter 28 of this rule is illustrative of those in earlier rules. It describes the steps that a superior must follow in correcting a wayward subject: namely, (a) two secret warnings, (b) public reproof, (c) excommunication, (d) fast, (e) corporal chastisement, (f) prayer.[5] But if these failed to produce the desired fruit, and the subject still continued to be rebellious and contumacious, he was to be expelled from the monastery, lest his evil ways infect the other religious and cause harm to the common good of the community.[6]

The rule of St. Benedict is also typical of other early rules concerning the manner of receiving again those monks who had been expelled from the monastery, or who had left through their own fault:

—*MPL,* LXVI, 519–520; St. Columban (d. 615), C. 10—*MPL,* LXXX, 223; Seebass, "Regula Coenobilis Sancti Columbani Abbatis," *Zeitschrift für Kirchengeschichte* (Gotha: F. A. Perthes, 1876—), XVII (1897), 233; St. Isidore of Seville (d. 636),—*MPL,* LXXXIII, 884–885; *MPL,* CIII, 567–568, 1033.

[4] *S. P. Benedicti Regula—MPL,* LXVI, 215 sqq.; cf. *Sancti Benedicti Regula Monasteriorum* (ed. critico-practica, Cuthbert Butler, Friburgi Brisgoviae, 1912).

[5] Cf. Bastien, "De Evolutione Historico-Iuridica Processus Dimissionis," —*Jus Pontificium* (Romae, 1921—), XI (1931), 20.

[6] *S. Benedicti Regula,* cap. XXVIII: "Si quis frater frequenter correptus pro qualibet culpa, si etiam excommunicatus, non emendaverit, acrior ei accedat correptio, id est, ut verberum vindicta in eum procedat. Quod si nec ita correxerit, aut forte (quod absit) in superbiam elatus, etiam defendere voluerit opera sua, tunc abbas faciat quod sapiens medicus. Si exhibuit fomenta, si unguenta adhortationum, si medicamina Scripturarum divinarum, si ad ultimum ustionem excommunicationis, vel plagas virgarum, etiam si viderit nihil suam praevalere industriam: adhibeat etiam (quod maius est) suam et omnium fratrum pro eo orationem: ut Dominus, qui omnia potest, operetur salutem circa infirmum fratrem. Quod si *nec isto modo sanatus fuerit,* tunc iam utatur abbas *ferro abscissionis,* ut ait Apostolus: 'Auferte malum ex vobis.' Et iterum: 'Infidelis si discedit, discedat; ne una ovis morbida omnem gregem contaminet."—*MPL,* LXVI, 519–520; I Cor. V, 15; I Cor. VII, 15. Italics inserted by the present writer.

> *Frater qui proprio vitio egreditur aut projicitur de monasterio, si reverti voluerit, spondeat prius omnem emendationem vitii pro quo egressus est; et sic in ultimo gradu recipiatur. . . . Quod si denuo exierit, usque tertio ita recipiatur. Jam postea sciens omnem sibi reversionis aditum denegari.*[7]

It seems that throughout this entire period the discipline of dismissal was provided for almost entirely by monastic rules, rather than by conciliar legislation. The above-mentioned rules did not state any explicit transgression or delict that warranted the offender's discharge from religion, but provided only a general norm on the manner of proceedings that might lead to expulsion. The prevalent attitude of the monastic institute intimated

---

[7] *S. Benedicti Regula,* cap. XXIX—*MPL,* LXVI, 523-524. The words "aut projicitur" are found in this text, but in Butler, *Sancti Benedicti Regula Monasteriorum,* p. 60. they are omitted. Delatte (*Commentary on the Rule of St. Benedict* [New York: Benziger Brothers, 1921], p. 228, note 1, makes note of Butler's text, but is not in agreement, and adds: "Without disputing the authority of the Carlovingian and Cassinese tradition, it is, however, possible to give a probable sense to our text. Why should an expelled monk not come to a better mind? Do not the arrangements of this chapter appear to be a natural consequence of what precedes?" Martène (*S.P. Benedicti Regula Commentata—MPL,* LXVI, 524-525) devoted some time to giving views of earlier commentators on the words "proprio vitio," and summed up the causes for which one might leave the monastery, and at the end gave application as to how such should be received back: ". . . 1°. Quidem propter relaxatam in proprio coenobio vitae regularis disciplinam exeunt, ad aliud observantiae strictioris transituri. 2°. Alii, studio majoris perfectionis aut contemplationis, eremum appetunt. 3°. Alii levitate et inconstantia, aut timore disciplinae egrediuntur. 4°. Alii propter superbiam, contumaciam aut aliud vitium projiciuntur, aut propria temeritate exeunt. 5°. Denique propter vitium contagiosum, hoc est commune, pro quo cum alio expelluntur. Et primi quidem et secundi non solum, si revertuntur, suscipiendi, sed etiam cum honore et amore amplectendi, ut eorum exemplo alii aedificentur. *Tertii et quarti eo modo recipiendi, quem hic describit S. Benedictus.* De contagiosis (5°) omnino silere S. Benedictum docent Hildemarus et Bernardus Cassinensis. . . ." (Italics inserted by present writer.) It may be noted that the authors considered 4° as coming well within the scope of cap. 29, and that only of 5° did they hold that St. Benedict was silent regarding the obligation of receiving back the one who had been expelled.

that a member should not always be expelled for even a grievous fault.

Other medicinal punishments should first be administered and tried in all ways for his amendment; this was considered in perfect accordance with the religious state, which is a school of virtue and perfection, and to which it belongs not only to promote virtue but also to correct faults, and especially to cure the spiritually weak member. Consequently the monastic founders deemed it foreign to their spirit to despair hastily of curing such a member, and this would have been done by expelling him without previous corrective treatment.

If, however, he did not amend after having been repeatedly corrected, but rather relapsed again and again, he was held to be incorrigible. Briefly, two conditions were required for expulsion, incorrigibility and contumacy: the latter evidencing culpable resistance of the will to correction, so that expulsion was deemed morally necessary, not so much as a medicinal remedy, but as a vindicative measure, and as a means to safeguard the common good, *lest the infected member contaminate the others: ne modicum fermentum totam massam corrumpat.*[8]

Apart from the monastic rules, the first juridical reference to *dismissal* seems to be that which is contained in the rescript of Pope Siricius (385) to Himerius, Bishop of Tarragona (Spain), in which the Pope ordered *expulsion* from the religious life, in addition to separation of the parties, and deprivation of communion until the hour of death, as the sanction for monks and nuns who contracted a sacrilegious marriage subsequent to profession.[9]

---

[8] S. Basilius, *Regulae Brevius Tractatae, XLIV—MPG,* XXXI, 1110-1111; *S. P. Benedicti Regula,* cap. XXVIII. *De iis qui saepius correpti non emendaverint—MPL,* LXVI, 519-520.

[9] Jaffé, *Regesta pontificum Romanorum ab condita Ecclesia ad annum post Christum natum MCXCVIII* (2. ed., correctam et auctam auspiciis Gulielmi Wattenbach curaverunt S. Loewenfeld, F. Kaltenbrunner, P. Ewald, 2 vols. in 1, Lipsiae, 1885–1888), (hereafter cited as "J" along with the initial of the author of the part in question), JK, n. 255; cf. Van Espen, *Jus Ecclesiasticum Universum* (4 tomes, Lugduni, 1778), Tom. I, pars I, tit. XXVII, c. VII.

Article 2. Justinian Legislation

The contribution of Roman Law to the canonical institute of the *dismissal of religious* was very limited. Justinian, it is true, included in his codification many laws that dealt with the Church, and among these some that touched upon the religious life,[10] but it is only in the Novels that he contemplated two cases of expulsion. The first[11] was applicable to both monks and nuns. It ordered expulsion for those guilty of very grave faults, when the corrective efforts of superiors proved fruitless on account of the persistent contumacy of the offenders. The second instance[12] was more specific. It concerned only monks, namely, those regarding whom it was established that they had frequented a tavern. The culprit was to be delivered up immediately to the defenders of the district, or to the Prefect of the city, and, after conviction, to be punished. Notice was to be sent to the abbot in order that the latter might expel him from the monastery, as one who had exchanged an angelic life for one that was discreditable.[13]

Article 3. Letters of St. Gregory the Great

During this period of the Church's history many of the bishops were selected from the monasteries. In the year 590 Gregory, a

[10] Cf. Schaefer, "Justinianus I et Vita Monachica,"—*Acta Congressus Iuridici Internationalis,* I (1935), 173–188; Tabera, "De Ordinatione Status Monachalis in Fontibus Iustinianeis,"—*CpR,* XIV (1933), 87–95, 199–206; Chapman, *St. Benedict and the Sixth Century* (London: Sheed and Ward, 1929), chap. IV, "The Laws of Justinian and the Holy Rule," pp. 57–74.

[11] Nov. (133.5) 1—*Corpus Iuris Civilis,* 3 vols., *Institutiones,* quas recognovit P. Krueger; *Digesta,* quae recognovit T. Mommsen, et retractavit P. Krueger; *Codex, Iustinianus,* quem recognovit et rectractavit P. Krueger; *Novellae,* quas recognovit R. Schoell, et absolvit G. Kroll (Berolini, 1928–1929).

[12] Nov. (133.6).

[13] Justinian in his *Codex,* C. (1.1) 7, gave to Ecclesiastical Legislation the approval and sanction of the Imperial Roman Law System. Hence at various points he directed the secular arm to come to the aid of the Church in the enforcement of her laws. With time such recourse became so much the normal way of acting that a gloss to Gratian (c. 4, D. XVII) stated this general rule: "Item habes hic, quod ubicumque deficit ecclesiastica potestas, semper recurritur ad brachium saeculare."

monk of the Monastery of St. Andrew in Rome, was chosen as the first monk to rule in the Chair of Peter. Forced to leave the cloister which he loved, Gregory I (590–604) was ever solicitous for the monastic state. Many of his letters were addressed to ecclesiastical authorities and civil magistrates,[14] directing them to bring back and enclose in the monastery those who had abandoned the monastic state; and in doing so the pope was particularly insistent on the part that the secular power was to exercise to bring about the desired effect.[15]

Article 4. Particular Legislation

For the next few centuries there is no evidence of legislation concerning dismissal until the year 845, when the Council of Meaux decreed that no monk be expelled from the monastery without the consent or presence of the local ordinary or his delegate;[16] the final judgment in this matter, as well as the future status of the religious, if discharged, was to be subject to the discretion and authority of the bishop.[17] This law apparently indicated a change in the discipline of dismissal as having been no

---

[14] Ep. I, 40(42)—c. 39, C. XXVII, q. 1.; Mansi, *Sacrorum Conciliorum Nova et Amplissima Collectio* (53 vols. in 60, Florentiae, Parisiis, Arnhem et Leipzig, 1901–1927), IX, 1058 (hereafter cited Mansi); *MPL,* LXXVII, 495; *Monumenta Germaniae Historica, Epistolae* (3 tomes, ed. P. Ewald et L. Hartmann, Berolini, 1867–1899), Tom. I, pars II (1891), p. 55 (hereafter cited *MGH*); JE, n. 1110.

Ep. I, 40(42)—c. 5, X, *de regularibus et transeuntibus ad religionem,* III, 31; Mansi, *MPL, MGH,* and JE, *loc. cit.*

Ep. III, 9—c. 28, C. XXVII, q. 1; *MGH, Epistolae* (N. B. Ep. IV, 9), Tom. I, pars II, p. 241; JE, n. 1281.

Ep. VIII, 8, 9—c. 18, 19, C. XXVII, q. 1; *MPL,* LXXVII, 912, 913; *MGH, Epistolae,* Tom. II, pars I (1893), pp. 10, 11; JE, nn. 1495, 1496.

Ep. X, 3(8)—c. 15, C. XXVII, q. 1; *MPL,* LXXVII, 1071, 1072; *MGH, Epistolae,* Tom. II, pars II (1895), p. 238; JE, n. 1770.

[15] Gloss to c. 19, C. XXVII, q. 1, gives this rule: "Gladius materialis spiritualem adiuvare debet."

[16] "The intervention of the bishop at that time was justified in view of the subjection which monasteries owed to the bishop, since they did not then enjoy the privilege of exemption"—apud Bastien, "De Evolutione Hictorico-Iuridica Processus Dimissionis,"—*Jus Pontificium,* XI (1931), 22.

[17] C. 59—*MGH,* Legum Sectio II, *Capitularia Regum Francorum* (2 tom. in 5 vols.; ed. A. Boretius et V. Krause, Hannoverae: 1883–1897), II, 412.

longer exclusively within the competence of religious superiors, at least in that particular locality.

In 895, the Council of Tribur re-enacted the substance of Siricius' rescript, already cited. Both of these are contained in the *Decree* of Gratian, and are noteworthy as the only two indications of dismissal to be incorporated in Gratian's work; still he does not discuss dismissal from the viewpoint of a legal institute or concept.[18]

The above-mentioned comprise the entire juridical treatment on the institute of *dismissal* for this period; no further legislation was forthcoming up to the time of Gregory IX (1227–1241).

[18] Cc. 11, 17, C. XXVII, q. 1; *MGH,* Legum Sectio II, *Capitularia Regum Francorum,* II, 225, 228.

CHAPTER III

GREGORY IX TO URBAN VIII

Article 1. Decretals of Gregory IX

For the sake of a clearer understanding of the Decretals of Gregory IX, it seems fitting that a brief mention should be made of the fact that both canonical legislation and the religious state underwent an amplification period around this time. The former was attributable to the enactments of the canonist Popes: chiefly Alexander III (1159–1181) and Innocent III (1198–1216). As to the religious life, the bond of its original stability had expanded into various forms of institutes, in addition to the monastic. Besides the Canons Regular, the Knights Templar had come into existence only a few years before the publication of the Decree of Gratian; these were followed in the succeeding decades of the twelfth century by other Military Orders, and, in the thirteenth century, by several orders for the ransom of captives, as well as by the Mendicant Friars.[1]

The purpose of the Decretals of Gregory IX (promulgated September 5, 1234, by means of the papal Constitution *Rex Pacificus*) was not that of supplanting the *Decree* of Gratian, but rather of supplementing it by means of a definitive redaction and authentic promulgation of the various decretals already existing in post-Gratian collections. Whereas inclusion in the *Decree* gave the laws it contained no other binding force than they had of themselves when promulgated, the collection of Gregory IX had the force of universal law, so that every law therein became universal, even those originally issued for particular cases, or derived from non-authentic sources.[2]

---

[1] Cf. Alzog, *Manual of Universal Church History* (3 vols., Cincinnati, 1903), Vol. II (Sixth Impression), Chap. IV, pp. 681–727; Funk, *A Manual of Church History, Authorized Translation of 5th German Edition* (2 vols., Luigi Cappadelta, St. Louis, 1910), I, 368–378.

[2] Jeličić, "De Mente Gregorii IX in adornanda Collectione Decretalium,"

It has been shown that up to the ninth century the discipline of *dismissal* was almost exclusively in the hands of monastic superiors. Then it was restricted, to some extent, by the particular councils of Meaux (845) and Tribur (895).[3] Outside of these localities, *expulsion* seems to have been confined to the provisions of religious rules rather than contemplated as an object of legislation.[4]

However, as time went on, it became increasingly evident that some superiors of regulars were too inclined to expel their monks, and hence the latter had the occasion to wander about with evident detriment to their own salvation and with public scandal to the faithful. In these circumstances something had to be done to enforce the return of such monks to their monasteries.[5] A remedy was provided in the *Decretals of Gregory IX,* which in effect or indirectly may be considered as furnishing the first general law on the dismissal of religious.

The Gregorian Decretals contain four references to expulsion. Two were simply applications of the general monastic norm on incorrigibility to particular offenses of certain monks. The second of these references extended the sanction of expulsion also to nuns who persisted in being incorrigible.[6] The third is an act

---

Acta Congressus Iuridici Internationalis, III (1936), 1–20; Serédi, "De Relatione inter Decretales Gregorii Papae IX et Codicem iuris canonici," *Acta Congressus Iuridici Internationalis,* IV (1937), 11–26.

[3] Cf. *supra,* pp. 24–25.

[4] Cf. in re Ordinis S. Dominici—*Constitutiones* (ed. nova, Parisiis, 1886), dist. I, c. XIX; in re Ord. S. Francisci—Horoy, *Bibliotheca Patristica Medii Aevii—ab anno MCCXVI usque ad Conc. Trident.* (Series Prima, Paris, 1880), Tomus Sextus, *S. Francisci Assiss. Opuscula,* Regula Prima, cap. XIII, col. 274; Regula Tertiariorum, cap. XVI, col. 313; Butler, *S. Benedicti Regula Monasteriorum,* c. XXVIII.—These norms agree substantially with those of other rules on this matter.

[5] Van Espen, *Jus Ecclesiasticum Universum,* Tom. I, pars I, tit. XXVII, cap. VII, n. V.

[6] Innocent III: "Si vero . . . proprietatem aliquam fuerit (monachus) deprehensus habere, regulari monitione praemissa de monasterio expellatur; nec recipiatur ulterius, nisi poeniteat secundum monasticam disciplinam . . ." —c. 6, X, *de statu monachorum,* III, 35; Potthast, *Regesta Pontificum Romanorum inde ab A. post Christum natum MCXCVIII ad A. MCCCIV* (2 vols., Berolini, 1874–1875), n. 1734 (hereafter cited Potthast); Honorius

of Innocent III sent to the abbots of the monasteries of St. Stephen and of St. Proculus in Bologna. The practice found therein is in keeping with that observed in monastic circles during the preceding centuries. The pope first disposed of the matter at hand—four canons regular who refused obedience to their superior—and then laid down a rule for the canons to follow.[7]

The fourth reference is an enactment of Gregory himself, and is the general law spoken of above as answering the needs of the times. It ordered all religious superiors to search, with all possible diligence, for *expelled* monks, as well as fugitives, which search was to be instituted *annually*. The delinquents, when found to be sufficiently docile and repentant, were to be taken back to the monastery; if not, notice of their condition had to be sent to the local ordinary.[8]

III: "Ipsi . . . monachos quos contumaces et rebelles invenerint . . . regulari censura percellant . . . non parcendo . . . quin ovem morbidam eiiciant ab ovili, ne inficiat sanas oves. . . . Haec autem omnia . . . necnon in monasteriis monialium, praecipimus observari."—c. 8, X, *de statu monachorum,* III, 35; Potthast, n. 7817.

[7] Innocent III: ". . . universis canonicis dedimus firmiter in mandatis, ut priori suo in his, quae ad eum pertinent, obedirent . . . alioquin eos de fratrum *ipsorum* [sic] consortio penitus excludatis."—c. 10, X, *de maioritate et obedienta,* I, 33; Potthast, n. 5030. The summary of this chapter is: "Canonici regulares inobedientes priori suo per ipsum excommunicari possunt, et, si fuerint incorrigibiles, de fratrum consortio expelli debent."

[8] Gregory IX—"Ne religiosi, vagandi occasionem habentes, salutis propriae detrimentum incurrant, et sanguis eorum de praelatorum manibus requiratur: statuimus, ut praesidentes capitulis celebrandis secundum statutum concilii generalis, seu patres, abbates, seu priores fugitivos suos et eiectos de ordine suo requirant sollicite annuatim. Qui si in monasteriis suis recipi possunt secundum ordinem regularem, abbates seu priores eorum monitione praevia per censuram ecclesiasticam compellantur ad receptionem ipsorum, salva ordinis disciplina. Quod si hoc regularis ordo non patitur, auctoritate nostra provideant, ut apud eadem monasteria in locis competentibus, si absque gravi scandalo fieri poterit, alioquin in aliis religiosis domibus eiusdem ordinis ad agendam ibi poenitentiam talibus vitae necessaria ministrentur. Si vero huiusmodi fugitivos vel eiectos inobedientes invenerint, eos excommunicent, et tamdiu faciant ab ecclesiarum praelatis excommunicatos publice nunciari, donec ad mandatum ipsorum humiliter revertantur."—c. 24 (fin.), X, *de regularibus et transeuntibus ad religionem,* III, 31; Potthast, n. 9651.

Article 2. The Decretalists

In the course of their lecture or commentary the decretalists considered the ejection or expulsion of religious in connection with c. 24, X, *de regularibus et transeuntibus ad religionem,* III, 31. After a brief summary of content, they immediately divided the constitution into its component parts,[9] and then proceeded to comment on the words which, as they felt, needed a fuller explanation.

Hostiensis (Henry of Segusia, d. 1271) viewed this norm of Gregory IX in the light of the Rule of St. Benedict, and found it quite consonant with the practice as insinuated there and in other monastic rules.[10] He mentioned in order the seven degrees for the correcting of a delinquent monk, as found listed in the Rule of St. Benedict,[11] and was in full accord with the provision that the monk be received back even a third time, but no oftener.[12] In fact, he stated that after the third time such a one was to be presumed incorrigible, and hence was to be deprived of all privileges and handed over to the secular power.[13] He implied the rule that one thrice reconciled, and yet not corrected, was to be cast forth from the monastery; and only if he promised to do penance was an exception allowed, in which case he was to be detained in a house of correction.[14]

---

[9] 1. Purpose of constitution—*Ne religiosi.*
 2. The constitution proper—two parts
 a. provisions with regard to ejected and fugitives—*Statuimus.*
 b. further measures if the foregoing (a) should be found unwilling to obey—*Si vero.*

[10] Hostiensis, *Commentaria in Quinque Libros Decretalium* (5 vols. in 3, Venetiis, 1581), III, tit. *de regularibus et transeuntibus:* cap. 24, *Ne religiosi,* p. 116.

[11] *Ibid.*, n. 6, s.v. *disciplina;* cf. *S. Benedicti Regula,* cap. XXIII—*MPL,* LXVI, 501-502; cap. XXVIII—*MPL,* LXVI, 519-520; also *supra,* p. 20.

[12] Cf. *S. Benedicti Regula,* cap. XXIX—*MPL,* LXVI, 523-524.

[13] "Praesumitur enim postea incorrigibilis . . . omni privilegio denudatur et potestati traditur saeculari."—*Ibid.*, n. 7.

[14] "Sic et monachus, ex quo ter reconciliatus, non corrigitur, est de monasterio perpetuo eiciendus, vel si promitteret poenitentiam agere, esset in aliquo ergastulo recludendus."—*loc. cit.* Traces of this last resort are found in some earlier rules, especially that of St. Isidore, ". . . Quamvis frequentium, graviorumque vitiorum voragine sit quispiam immersus, non

Hostiensis adverted to this last mentioned remedy under the words "*locis competentibus*," and then discussed further details. First he noted that Innocent IV (1243–1254) had taken these words to mean a separation from the rest of the brethren, but seemed not altogether certain how this was to be done. Then Hostiensis offered his own teaching, which specified a definite meaning for the words. For him these words denoted a prison (house of correction) or a vaulted chamber, but, whatever it was, it was to be strong and secure.[15]

Moreover, he took the stand that one who had thrice gone out and thrice been reconciled, and yet had not amended, could not be received again in the same monastery, since regular order did not allow this.[16] He added, furthermore, that a custom seemed to have arisen that under similar circumstances a monk was not to be received back even after a second fruitless reconciliation.[17] In still another passage this same author made a similar statement regarding an apparently entrenched custom; yet he insisted that the provisions of the rule for the threefold opportunity of reconciliation constituted the law.[18]

Ioannes Andreae (1272–1348) gave the same consideration to

---

tamen est a monasterio projiciendus, sed juxta qualitatem coercendus, ne forte qui poterat per diuturnam poenitudinem emendari, dum projicitur, ore diaboli devoretur."—*Regula Monachorum,* cap. XVI. Yet Faustino Arevalo (d. 1824) in a footnote to this passage added that other Fathers were not in agreement with St. Isidore on this point, and that even St. Isidore made allowance for casting out those who were really incorrigible.—*MPL,* LXXXIII, 885.

[15] "Non cum aliis monachis, sed forte ad serviendum, vel alio modo, dominus noster (Innoc. IV) ; Tu dicas competentibus, puta, aliquibus ergastulis seu camerulis fortibus tamen, ne inde exire valeant"—*ibid.,* n. 9.

[16] "Quod recipiatur in eodem monasterio, regularis ordo non patitur, puta quia scilicet ter exivit, et ter reconciliatus fuit, nec corrigitur, ut in regula supradicta"—*ibid.,* n. 8.

[17] ". . . nam ex quo etiam bis tantum exivit, videtur hoc in consuetudinem deduxisse . . ."—*ibid.,* n. 9.

[18] "Si vero bis exierit, recipere non cogitur ipsum abbas, sicut innuit hic in fin. versi. alioquin, et in regula continetur, secundum Goffre imo dicit regula, ex quo ter exivit. quod dic. ut ne. infra de regulari cap. fin."—*op. cit.,* Lib. I, tit. *de maioritate et obedientia,* c. 10, *Cum in ecclesiis,* n. 8, s.v. *Redeuntes.*

the Rule of St. Benedict, and quoted Hostiensis in regard to the degrees of punishment, and in relation to the treatment of the one who had departed for the third time.[19] He adduced the latter's example of the case that implied grave scandal, which case had special significance in his eyes because of the element of personal knowledge involved;[20] and he then added that those in charge could force another monastery to receive such a monk, even if it were unwilling, in virtue of the words "*auctoritate nostra,*" which otherwise would be devoid of meaning.[21] While this passage conveys the general impression that this author was opposed to complete expulsion, it was only in connection with c. 10, X, *de maioritate et obedientia,* I, 33, that he gave this view its clearest expression. There he stated that the punishment for incorrigibility was indeed separation from the brethren, but that this was to be understood only as regards the common life. For the rest, such members were to be imprisoned, lest disobedience be made an occasion to gain freedom to wander about.[22]

Panormitanus (Abbas Siculus, Nicolaus de Tudeschis, 1386–1453)[23] followed the general interpretation given by the preceding writers.[24] Moreover, he stated that the Constitution of Gregory IX abrogated the earlier provisions of Innocent III,[25] so that thenceforward a recalcitrant monk was subject to imprisonment rather than expulsion.[26]

---

[19] Andreae, *In Quinque Decretalium Libros Novella Commentaria* (4 vols., Venetiis: 1581), III, in c. fin. *de regularibus et trans.,* c. 24 (hereafter cited *Novella Commentaria*).

[20] ". . . forte tot et tanta commisit, quod fratres dicunt communiter quod exibunt, si ille ibi reducatur, ut dicit Hostiensis se de facto vidisse"—*Novella Commentaria, ibid.,* n. 4.

[21] ". . . quia alias esset elusoria, si coerctionem aliquam non haberet . . ." —*loc. cit.*

[22] ". . . quia non comedent cum aliis in refectorio, nec iacebunt in dormitorio, sed detrudentur in carcerem. Si enim de monasterio expellentur, volenti vagari facile esset se facere inobedientem, secundum Petrum et Abbatem"—*Novella Commentaria,* lib. I, tit. 33, c. 10, n. 9, s.v. Consortio.

[23] *Commentaria,* Lib. III, *de regularibus et trans.,* c. 24.

[24] It may here be noted that he furnished a definition of what was meant by "ejected": "Eiectus vero dicitur, quod a suo superiore fuit eiectus a monasterio culpa sua forte exigente."—*Commentaria, ibid.,* n. 2.

[25] c. 6, X, *de statu monachorum,* III, 35; cf. *supra,* p. 27, note 6.

[26] "Credo quod hodie non habet locum haec expulsio a monasterio, c. 6,

In connection with this constitution Panormitanus raised a particular question, perhaps in view of his earlier status as an abbot. It had to do with the words "*eiusdem ordinis,*"[27] and he treated this matter at some length. He granted that the principle announced in these words was easy of application in a centralized group, but pointed out that it was not so in the Benedictine family. For in the latter the various forms of autonomy of the single houses had to be taken into consideration.

Some (e.g., Cistercians, Olivetans, Vallambrosians; and among non-Benedictines: the Canons Regular, especially the Premonstratensians; and Carthusians) already had a certain degree of centralization, so that they became in a stricter sense an order. They had united, and in their statutes placed one head, an abbot or prior general, over the whole institute. Yet, for the most part, *de iure communi,* each monastery had its own independent regimen, and abbot was not subject to abbot. This group offered no difficulty with regard to the understanding of the constitution, for it expressly gave power to such as these to act.[28]

Outside the fold of monastic congregations were a great number of other monasteries—mostly of those religious who were termed "Black Monks" by reason of the color of their habit—not so united as those above, but each an independent unit in itself.[29]

X, *de statu monachorum,* III, 35, sed sit procedendum, prout dicitur in d. c. fi. de reg. Nam illud c. fuit posterius, cum sit Gregorii Noni, et providet circa eiectos, et fugitivos, ut saltem casu, quo licita est expulsio, deputentur tales in ergastulo intra septa monasterii, ne detur occasio vagandi, et dic. ut ibi."—*Commentaria,* Lib. III, tit. *de statu monachorum,* c. 6, n. 13.

[27] Cf. Butler, *Benedictine Monachism* (2. ed., with supplementary notes, New York: Longmans, Green & Co., 1924), chap. XVI, "The Order of St. Benedict," pp. 258–274.

[28] The same was true for those who, though they do not have abbots or priors for superiors, were governed by general chapters. For the Pope gave to those presiding at these chapters the same power as was given to the aforesaid superiors by virtue of the fact that they were at the head of a congregation.—". . . haec litera non solum dat potestatem abbatibus generalibus, sed etiam praesidentibus capitulo."—*Commentaria,* Lib. III, tit. *de regularibus et trans.,* c. 24, n. 2. No doubt the wording was such as to include other forms of religious life emerging at that time. Cf. Funk, *A Manual of Church History,* I, 372–378.

[29] Today most Benedictine Abbeys belong to some Monastic Congregation.

It was in this group that Panormitanus saw a condition that rendered almost impossible the fulfillment of a part of the Pope's command. He stated that the text alone did not offer a solution for the problem, and hence he maintained only what was certain in the matter, offering nothing more than an indication as to the rest.

Every abbot could and had to fulfill the provisions of law as to the seeking out and bringing back of his fugitive or ejected monks,[30] but the abbot of an entirely independent monastery encountered difficulty with certain other provisions of the constitution. For he could not compel the monks of another monastery to receive those who could not be brought back to his own monastery for fear of scandal. Then, too, there was always the added danger in view of these conditions that such an abbot would not always exercise due care in the seeking out of those who had left the monastery or been ejected from it.

Thus Panormitanus made mention of the legal plight which confronted the abbot of an unaffiliated monastery, and stated that his obligation was the same as that of other superiors. While this author did not directly solve the difficulty in the question raised, yet he seemed to think that these very circumstances prompted the Pope to make mention of the abbot general.[31] Thus he hinted that the desirable solution might lie in the forming of monastic congregations, so that in such matters the abbot general would act by authority of the Pope and as his delegate.[32]

For further details on the position of an autonomous monastery in the framework of the congregation cf. Augustine, *A Commentary,* pp. 111–114; Beste, *Introductio in Codicem,* pp. 327–329, under c. 501, n. 3. Cf. also Butler, *Benedictine Monachism,* chap. XV, "Benedictine Polity," pp. 234–257; Bastien, "Conspectus Historico-Juridicus de Regimine Monasterii in Ordine Sancti Benedicti"—*Jus Pontificium,* IX (1929), 296–305; X (1930), 44–55.

30 ". . . nunquid quilibet abbas sui monasterii possit facere contenta hic? Dic, quod potest et debet revocare fugitivos . . . et credo eum peccare, nisi revocet, quamvis hoc non patiatur, quia mens huius constitutionis vendicat sibi locum in quolibet monasterio."—*Commentaria,* Lib. III, tit. *de regularibus et trans.*, c. 24, n. 3.

31 "Sed ideo papa facit mentionem de generale abbate . . ."—*loc. cit.*

32 ". . . sed hoc facit abbas generalis auctoritate domini papae, et sic tamquam delegatus eius . . ."—*loc. cit.*

Attention must be given to the fact that Panormitanus, throughout his treatment of this matter, made frequent mention of an *abbot general.* He even made it appear that the Pope had done the same. But a brief glance at the document [33] will give no evidence of the mention of such an official. Panormitanus did not refer to such an official in his brief treatment of the component parts of the constitution, but he consistently used the title "*abbas generalis*" in his commentary. He offered no explanation for the use of the terminology, and cited no authority. He seemed simply to take it as a matter of common parlance and understanding. Opportunity offered itself in the form of the words "*secundum statutum concilii generalis,*" but he passed it by without comment. Hostiensis, on the other hand, had noted that he would speak more at length on it when he would come to consider that very "*statutum*" which had been included in Gregory's Decretals.[34]

It has already been intimated that centuries came and went without any attempt on a large scale to modify the primeval isolation of the individual houses of the Black Monks. The only general legislation of the Church concerning the formation and organization of monastic congregations on the part of Black Monk monasteries came in the IV General Council of the Lateran, held under Innocent III in 1215. In canon 12 (*In singulis*)[35] it decreed that in each kingdom or province the Black Monks' abbots or conventual priors should every three years meet together in chapter.

Four abbots were to be chosen as presidents of the chapter, with a special provision that none should take upon himself any authority of superior. The agenda of the meeting were to be centered on matters of improvement regarding the regular observance. Whatever was agreed upon, provided that it met the approval of all the presidents, was to be observed without appeal. Provisions were also made for visitations and corrections. This system sketched out by the Council satisfied a need long felt as

[33] Cf. *supra,* p. 28, note 8.

[34] Hostiensis—*Commentaria in Quinque Libros Decretalium,* Lib. III, cap. VII, *de statu monachorum, etc.,* pp. 134–135.

[35] Mansi, XXII, 999–1002; taken into the Decretals of Gregory in c. 7, X, *de statu monachorum, etc.,* III, 35.

the outcome of practical experience. Such a loose union, whilst preserving for each monastery the ancient Benedictine principle of family autonomy, was able to do much for mutual support and assistance.[36]

Somewhat later (1336) the Bull of Benedict XII, *Summi Magistri,*[37] commonly but incorrectly termed "*Benedictina,*" supplemented the Council's enactment as to working details, but left principles untouched. However, this plan did not furnish much hope of success on the continent, though it fared better in England.[38] Yet, antedating these enactments by a whole century, certain monastic congregations, forerunners of the modern, were working for a closer bond of union. So it may be that Panormitanus belonged to this latter group, and as a consequence used terms common in their ranks. While he recognized the difficulties of those monasteries which were not centrally organized, it was but natural that he should suggest the use of such means as proved feasible for confederated monasteries.

Panormitanus further pointed out that there were cases in which an ejected monk was no longer to be received back in the same monastery. He cited as an example the norm in chapter 29 of St. Benedict's Rule, namely, that one who had departed three times was no longer to be received back into the monastic family.[39] However, he added that Gregory's norm *changed* this in that the monk was to be received back, but not as before, for no longer was he to be with the rest of the monks, but in a place apart, where he would have no opportunity for wandering about or for becoming a source of infection for others.[40]

---

[36] Butler, *Benedictine Monachism,* chap. XV, "Benedictine Polity."

[37] Benedictus XII, bulla *Summi Magistri,* 20 iun. 1336—*Bullarum Diplomatum et Privilegiorum Sanctorum Romanorum Pontificum Taurinensis Editio* (24 tomes in 25 vols., Augustae Taurinorum, 1857–1872), IV, 347–387 (hereafter cited *BRT*).

[38] Butler, *Benedictine Monachism,* p. 241.

[39] "Nam in certo casu fugitivi et eiecti non debent recipi amplius in eisdem monasteriis. Pone exemplum in ordine S. Benedicti: nam ter fugiens, non est amplius recipiendus. Sed iste textus providet ne habeat occasionem vagandi; quod recipiatur in proprio monasterio, non tamen quod vivat cum aliis, sed stabit in arcto loco, ut in ergastulo seu in arcta camera."—*Commentaria,* Lib. III, tit. *de regularibus et trans.,* c. 24, n. 1.

[40] Bastien ("De Evolutione Historico-Juridica Processus Dimissionis,"

In conclusion, Panormitanus laid special stress on the words "*Auctoritate nostra,*"[41] which in his estimation had been added to take care of the particular case in which the provisions of the rule would not allow one to be taken back again. Only in this case was it necessary to recur to the authority of the Pope, since the provisions of the rules remained in force and were left unchanged as to other matters. Thus he limited the extension of these words to the setting in which they were found in Gregory's Constitution, and assured superiors that, with this one exception, their powers remained the same as they had been before, regardless of the interpretation some authors had given to these words.

Article 3. Constitutions, Privileges, and Later Writers

Though the sources are lacking in general norms by which the discipline of dismissal would be set in order as a legal institute, nevertheless this discipline was being firmly established, either through papal approbation of the constitutions of religious orders,[42] or through papal indults granting privileges of expulsion to certain orders. These privileges were afterwards shared by other institutes on the basis of the general intercommunication of privileges.[43] Chief among these privileges were those given to

---

Jus Pontificium, XI, 1931, 23) makes the following observation: "Attamen circa saec. XIII alia invaluit iurisprudentia, scilicet non expellendi incorrigibiles, sed potius eos incarcerandi in ergastulo . . . ," and a little farther on adds: "Aliud testimonium praebent *Statuta Nova Ordinis Cartusiensis, an. 1368*—p. II, c. IX, n. 5: 'Nullus pro quocumque crimine de Ordine expellatur, sed pro modo criminis et delicti carceri perpetuo vel ad tempus intrudatur,'—and in a footnote—'Ad haec D. Le Masson, *Disciplina Ordinis Cartusiensis,* editio Monstralii, 1894, animadvertit: 'Hic mutari incipit usus antiquus expellendi ab ordine eos, qui in crimen aliquod inciderent. Unde coniicimus circa illa tempora mutari etiam coepisse in Ecclesia usum illum expulsionis e monasterio.'"

[41] "Et pondera, quia haec verba fuerunt adiecta solum in eo casu, quo non poterant isti recipi secundum provisionem regulae; unde fuit opus, quod auctoritas Papae intercederet, reliqua vero puto, quod iure ipsorum possunt superiores hoc facere, per iura superius allegata et sic tempera dicta Doctorum hic."—*Commentaria,* Lib. III, tit. *de regularibus et trans.,* c. 24, n. 4.

[42] E.g., Dominicans, Franciscans, Carthusians. Cf. *supra,* pp. 26–27.

[43] Cf. J. B. Confettio, *Privilegiorum Sacrorum Ordinum Fratrum Mendicantium et non Mendicantium Collectio* (Postrema Editio, Venetiis, 1616),

the Friars Minor by Popes Innocent IV (1243–1254)[44] and Alexander VI (1492–1503).[45]

The latter's concession to the General and Provincial Superiors of the Friars Minor marked an important stage of the development of dismissal. By this indult the power of discharging incorrigible subjects was granted not only to the supreme moderator and his vicar (as provided by Innocent IV), but also to provincial superiors when these had the consent of the majority of their consulters.[46] Through the factor of the intercommunication of privileges this norm resulted in a kind of common discipline among numerous other institutes, so that it soon obtained the force of a general practice with some degree of canonical sanction.[47]

The Council of Trent (1545–1563) in Session XXV, *de regularibus et monialibus,* issued a number of decrees on the reform of religious life, but it remained silent on the matter of dismissal. However, during this time under Pius IV (1559–1565) the Sacred Congregation of the Council issued several decrees to the Procurators General of the Orders of Regulars, stating that they should imprison delinquent monks within the monastery, and *not expel* them, even when their correction was despaired of.[48] Soon

---

cap. V, *De Communione privilegiorum inter omnes Mendicantium Ordines,* pp. 294–296 (hereafter cited *Privilegiorum Collectio*); Matulenas, *Communication, A Source of Privilege,* The Catholic University of America Canon Law Studies, n. 183 (Washington, D. C.: The Catholic University of America Press, 1943).

[44] Innocentius IV, const. *Ordinem vestrum,* 14 nov. 1245—*BRT,* III, 520.

[45] Cf. Roderico, *Quaestiones Regulares seu Resolutiones Quaestionum Regularium* (Lugduni, 1634), Resolutio LVII, *De Eiectis, seu Expulsis a Religione,* pp. 415 sq. (hereafter cited *Quaestiones Regulares*); Tabera, "De Dimissione Religiosorum,"—*CpR,* XI (1930), 280, nota 29.

[46] Alexander VI, litt. apost., *Cum sicut nobis,* 15 iun. 1501—apud Confettio, *Privilegiorum Collectio,* p. 92.

[47] Cf. Tabera, "De Dimissione Religiosorum,"—*CpR,* XI (1930), 280.

[48] Cf. S. Pallottini, *Collectio Omnium Conclusionum et Resolutionum Quae in Causis Propositis apud Sacram Congregationem Cardinalium S. Concilii Tridentini Interpretum Prodierunt ab eius institutione anno MDLXIV ad MDCCLX, distinctis titulis alphabetico ordine per materias* digestas (18 vols., Romae: 1868–1895), XV, s.v. "Regulares," § I—"Quoad Eiectionem," n. 35 (hereafter cited Pallottini); Fagnanus, *Commentaria in Quinque Libros Decretalium* (4 vols., Venetiis, 1709), Lib. III,

afterwards the Friars Minor Conventual, in a general chapter held for the reform of their order, adopted this provision in a declaration on chapter VII of their rule, and as such it received the approbation of Pius IV.[49]

However, the difficulties that soon arose with such a system again prompted the religious superiors to petition the Holy See for certain privileges in the matter of expulsion. Thus, Pius V (1566–1572), the immediate successor of Pius IV, in the very first year of his pontificate granted such a privilege to the Order of St. Jerome in Spain. This indult was not as liberal as those granted before the time of Pius IV. Though it again conceded prelates the right to cast out incorrigibles, it now limited the exercise of this power to the *Prior General* under the condition that he proceed with the counsel of the brethren.

The concession was made in view of the constitutions which provided that the said superior should have outside of the general chapter the same powers which that body had when it was in session.[50] No mention was made of other lesser prelates—provincials, priors, guardians, etc.—and so *ex iure communi* they were powerless in this matter. They could be delegated by the Prior General. Nevertheless, no general rule can be given in this matter, for the special rights and privileges granted at this time to various religious groups must be considered separately. Each

tit. XXXI, c. 24, n. 36 (hereafter cited *Commentaria*); Benedictus XIV, *De Synodo Diocesana* (2. ed., 2 vols., Parmae, 1764), Lib. XIII, c. XI, n. XV.

[49] Pius IV, const. *Sedis Apostolicae copiosa benignitas,* 17 sept. 1565—". . . Incorrigibiles, in capitulis generalibus et provincialibus publice puniantur. Quod si neque hoc modo ad mentem revocari poterunt, ut bene honesteque vivere velint, suspendantur a divinis, et laicalem ducant vitam, ac serviant monasterio tamquam laici. *Et si perseveraverint incorrigibiles esse, perpetuis carceribus mancipentur.*"—*BRT,* VII, 411. Italics inserted by the present writer.

[50] Pius V, 1566—"Considerans quod Prior Generalis per constitutiones dicti ordinis habet omnimodam et ordinariam potestatem, quam ipsum Capitulum generale, tempore quo celebratur habet, Priori Generali concessit facultatem relegandi, dum tamen haec omnia faciat de consilio fratrum."—Apud Suarez, *De Religione,* tract. VIII, lib. III, c. IV, n. 19; cf. Roderico, *Quaestiones Regulares,* Resolutio LVII, n. 3.

community observed the institute approved for it by the Church.[51]

Finally, in 1596 the Holy See expressed its mind on this matter in stating that the right of expulsion should not be denied to religious superiors when they acted according to the norms of their rules which had been approved by the Apostolic See.[52]

Meanwhile, authors and commentators were forming and shaping an integral discipline on dismissal, though still disputing many relative points. Their conclusions were based on the privileges granted during this time by the Holy See, on the interpretations of the older monastic norms of expulsion, and on the fundamental notions of the religious life. It was their common opinion that religious could be expelled only in cases of incorrigibility; but what precisely constituted the nature and requisites of this incorrigibility was a controverted question. Practically all agreed that it was verified in those cases in which corrections and warnings had proved futile.

Thus, Suarez (d. 1617) stated that a just cause for expulsion was had when following conditions were present: (a) a grave, external sin, when of its very nature it occasioned scandal to others and brought infamy to religion; and (b) a previous warning. He further added that the element of correction, namely, of what nature it should be and how often to be administered, was left to the judgment of the superior, since no definite and certain rule was in vogue.[53] In the commission of the more heinous delicts (generally those which in civil law were penalized with capital punishment), he also admitted a so-called ***presumed incorrigibility,*** for which the delinquent religious could be lawfully discharged immediately and without warning.[54]

---

[51] Suarez, *De Religione,* tract. VIII, lib. III, c. IV, n. 20.

[52] S. C. Ep. et Reg., *Lisbonen,* 22 ian. 1596—*Fontes,* n. 1547. According to the testimony of Bastien (1866–1940), this same Congregation instituted a criminal process for expelling the rebellious and contumacious: ". . . post Tridentinum tamen processus quidem criminalis, praesertim ob enormia delicta, institutus fuit, sed S. C. Episc. et Regul. reservatus, uti constat ex plurimis processibus in Tabulario huius S. Congregationis asservatis."—"De Dimissione Religiosorum," *Jus Pontificium,* XI (1931), 24.

[53] Suarez, *De Religione,* tract. VIII, lib. III, c. IV, nn. 9–10.

[54] Suarez, *De Religione,* tract. VIII, lib. III, c. IV, n. 11; Castropalao, *Opus Morale* (7 vols. in 3, noviss. ed., Lugduni, 1682), Pars Tertia, Tract.

Sanchez (d. 1610) not only held the doctrine regarding the requisite of incorrigibility in conformity with the other authors of his time,[55] but also showed its application to incorrigible *nuns*. As a result of his investigation he reached the conclusion that the ancient discipline was entirely opposed to the expulsion of nuns. While admitting that *in rigore iuris* nuns were just as much subject to expulsion as men religious, yet he found that *in praxi* this means was not used; accordingly he concluded that each case should be referred to the Holy See.[56]

XVI, Disput. IV, Punctum XIX, n. 7; cf. Tabera, "De Dimissione Religiosorum"—*CpR,* XI (1930), 411–412. Nevertheless this was never understood as an *ipso facto* effective dismissal, and later authors were fairly unanimous in denying this incorrigibility as being presumed by law.

[55] Sanchez, *Opus Morale in Praecepta Decalogi* (2 vols., Antverpiae, 1631-1637), lib. VI, c. 9, nn. 3–5.

[56] ". . . nullatenus auderem consulere Praelato alicui, ut id inconsulto Romano Pontifice, aut eius Nuntio efficeret, quod fit res nova et inusitata . . ."—Sanchez, *ibid.,* n. 6; Roderico, *Quaestiones Regulares,* Resolutio LVII, n. 3; *Collectanea in Usum Secretariae Sacrae Congregationis Episcoporum et Regularium* (ed. noviss. A. Bizzarri, Romae, 1885), p. 460 (hereafter cited *Collectanea*). The last two, Roderico and Bizzarri, made mention of a privilege granted to the Cistercians by Innocent IV, namely, to cast out nuns who proved incorrigible. Roderico mentioned it as a fact; but in Bizzarri the S. C. of Bishops and Regulars on Jan. 15, 1841, stated that such an indult could not have had any juridical force after the Council of Trent because of the stricter norm which the Council had enacted regarding the cloister of nuns.

CHAPTER IV

URBAN VIII TO PIUS IX

Article 1. The Decree "Sacra Congregatio" of Urban VIII

As has been intimated, the Decree of Pius IV[1] was not in favor among Regulars. Its provisions worked a great hardship on the religious superiors. In many cases the result that it was expected to achieve—the amendment of the delinquent—was not forthcoming. In fact, it opened the way to greater evils, namely, to despair on the part of the imprisoned on the one hand, and to laxity on the part of superiors who tired of constant vigilance and inconveniences on the other. Moreover, at the turn of the century, a bitter controversy raged as to whether the Decretal of Gregory IX and the Decree of Pius IV had ever been received in use, and if not, whether it was fitting that they should be urged in practice.

The Regulars adduced many reasons against such a use both in the past and also for the present. In these circumstances the Procurators General of the Orders presented new petitions, asking that the condition of the incorrigibles and the burdens imposed on superiors in regard to vigilance should both be taken care of in some more befitting manner. The Sacred Congregation of the Council, having maturely and diligently discussed the matter, and with the approval of Pope Urban VIII (1623–1644), issued the Decree *Sacra Congregatio* on Sept. 21, 1624.[2]

This decree had the effect of reorganizing, in an authentic manner, the mass of norms concerning dismissal that had evolved from particular constitutions and privileges. Thenceforth no member of an order could be expelled unless all the conditions postulated by the *common*[3] law for proving him truly incor-

[1] Cf. *supra*, p. 38.

[2] Van Espen, *Jus Ecclesiasticum Universum*, Tom. I, pars I, tit. XXVII, cap. VII, nn. VIII–IX.

[3] Cf. *supra*, p. 39.

rigible were verified, and, in addition, a one year period of incarceration, spent in fasting and penance within the monastery confines, had been observed.[4]

Only after a use of this latter means had shown a monk's persistent contumacy, could a formal trial be held to determine whether the guilty religious might be expelled. There was no obligation to expel such a one; and so it was left to the option of the superior either to continue to detain him in prison, or to proceed to expulsion. This power to expel incorrigibles was restricted to the general, who in this matter had to act with the counsel and assent of six fathers chosen from among the seniors in attendance at the chapter.[5]

The decree renewed the Constitution of Gregory IX, which demanded that the superiors search for their expelled subjects at least annually.[6] Moreover, it declared that this Constitution was of obligation even as regards those who had been justly and finally expelled according to the juridic norms, as long as there was evident hope of their emendation, based at least on the testimonial letters of the ordinary. The Sacred Congregation also imposed a serious obligation on the consciences of the ordinaries to respect truthfulness in the granting of these testimonial letters.[7]

The decree concluded by stating that no matter what was said in the constitutions of the various religious orders, whether mendicant or non-mendicant, no matter what was said in the constitu-

---

[4] S. C. C., decr. *Sacra Congregatio,* 21 sept. 1624, § 6: "Ad haec, ut imposterum e Religionibus nullus legitime professus eiici possit, nisi sit vere incorrigibilis: vere autem incorrigibilis minime censeatur, nisi non solum concurrant ea omnia, quae ad hoc ex iuris communis dispositione requiruntur, sublatis hac in parte Statutis, et Constitutionibus cuiusque Religionis, et Ordinis, etiam a Sede Apostolica approbatis, et confirmatis: verum etiam unius anni spatio in ieiunio, et poenitentia probetur in carceribus; proindeque unaquaeque Religio privatos habeat carceres in qualibet saltem Provincia."—*Fontes,* n. 2454; Ferraris, *Prompta Bibliotheca,* s.v. "Ejicere, eiecti a religione," n. 2.

[5] S. C. C., *loc. cit.:* "Elapso autem anno . . . eiici tandem potest, sed ab ipsomet Generali tantum de consilio, et assensu sex Patrum ex gravioribus Religionis eligendis in singulis Capitulis, vel congregationibus generalibus; . . ."—*Fontes,* n. 2454.

[6] Cf. *supra,* p. 28.

[7] S. C. C., decr. *Sacra Congregatio,* 21 sept. 1624, § 11.—*Fontes,* n. 2454.

tions of monastic congregations, of convents, of houses, or of any of the places of regulars, all were bound to follow its regulations, notwithstanding any contrary customs, exemptions, indults and privileges, however they might have been approved. As an added precaution it enacted that if anyone did anything contrary to the prescripts of this decree, or altered them in any way, or undermined them, he *ipso facto* incurred the privation of all offices, of both active and passive electoral rights, and the perpetual incapacity for these in the future. The remission of these penalties was reserved to the Holy See, and no religious superior had any power to dispense from them.[8]

This decree was in turn the subject of further interpretations on the part of the same Sacred Congregation.[9] Thus, in the very next year the Sacred Congregation, in answer to a doubt, stated that an incorrigible religious was not to be cast out immediately at the completion of the year of imprisonment, but only then if at length he did not come to a better state of mind, and obdurately persisted in his contumacy.[10]

Soon after the appearance of this decree, various opinions were advanced as to the sense in which a year of imprisonment should be understood. In answer to the inquiry of the General of the Minims, the Sacred Congregation replied on November 13, 1632, that the year must be entire;[11] and a year later stated that a religious who had fled from prison could not for that reason be cast out, but was to be punished for this delict, by being brought back to prison to be detained in irons.[12]

Further, in 1648 the Sacred Congregation decreed that the year of imprisonment could not be curtailed, and hence no moderation was to be sought or undertaken.[13] In 1653 it again took up this matter and stated that the year of imprisonment had to be con-

---

[8] *Ibid.*, § 14.—*Fontes*, n. 2454.

[9] Cf. S. C. C. in re particular cases—Pallottini, XV, s.v. "Regulares," § I—"Quoad Eiectionem," n. 1 *sqq.*

[10] S. C. C., *Dubium*—9 aug. 1625—Pallottini, *ibid.*, n. 23.

[11] S. C. C., *in Minimorum,* 13 nov. 1632—Pallottini, *ibid.*, n. 24.

[12] S. C. C., *in Minimorum,* 13 nov. 1633—Pallottini, *ibid.*, n. 19.

[13] S. C. C., *in Hispaniorum et Indiarum,* 16 aug. 1648—Pallottini, *ibid.*, n. 25.

tinuous, and hence it did not suffice that one had been detained in prison at various times for the combined length of a year.[14] Finally, in 1689 it added that a religious could not be cast out as incorrigible, even if all other presuppositions were present, if an entire continuous year had not been served before the flight of the imprisoned one.[15]

The Sacred Congregation also issued replies with regard to the superior competent in the matter of effecting the imprisonment and the dismissal. Thus, in 1653 it denied the generals the right to delegate to their provincials, commissaries or vicars general the power of effecting the dismissal.[16] In the same decree it further stated that the six members of the monastic chapter who were to pass the sentence of dismissal on an incorrigible religious along with the general could not be elected outside the general chapter. If nevertheless they were so elected, then recourse to the Holy See became necessary if a dismissal of the incorrigible religious was contemplated.[17]

Article 2. The Canonists of the Classical Period

In the period between the Council of Trent and the end of the eighteenth century, the authors continued to comment on the Decretals of Gregory IX, but in doing so they gradually evolved a divergent doctrine. This divergency was occasioned by the later developments in the law which called for a new interpretation in the light of the altered application of the principles involved.[18]

In their treatment of c. 24, X, *de regularibus et transeuntibus ad religionem,* III, 31, these authors made brief references to the teaching of the earlier decretalists.[19] These latter were under-

[14] S. C. C., *in Ordinis Captivorum,* 21 iun. 1653—Pallottini, *ibid.,* n. 27.

[15] S. C. C., *Dubium Eiectionis Incorrigibilium,* 17 dec. 1689—Pallottini, *ibid.,* n. 20.

[16] S. C. C., *in Regularium Ord. Captivorum,* 21 iun. 1653—Pallottini, *ibid.,* n. 17.

[17] S. C. C., *in Regularium Ord. Captivorum,* 21 iun. 1653—Pallottini, *ibid.,* n. 28.

[18] Wernz, *Ius Decretalium,* I, n. 314 sq.; Maroto, *Institutiones Iuris Canonici ad Normam Novi Codicis* (2 vols., Romae, 1918–1919), I, n. 140 (hereafter cited *Institutiones*).

[19] Cf. *supra,* Chapter III, Article 2, pp. 29–36.

stood by them to have considered this law as an innovation in regard to the norm for dismissal as previously observed in accordance with the prescriptions of monastic rules, so that a religious who in line with the earlier discipline was to be cast out, thereafter was rather to be placed in confinement.[20] However, it should be noted that, though the earlier decretalists implied that this norm of Gregory IX was quite consonant with the practice of St. Benedict and the other monastic rules,[21] Fagnanus (1598–1678)[22] and Van Espen (1646–1728),[23] on the contrary, interpreted it as taking away the provisions of the rule.[24]

Some of the authors[25] held that the Constitution of Gregory IX applied only to those who were *unjustly* ejected or who had

---

[20] Cf. Barbosa, *Collectanea Doctorum tam veterum quam Recentiorum in Ius Pontificium Universum* (6 vols., Lugduni, 1669), Lib. III, tit. XXXV, c. 6, n. 6 (hereafter cited *Collectanea Doctorum*); Gonzalez-Tellez, *Commentaria Perpetua in Singulos Textus quinque Librorum Decretalium* (5 tomes in 4 vols., Venetiis, 1699), lib. III, tit. XXXI, c. XXIV, n. 7 (hereafter cited *Commentaria Perpetua*); Fagnanus, *Commentaria*, Lib. III, tit. XXXI, c. 24, nn. 37–38. In n. 38 Fagnanus summed up his findings as follows: "Ex quibus patet jura loquentia de expulsione Regularium non esse accipienda de expulsione e monasterio, seu ab ordine, ita ut in saeculo vivant; sed a communione et commercio aliorum regularium tantum." Cf. also Reiffenstuel, *Jus Canonicum Universum*, lib. III, tit. XXXI, n. 226; Van Espen, *Jus Ecclesiasticum Universum*, Tom. I, pars I, tit. XXVII, c. VII, n. VI; Schmalzgrueber, *Ius Ecclesiasticum Universum*, lib. III, tit. XXXI, n. 245.

[21] Cf. *supra*, p. 29–31.

[22] *Commentaria*, Lib. III, tit. XXXI, c. 24, n. 43.

[23] *Jus Ecclesiasticum Universum*, Tom. I, pars I, tit. XXVII, c. VII, n. 7; tit. XXXI, c. III, n. 32.

[24] Van Espen (*Jus Ecclesiasticum Universum*, Tom. I, pars I, tit. XXXI, c. III, n. XXXII) quoted with approval the words of Bohier (d. 1380): "'Oportet supplere hodie ubicumque invenitur in Regula, *Monachus projicitur vel expellatur a monasterio:* id est *retrudatur in ergastulum,* sive in carcerem, sive in aliud monasterium ad agendam poenitentiam transmittatur.'"

[25] E.g., Barbosa, *Collectanea Doctorum*, Lib. III, tit. XXXI, c. 24, n. 3; Gonzalez-Tellez, *Commentaria Perpetua*, lib. III, tit. XXXI, c. XXIV, n. 9; Engel, *Collegium Universi Iuris Canonici* (ed. nona; post omnes alias recognita et locupletata; cui nunc primum adjectae sunt annotationes Caspari Barthel, Beneventi, 1760), Lib. III, tit. XXXI, n. 56.

shown sufficient emendation; but Fagnanus [26] vigorously opposed this view, and strove to show that the only logical application could be in regard to those who had been *justly* cast forth. He based his argument on the contention that superiors are always in justice bound to seek out those who were unjustly dismissed, and to do so at once; hence the law could not have reference to the obligation of seeking out and recalling this latter class.

Fagnanus, as Secretary of the Sacred Congregation of the Council, was also active in the controversy of the Regulars concerning the Constitution of Gregory IX.[27] He was painstaking in his presentation and consideration of the arguments adduced by the Regulars, but he felt constrained to rebuke them for their way of reasoning. For he maintained that the canons dealt only with separation from the common life, and not at all with the expulsion from the monastery, as the Regulars interpreted it.[28] His entire treatise on this point is a review of opinions of the past [29] and an account of the concessions and compromises made by both sides in the preparation of the decree *Sacra Congregatio* of Urban VIII (1623–1644).[30] With the appearance of this decree the controversy came to an end.[31]

Once again the teaching that even a professed religious could be expelled from the order for a legitimate cause became unanimous.[32] Hence the authors again sought to establish just

[26] *Commentaria,* Lib. III, tit. XXXI, c. 24, nn. 17–36, especially nn. 17 and 31.

[27] Cf. *supra,* p. 41.

[28] Fagnanus, *Commentaria,* lib. III, tit. XXXI, c. 24, n. 37: "Videntur maximi ponderis quae a Regularibus objiciuntur, sed facile diluuntur omnia, si haec materia ejectionis, seu expulsionis religiosorum intelligatur juxta mentem Sacrorum Canonum, non autem eo modo, quo eam accipiunt Regulares. Nam ex juris dispositione quotiescumque permittitur, ut Regulares ejiciantur, hoc est intelligendum de illa ejectione, quae fit a societate et consortio aliorum Regularium, non autem de expulsione a Monasterio, seu a Religione, quemadmodum Regulares intelligunt."

[29] *Ibid.,* nn. 1–50.

[30] *Ibid.,* nn. 52–70.

[31] Reiffenstuel, *Jus Canonicum Universum,* lib. III, tit. XXXI, n. 227.

[32] Barbosa, *Collectanea Doctorum,* lib. III, tit. XXXI, c. 24, nn. 5 and 23; Gonzalez-Tellez, *Commentaria Perpetua,* lib. III, tit. XXXI, c. XXIV, n. 9; Engel, *Collegium Universi Iuris Canonici,* Lib. III, tit. XXXI, n. 56;

what was needed to constitute the incorrigibility postulated in the law. Thus Reiffenstuel (1642–1703)[33] noted three points: (a) a grave delict; (b) a public delict, that is, one of such a nature that it be known not only among the fellow religious, but also to outsiders, so that such a one could not, without infamy to the monastery, be kept in the community; and (c) a threefold admonition, correction and punishment. Special stress was laid on the last point as the only means for gauging the presence of a real incorrigibility. Schmalzgrueber (1663–1735)[34] likewise required an incorrigibility that was notorious, and one that stood revealed as such by *three* admonitions which had remained without the desired results.

Van Espen,[35] on the other hand, in keeping with his earlier leanings as indicated above, denied altogether the right of an institute to expel an incorrigible member,[36] and indicated rather that the remedy for the evil lay in stricter requirements for *admission* to the religious state.[37] From what has been said above,[38] it is evident that he was wrong in denying to an institute the right to expel incorrigible monks. However, while he was following the general teaching in insisting on stricter requirements for entrance to the novitiate and profession, he failed to give credit where it was due. This last mentioned matter was always insisted upon by the Sacred Congregation of the Council.

Fagnanus, *Commentaria,* lib. III, tit. XXXI, c. 24, nn. 59–60; Reiffenstuel, *Jus Canonicum Universum,* lib. III, tit. XXXI, n. 226; Van Espen, *Jus Ecclesiasticum Universum,* Tom. I, pars I, tit. XXVII, c. VII, n. 9, though in n. 10 he states that he doubts whether it is suited to the customs of the times, or at least to his own regions; Schmalzgrueber, *Ius Ecclesiasticum Universum,* Lib. III, tit. XXXI, c. III, n. 246.

[33] *Jus Canonicum Universum,* lib. III, tit. XXXI, nn. 228–230.

[34] *Ius Ecclesiasticum Universum,* Lib. III, tit. XXXI, n. 247.

[35] *Jus Ecclesiasticum Universum,* Tom. I, pars I, tit. XXVII, c. VII, n. 14.

[36] "Denique cum moderna disciplina non permittat monachos rebelles ipsamque Religionem quantumcumque turbantes expellere, et a Congregatione omnino dimittere . . ."—*loc. cit.*

[37] ". . . major merito hodie in recipiendis ad monasticam professionem cura, diligentiusque atque exactius examen et probatio adhibenda sunt quam olim, dum similis e Monasterio ejicere licebat. . . ."—*Ibid.,* n. 14.

[38] Cf. *supra,* p. 46.

In fact, in issuing the decree of Urban VIII, the Sacred Congregation made it a matter of primary concern to renew the decrees of Clement VIII on the novitiate.[39]

Article 3. The Decree "Instantibus" of Innocent XII

The norms set down by Urban VIII in his decree *Sacra Congregatio* were slightly altered, after a period of seventy years, by Innocent XII (1691–1700). Individual groups had obtained some mitigations earlier, but at this time the procurators general of the religious orders in a concerted effort petitioned the Sacred Congregation to modify the provisions of Urban's decree. It was their avowed purpose to obtain an easier manner of casting out incorrigible religious, and the reasons advanced were similar to those presented under Urban VIII. The Sacred Congregation, upon mature deliberation and with the approval and authority of the pope, acceded to their wishes in the decree *Instantibus* of July 24, 1694.[40]

This decree[41] renewed for the most part the earlier legislation of the decree *Sacra Congregatio,* but it also introduced some opportune changes in the matter of expulsion. Thus, (a) the year of incarceration to prove incorrigibility was reduced to a period of six months;[42] (b) the faculty of trying cases of expulsion was extended to the provincial superiors, who in this matter were

---

[39] S. C. C., decr. *Sacra Congregatio,* 21 sept. 1624, § 1—*Fontes,* n. 2454. The decrees of Clement VIII in question are: Const. *Regularis disciplinae,* 12 mart. 1596—*Fontes,* n. 183; decr. *Sanctissimus,* 20 iun. 1599—*Fontes,* n. 186; decr. *Nullus omnino,* 25 iul. 1599—*Fontes,* n. 187; const. *Cum ad regularem,* 19 mart. 1603—*Fontes,* n. 189.

[40] S. C. C., decr. *Instantibus,* 24 iul. 1694—*Fontes,* n. 2942; Ferraris, *Prompta Bibliotheca,* s.v. "Ejecti a Religione," n. 3. It may here be noted that several authors give March 1, 1693, as the date of this decree: thus, Pallottini, *XV, n. I Regulares quoad Eiectionem, 26, 29;* De Ameno, *Opera Omnia* (3 tomes, Romae, 1753–54), Tom. II, *De Incorrigibilium Expulsione,* Pars I, *De Incorrigibili expellendo,* Pars II, *Formularium Processus,* Pars III, *De Statu Expulsorum*—Pars I, nn. 30–35, *Decretum de Ejectis et Eijiciendis* (hereafter cited *De Incorrigibilium Expulsione*), though at the end of the decree he gives as the date 24 iul. 1694; Benedictus XIV, *De Synodo Dioecesana,* lib. XIII, c. XI, n. XVI.

[41] *Ibid.,* nn. 1 and 5.

[42] *Ibid.,* n. 2.

required to act with the counsel and consent of six religious of their province chosen in the chapter and approved by the general;[43] and (c) for the future the process was to be regulated according to the laws and usages of the respective orders, until such time that the Sacred Congregation should provide otherwise.[44]

Later pontiffs did indeed grant indults to certain institutes for an easier and more expeditious method of expulsion; nevertheless the substance of the law of Innocent XII remained unchanged.[45]

The authors of the eighteenth century raised many questions in regard to the interpretation of the decrees of Urban VIII and Innocent XII. De Ameno in his treatise had the set purpose of giving religious superiors a thorough understanding not only of the practice of expulsion, but also of the theory, so that they might do all things in accordance with the requirements of law, and thus more easily render an account for their acts.[46] Accordingly he outlined the teaching of the common law along with the new decrees of the Apostolic See and the rescripts of the Sacred Congregation,[47] and then presented a full exposition of the various formularies that had to be used in the process of dismissal as demanded by the decree of Innocent XII.[48]

De Ameno, Ferraris (d. ca. 1763), and others quoted by them, were in agreement in assigning five requisites for establishing the incorrigibility that was postulated as a condition for expulsion.[49] The first was the relapse into a grave crime on the part of the one to be expelled; the second was the repeated warning and repeated punishment inflicted on the guilty party for his correction; the third was the strict adherence to the procedural form as instituted according to the Order's constitutions on expulsion; the fourth was the formal imprisonment accompanied with fast-

---

[43] *Ibid.*, n. 3.

[44] *Ibid.*, n. 4.

[45] Benedictus XIV, *De Synodo Dioecesana,* lib. XIII, c. XI, n. XIX.

[46] De Ameno, *De Incorrigibilium Expulsione,* Pars I, n. 1.

[47] *Ibid.*, Pars I.

[48] *Ibid.*, Pars II.

[49] De Ameno, *De Incorrigibilium Expulsione,* Pars I, q. IV; Ferraris, *Prompta Bibliotheca,* s.v. "Ejecti a Religione," n. 4.

ing and penance; and the fifth was the eventual but evident incorrigibility in the delict.[50]

According to these authors, a relapse was manifested not only when a religious lapsed time upon time into the same crime, but also when he fell repeatedly into crimes specifically distinct from one another.[51] Moreover, the warning and the punishment had to be three times administered in due form, *de forma legis* as De Ameno insisted, and only after this could the superiors resort to the imprisonment of the delinquent monk.[52] Hence superiors could not immediately invoke the process which was instituted in law for the sake of establishing the fact of incorrigibility, but first had to be certain—through documents or otherwise—of the presence of crimes and of the corrections administered to their perpetrators.

If evidence of these facts was had, then the competent superior together with his co-judges further had to investigate whether there was a moral continuance in the subject's evil ways, which continuity would indicate a lack of betterment in the delinquent's morals, and the consequent need of separating him from the other members of the community.[53] If matters were found to be so, then the superiors were to test his incorrigibility through six months of incarceration. This was not understood to imply nothing more than a mere detention; rather, the imprisonment was to be accompanied with positive elements of trial.

The necessarily continuous and complete lapse of this time was fully discussed by the authors.[54] Yet, even at completion of the term of imprisonment the delinquent's expulsion was not to take place immediately; some additional time was to be allowed to pass before his incorrigibility was to be established definitively. Finally, if even the means of imprisonment failed in its desired result, then the subject not only could be, but also was to be, expelled by the competent superiors observing the due form in this procedure.[55]

---

[50] *Loc. cit.*

[51] De Ameno, *ibid.*, q. VII; Ferraris, *ibid.*, n. 5.

[52] De Ameno, *ibid.*, p. VI, nn. 62, 64, q. IX, n. 91; Ferraris, *ibid.*, nn. 6, 14.

[53] De Ameno, *ibid.*, qq. VIII–XII; Ferraris, *ibid.*, nn. 7, 31–37.

[54] De Ameno, *ibid.*, q. XIII; Ferraris, *ibid.*, nn. 8–12.

[55] De Ameno, *ibid.*, q. XIV; Ferraris, *ibid.*, nn. 16–17.

Thus the authors considered a religious who had been convicted of three grave crimes, thrice punished, and tried for six months in prison, and still had not amended his life inasmuch as he continued to persist in his obstinacy, to be truly incorrigible, and as such to become a subject for necessary expulsion from his monastery.[56]

[56] De Ameno, *ibid.*, Pars II, nn. 1–5; Ferraris, *ibid.*, n. 13.

CHAPTER V

PIUS IX TO THE DECREE "QUUM SINGULAE" OF PIUS X

ARTICLE 1. THE DECREE "SANCTISSIMUS" OF PIUS IX

From the end of the seventeenth century until the year 1911 the norms of the general law concerning the discharge of the members of Orders remained quite stable.[1] However, the norms set down by Urban VIII and Innocent XII could not always be observed in their entirety without a certain amount of difficulty. This was particularly true, during the eighteenth and nineteenth centuries, in regard to the imprisonment of incorrigible religious.[2]

In 1841 the Sacred Congregation of Bishops and Regulars made reference to the difficulties of the times. Ecclesiastical power was often impeded in its operation. Accordingly, it perceived that there could and would arise conditions in which even the expulsion of a nun would become necessary to restore peace and order to a community. Should circumstances in some locality demand such action, it should only be undertaken with the consent of the Holy See.[3]

A new norm appeared in 1857, to the effect that in all institutes of solemn vows, the prospective members were to make their first profession in simple vows for a minimum of three years, and only upon the lapse of this period were to be admitted to solemn vows.[4] However, it did not establish the nature and quality of these vows, nor the obligation and privileges of the

[1] Tabera, "De Dimissione Religiosorum"—*CpR,* XI (1930), 281.

[2] Tabera, *ibid.,* p. 282, nota 43.

[3] S. C. Ep. et Reg., *Incerti Loci,* 15 ian. 1841—Bizzarri, *Collectanea,* p. 460.

[4] S. C. super Statu Regularium, litt. encycl. *Neminem latet,* 19 mart. 1857—*Fontes,* n. 4381; S. C. Ep. et Reg., decr. 19 mart. 1857—*Fontes,* n. 1976.

religious thus professed. The desired clarification was given on June 12, 1858, in the declaration *Sanctissimus.*[5]

The vows were declared to be perpetual on the part of the religious,[6] and their dispensation reserved to the Roman Pontiff.[7] Nevertheless, these simple vows could be dissolved by the institute in the act of dismissal; for, with the fact of dismissal the bond and obligations of the vows ceased.[8] The power to dismiss a member from his community was to belong to the supreme moderator or general together with his council; in extraordinary cases this power could be subdelegated to certain approved religious, not less than three in number.[9]

If just and reasonable causes for the dismissal were verified, then the requisite steps were to be taken, but not through a formal process or trial; an informal proceeding was declared sufficient, as long as a due regard for prudence, for charity, and for expediency was observed.[10] Noteworthy is the declaration's use of the term "dismissal," and not "expulsion," to characterize the action of the community.[11] This declaration was originally given to the Superior General of the Dominicans, but was extended to the other orders,[12] so that it became the common law for all religious orders.

[5] S. C. super Statu Regularium, declar. *Sanctissimus,* 12 iun. 1858—*Fontes,* n. 4583.

[6] *Ibid.,* n. I.

[7] *Ibid,* n. II.

[8] *Ibid.,* n. III.

[9] *Ibid.,* n. IV.

[10] *Ibid.,* n. V; for further interpretations of the "just and reasonable cause" cf. S. C. Ep. et Reg., resp. 7 febr. 1862—Bizzarri, *Collectanea,* p. 861; S. C. Ep. et Reg. decr. *Cum Regulares,* 30 iul. 1881—*Acta Sanctae Sedis* (41 vols., Romae, 1865-1908), XIV (1881), 91 (hereafter cited *ASS*): S. C. Ep. et Reg., resp. 19 nov. 1886—Vermeersch, *De Religiosis Institutis et Personis* (2 vols., tomus prior, 1902, tomus alter, *Supplementa et Monumenta,* 3. ed., Brugis, 1904), II, n. 130 A; S. C. super Statu Regularium, resp. 15 dec. 1893—Vermeersch, *ibid.,* n. 130 B; S. C. Ep. et Reg., const. *Ordinis S. Benedicti,* 13 maii 1904—*Fontes,* n. 2048; S. C. de Religiosis, decr. *Inter reliquas,* 1 ian. 1911—*AAS,* III(1911), 39.

[11] Ried-Brig, *Manuale Practicum Juris Disciplinaris et Criminalis Regularium ad usum Ff. Minorum Capuccinorum exaratum* (Romae, 1902), n. 260.

[12] S. C. super Statu Regularium, resp., 7 febr. 1862—*Fontes,* n. 4387; Bizzarri, *Collectanea,* p. 857, N.B.

Bouix (1808–1870) in particular made mention of the elements which in his day militated against the penalty of imprisonment. For either the state did not recognize religious as such, or refused the aid of the secular arm to enforce Church law, or itself would proceed against superiors who resorted to this punishment. Though he was of the opinion that in such circumstances the law did not apply, and that correspondingly an incorrigible religious could be expelled without the formality of incarceration, yet, for the sake of obviating other inconveniences that would or could arise, he deemed it more advantageous to have recourse to the Sacred Congregation of the Council, or to the Sacred Congregation of Bishops and Regulars.[13]

In 1886 the Sacred Congregation for the Discipline of Regulars settled the matter by deciding that a pontifical indult had to be obtained, in individual cases, for omitting the imprisonment of incorrigible religious, and for expelling them after only a summary process.[14] This same decree also required the permission of the Holy See for the readmission of a religious who had repented satisfactorily after expulsion.

Article 2. The Decrees of Leo XIII

Correlative to the declaration *Sanctissimus* of 1858 was the decree *Auctis admodum* of 1892.[15] The latter did not derogate in any way from the former, since it legislated solely for the dismissal of those who were professed in institutes of simple vows.[16] Congregations of simple vows had their rise in the sixteenth century, and enjoyed a remarkable increase in the following centuries.

---

[13] Bouix, *Tractatus De Jure Regularium* (2 vols., 3. ed., Parisiis, 1882–1883), II, 482.

[14] S. C. super Disciplina Regulari, resp. *Congressus,* 22 ian. 1886—Vermeersch, *Supplementa et Monumenta,* II, n. 128. In accordance with this Craisson (d. 1881) taught: "Ubi autem huic incarcerationi obstant leges civiles, ut in Gallia, ad sacram Congregationem Regularium est recurrendum."—*Elementa Juris Canonici ad usum Galliae Seminariorum* (ed. 7, . . . cum Supplemento de Statu Religioso, Parisiis, 1887), Supplementum (Lib. III), n. 1035.

[15] S. C. Ep. et Reg., decr. *Auctis admodum,* 4 nov. 1892—*Fontes,* n. 2020; cf. S. C. Ep. et Reg., resp. 27 febr. 1891—*ASS,* XXIV (1891), 565.

[16] *Ibid.,* n. III.

Nevertheless, they were not given official recognition, and so remained outside of the provisions of the common law. Since the Holy See did not establish any general laws for them, they were governed in all things by their own particular statutes. This was especially evident in the matter of dismissal. Due to their absolute freedom, the institutes readily proceeded to dismiss delinquent members. This action compelled bishops to receive and support those in sacred orders. At length no longer able to bear the added burden, the bishops appealed for some remedy.[17] Accordingly, the Sacred Congregation of Bishops and Regulars in this decree extended the method of expelling regulars to apply also to members of congregations under perpetual vows, and to religious who, though professed only with temporary vows, were in sacred orders.[18] This last case soon disappeared from the realm of possible occurrence, since nn. I and II of the decree *Auctis admodum* forbade a religious when only temporarily professed to receive sacred orders. The ordination had to follow after the profession of perpetual vows.

The fact of incorrigibility was considered verified after a threefold canonical warning and correction had been administered in vain. Then a process was to be instituted, with a due allowance of time for the accused to propose his defense, at least by proxy. The defendant was to be granted the right of redress against the sentence, with suspensive effect. If, however, the usual method of procedure could not be followed, recourse was to be made to the Holy See for permission to institute a summary process.[19]

Bachofen (1872–1943) held that this decree left the obligation of incarceration intact.[20] Vermeersch (1858–1936), on the other

---

[17] *Ibid.*, Introduction; Hippolytus a S. Familia, "De Dimissione Religiosorum"—*Analecta O. C. D.*, IV (1929), 105.

[18] *Ibid.*, n. III. The decree used the expression "*expellendis*" in reference to Regulars, and "*dimittendo*" for the rest.

[19] *Loc. cit.;* cf. S. C. Ep. et Reg., decr. *Abulen.*, 20 nov. 1895—*Fontes*, n. 2026; S. C. Ep. et Reg., resp. 4 iul. 1898—Vermeersch, *Supplementa et Monumenta*, II, n. 134.

[20] "De ista incarceratione silet quidem '*Auctis admodum*'; ast cum renovet decretum citatum '*Sacra Congregatio*' et insuper 'correctionem' requirat, non est illa incarceratio abolita dicenda. Si vero ex temporum adjunctis hoc plerumque fieri nequit, non eo ipso cessat potestas Superiorum

hand, stated that this added means of proof could now be omitted; but, to forestall doubt as to the validity of the expulsion, he deemed it best to obtain an indult to this effect.[21]

Leo XIII again touched upon the discipline of dismissal in the Constitution *Conditae a Christo* in 1900.[22] This dealt principally with the bishop's authority in this matter. Thus, in congregations of diocesan approval the superior properly authorized to dismiss members was the local ordinary.[23] In congregations of pontifical approval, however, the competent superior was the superior general of that institute. He had to follow the rules of the institute and the pontifical decrees.[24]

The next year (1901), by way of complement of the Constitution of Leo XIII, the Congregation of Bishops and Regulars published a set of *Normae* whose primary purpose was to outline a program for the formation of religious institutes, together with the method of obtaining authoritative approbation.[25] The *Normae* refer to dismissal in the 19th Chapter of Section II, Part I. It is true that no remarkable contribution is made by the *Normae* to the process of dismissal in institutes of men; rather, they faithfully restate the existing discipline.[26]

---

ad hanc poenitentiam infligendam."—Bachofen, *Compendium Juris Regularium* (New York: Benziger Brothers, 1903), c. VI, art. II, 3b, p. 356.

[21] Vermeersch, *De Religiosis Institutis et Personis,* I, n. 331, b, nota 2.

[22] Leo XIII, const. *Conditae a Christo,* 8 dec. 1900—*Fontes,* n. 644; *ASS,* XXXIII (1900), 341 sqq.

[23] Const. *Conditae a Christo,* 1, VIII: "Episcopo alumnas sodalitatum dioecesanarum professas dimittendi potestas est, votis perpetuis aeque ac temporariis remissis, uno dempto (ex auctoritate saltem propria) colendae perpetuo castitatis. Cavendum tamen ne istiusmodi remissione ius alienum laedatur; laedetur, autem, si insciis moderatoribus id fiat iusteque dissentientibus."—*Fontes,* n. 644.

[24] *Ibid.,* 2, I: "Praesidum similiter est familias singulas ordinare, tirones ac professos dimittere, iis tamen servatis quaecumque ex instituti legibus pontificiisque decretis servari oportet."—*Fontes,* n. 644.

[25] *Normae Secundum Quas Sacra Congregatio Episcoporum et Regularium Procedere Solet in Approbandis Novis Institutis Votorum Simplicium* (Romae, 1901) (hereafter cited as *Normae*); cf. *American Ecclesiastical Review* (Vols. I–XXXII, Philadelphia, 1889–1905; from 1905: *The Ecclesiastical Review* (Vols. XXXIII-CIX, Philadelphia, 1905–1943; from 1944: *The American Ecclesiastical Review,* Washington, D. C., Vol. CX, 1944–), XXVI (1902), 594 ff.

[26] *Normae,* Sectio Altera, pars prima, c. XIX, n. 201.

However, in regard to the congregations of sisters, the meager store of legislation on this process that originated especially from the *Conditae a Christo* was augmented by the *Normae.* In substance, the latter provided that no sister under temporary vows should be dismissed unless grave causes were verified, and the majority vote of the general council was obtained; for the sisters under perpetual vows more serious external reasons (physical infirmities were not to be considered under this concept) were required, to which reasons was added that of incorrigibility if it occasioned no prospect of reform, but rather threatened serious consequences to the institute. These conditions also were to be subject to the vote of the general council for their certification.[27] In every case the validity of the dismissal depended on the confirmation of the Holy See, namely the Sacred Congregation of Bishops and Regulars (after 1908 the Sacred Congregation of Religious).[28]

In 1902 the Sacred Congregation of Bishops and Regulars extended the provisions of the Encyclical *Neminem latet* (March 19, 1857) to all orders of women taking solemn vows. The nuns (*moniales*) were to take simple vows after the novitiate for a period of three years, and only then were to make their solemn profession.[29] This change was necessitated by the conditions of the time. The decree *Perpensis* also provided for dispensation from the vows and for dismissal from the order, both of which were reserved to the Holy See.[30]

---

[27] *Ibid.,* nn. 192–200.

[28] Pius X, const. *Sapienti consilio,* 29 iun. 1908, I, 5º—*AAS,* I (1909), 11.

[29] S. C. Ep. et Reg., decr. *Perpensis,* 3 maii 1902—*Fontes,* n. 2039.

[30] *Ibid.,* nn. 5 and 12. The norm for dismissal is couched as follows: "Ad dimittendas e monasterio praefatas votorum simplicium professas, recurrendum erit, in singulis casibus, ad S. Sedem, distincte exponendo graves causas, quae dimissionem suadere seu exigere videantur."

CHAPTER VI

JURIDICAL REFORMATION AND UNIFICATION OF THE INSTITUTE OF DISMISSAL

ARTICLE 1. THE DECREE "QUUM SINGULAE" OF PIUS X

The latest pre-Code decree of the Holy See touching on the dismissal of religious was the decree *Quum singulae,* issued under Pius X by the Sacred Congregation of Religious, May 16, 1911.[1] This re-adapted the manner of proceeding in the dismissal and expulsion of persons professed in Orders and other religious institutes and, at the same time, reduced the norms of law hitherto contained in various sources into one generic and uniform system.

The radical purpose for the alteration, as set forth in the prologue of the decree, was to provide some juridical adjustment in the discipline of dismissal through the enactment of definite, brief and expedite norms, since the prescriptions and solemnities of the former legislation, especially those stated in the decree of Urban VIII (Sept. 21, 1624), could no longer be observed under contemporary circumstances.[2] It was a definite contribution toward the final revision of existing laws as ordered by Pius X.[3]

The decree *Quum singulae* provided for:

(1) THE EXPULSION OR DISMISSAL OF "MALE" RELIGIOUS

a. *In Cases of Less Urgent Necessity*

The competent tribunal was to consist of the superior general, or abbot general, and at least four general councillors; in the event of the absence of any of the latter, the deficiency was to

[1] S. C. de Rel., decr., *Quum singulae,* 16 maii 1911—*AAS,* III (1911), 235, 238; *Fontes,* n. 4409.

[2] Cf. Vermeersch, "Forma Expellendi vel Dimittendi Religiosos et Moniales," Annotatio I—*Periodica,* VI (1912), 47.

[3] Hippolytus a S. Familia, "De Dimissione Religiosorum"—*Analecta* O. C. D., IV (1929), 106.

be supplied by another religious selected by the head of the tribunal, with the consent of the other councillors. If an abbey did not belong to a monastic congregation, recourse had to be made to the Holy See in every case. In every tribunal a religious of the respective institute was to be designated as promoter of justice by the general council.[4]

For the future only a *summary* process was to be followed for the expulsion of regulars in solemn vows; likewise for the dismissal of members of other institutes in perpetual vows, and for clerics in major orders who had only temporary vows. Nevertheless, special privileges granted to certain institutes could remain in force.[5]

The decree then outlined what necessarily had to precede a trial: upon what grounds it could be begun; how it was to be conducted.[6] A threefold canonical warning had to be given, by a competent superior, which meant that it had to proceed in some way from the authority of the provincial or quasi-provincial; consequently, the local superior, if he actually gave the warnings, required the provincial's leave to do so. Three grave transgressions had to be realized, and they had to be of the same species. If of different species, they were to be such that, considered collectively, they disclosed the obstinately perverse will of the offender. Even one crime could suffice, provided that it was continuous, and rendered virtually threefold through culpable neglect after three warnings. The threat of expulsion or of dismissal could be added to the last warning, if the superior saw fit to do so; but this threat did not necessarily have to be made. A warning was not to be repeated unless the transgression was repeated; or, in the case of a continuous transgression, only after the lapse of two complete days. Six days had to pass, after a third warning, before the process could be started.

Sufficient proofs had to be verified in regard to: the guilt of

---

[4] S. C. de Rel., decr. *Quum singulae,* 16 maii 1911, nn. 1–2—*AAS,* III (1911), 235.

[5] *Ibid.,* n. 3. N.B. The decree used the term "expulsion" in reference to institutes of solemn vows, and the term "dismissal" in reference to institutes of simple vows.

[6] *Ibid.,* nn. 4–16.

the religious; the gravity and number of his offenses; his pertinacity subsequent to the three warnings. His guilt could be proved by the culprit's confession, by authentic documents, or by the sworn testimony of at least two witnesses. The gravity of the offenses presupposed gravity on the side of the obligation of the violated law itself, especially in regard to its sanction; the "*dolus*" of the transgressor, and the material or moral harm to the community, were also to be considered.

Concerning the threefold warning, an authentic document had to be in evidence, that is, one containing the signatures of two witnesses to the warning; but a registered letter also sufficed, inasmuch as the written receipt of the postal officials reliably attested the acceptance or refusal on the part of the religious in question. Before such a letter was sent, a copy was to be made and signed by two witnesses. Finally, the fact that the condition of a sufficient warning was verified was to be recorded in the archives of the community.

When the action was begun, all necessary documents were to be forwarded by the provincial to the superior general, who in turn was to hand them over to the promoter of justice. The latter's accusations and the fact that action had commenced were to be communicated to the accused, in order to give him opportunity to prepare his defense, but within the time designated by the judge. The accused could defend himself personally, or by means of a proxy of the same institute; if he did neither, the tribunal *ex officio* had to appoint another religious of the institute to defend the case.

If the tribunal passed a sentence of expulsion or dismissal, the defendant could, within ten days, appeal, with suspensive effect, to the Sacred Congregation of Religious. If, however, the continued presence of the delinquent was an occasion of very serious scandal, or of grave harm to the community or its members, the superior general, with the consent of the chapter or of his council, could, despite the appeal, send him away, *dimisso habitu.*[7]

When the dismissal was that of a major cleric, prompt notice

---

[7] *Loc. cit.*

of the sentence was to be sent to the ordinary of his place of origin, and of the place where he would most likely reside.[8]

b. *In Cases of More Urgent Necessity*

If a religious was certainly guilty of a delict so heinous as to cause danger of grave scandal, or very grave detriment to the community, and the case admitted of no delay, even the provincial superior or the local abbot could discharge the delinquent immediately.[9] In this case the process of dismissal or expulsion was to be begun at once, and, until the final sentence was passed, the religious was not held to be formally expelled or dismissed. He could also appeal to the Sacred Congregation of Religious, but only with a non-suspensive effect.

The cases considered thus far all furnished a basis of simply *ferendae sententiae* penalties. However, the decree *Quum singulae* also introduced a *latae sententiae* penalty.[10] It stated that certain public crimes entailed the penalty of expulsion or dismissal, so that a declaratory sentence of the fact sufficed for the effect. Either the general or the provincial superior, with their respective councils, could make this declaration. Moreover, the delicts to which this penalty was attached were: public apostasy from the Catholic faith; apostasy from an order of regulars or from an institute, upon the lapse of a three months' absence; flight from the monastery when undertaken in the company of a woman; a civil contract of marriage, the attempt to contract marriage, or also the celebration of a marriage, which a religious if professed with merely simple vows could validly contract.[11]

---

8 *Ibid.*, n. 19.

9 ". . . poterit . . . ad saeculum item remitti, habito religioso illico deposito. . . ."—*ibid.*, n. 17.

10 Vermeersch, "Forma expellendi vel Dimittendi Religiosos et Moniales," Annotatio II—*Periodica,* VI (1912), 47; "art. cit.," Annotatio III, 1, c.)—*Periodica,* VI (1912), 51.

11 S. C. de Rel., decr. *Quum singulae,* 16 maii 1911, n. 18: "Item contra quaedam delicta censetur veluti lata a iure poena expulsionis vel dimissionis. Quae delicta sunt:

(a) publica apostasia a Fide Catholica;

(b) apostasia ab Ordine vel Instituto, nisi intra tres menses Religiosus redierit;

The decree stated that, after the expulsion or dismissal, clerics in major orders were perpetually suspended; those in minor orders were forbidden to receive higher orders without the permission of the Holy See. Similar permission was required in case the discharged religious was after a proper reformation of his ways to be admitted into his former institute, or received into another.[12] Vermeersch,[13] in regard to the minor clerics mentioned above, taught that they were not to be considered irregular, but simply were to be withheld from the reception of higher orders; also that the permission required to receive higher orders was not to be confused with a dispensation from irregularity.[14]

(II) THE EXPULSION OR DISMISSAL OF "WOMEN" RELIGIOUS

The decree also determined what norms were to be employed for women religious in the matter of their expulsion or dismissal. The rules found in this part of the decree were drawn from the decree *Perpensis* and from the *Normae.* Four classifications of these religious were mentioned: (1) Nuns, that is, those who had taken solemn vows in an order; (2) those who had made simple profession preparatory to a later solemn profession; (3) sisters, with perpetual vows in an institute of simple vows; and (4) sisters of religious *orders,* i.e., "lay-sisters" (*quasi monialibus adiunctae*) whose constitutions prescribed simple perpetual vows.

For the expulsion or dismissal of (1), (2), and (3), grave external causes, joined with incorrigibility and detriment to the community, were required. Less serious causes sufficed in the case of (4).

(c) fuga a monasterio, suscepta secum muliere;

(d) et multo magis contractus, ut aiunt, civilis, vel attentatio aut celebratio matrimonii, etiam validi, seu quando vota non sint solemnia vel non habeant solemnium effectum.

Sufficit in istis casibus, ut Superior Generalis vel Provincialis cum suo respective Consilio emittat sententiam declaratoriam facti."—*AAS,* III (1911), 237.

[12] *Ibid.,* n. 20.

[13] "Forma Expellendi vel Dimittendi Religiosos et Moniales," Annotatio III, 6—*Periodica,* VI (1912), 52.

[14] ". . . neque odiosa est seu stricti iuris."—Vermeersch, *loc. cit.*

The respective causes were to be judged by the abbess or superioress together with her council. When sufficient experiment indicated no further hope of emendation, but rather an imminent serious harm to the institute on account of the continued incorrigible faults (at least through two such instances) of the nun or sister, the abbess or superioress and her council were to vote secretly, in order to determine whether the facts of the case constituted causes sufficient to warrant a discharge from the institute. These causes were then submitted to the local ordinary (also to the superior of regulars, if the community of nuns was subject to him). Confirmation on the part of the Holy See had to be obtained before the expulsion or dismissal could be rendered effective. However, in the case of grave external scandal, a nun or sister could be sent away immediately; but the case was to be reported to the Holy See without delay.[15]

It is to be remarked that the decree, for the most part, dealt with the dismissal of men religious in solemn or perpetual vows, and that it touched upon the dismissal of women religious with vows of the same degree only in the last number. It did not treat of the dismissal of men or women religious in temporary vows,[16] since these were not considered subject to discharge through a *formal* process. They could be dismissed according to earlier norms; still, even in these cases grave causes had to be verified and subjected to the majority vote of the supreme moderator and his council.

That the decree *Quum singulae* introduced changes in the discipline of dismissal is quite evident from a comparison with the norms earlier prevalent. It did not usher in a complete change; but rather altered the older provisions in order to remedy the more crying needs. Incarceration as a prelude to expulsion was

---

[15] S. C. de Rel., decr. *Quum singulae,* 16 maii 1911, n. 21—*AAS,* III (1911), 238.

[16] Cf. *ibid.,* nn. 3, 20, 21—*AAS,* III (1911), 235, 238; Vermeersch, "Forma Expellendi vel Dimittendi Religiosos et Moniales," Annotatio II, A, 1, c), B); Annotatio II, B, 1, c); Annotatio III, 9, e)—*Periodica,* VI (1912), 48, 50, 53; Villien, "La Procédure Canonique pour L'Expulsion des Religieux"—*Le Canoniste Contemporain* (45 vols., Paris, 1878–1922 [later *Le Canoniste,* Paris, 1924–1926]), XXXV (1912), 714.

suppressed; and other delays notably reduced.[17] In cases of urgent necessity, the formal power to discharge the offender was given to superiors. Although the Constitution *Sapienti consilio* (June 29, 1908)[18] stated that the judicial matters concerning religious must be referred to the S. R. Rota, the decree *Quum singulae* allowed a religious to appeal to the Sacred Congregation of Religious, against the sentence of expulsion or dismissal passed by the tribunal of his institute.[19] Moreover, whereas previously an expelled religious, when he had shown proper indications as to the emendation of his ways, was to be re-admitted to his order, the new decree prescribed that permission for this was to be obtained from the Holy See.

The decree contained, apparently, an unusual innovation in this that it seemed to grant ecclesiastical jurisdiction to persons who do not have the power of orders,[20] for, in prescribing the *process* for the expulsion and dismissal of religious, no distinction was made between clerical and lay institutes. Moreover, the decree stated that general superiors with their council were to constitute the *tribunal;* and from the *sentence* of this tribunal the right to *appeal* was granted. These terms seem to have presupposed that such a tribunal had ecclesiastical jurisdiction. In a lay institute the members of the prescribed tribunal obviously were lay religious, and previously the law had not granted ecclesiastical jurisdiction to lay persons, even if they were religious.

Article 2. The Penalty of Expulsion or Dismissal "Veluti lata a iure"

Another notable innovation was the introduction, for the first time in ecclesiastical legislation, of the institute of an *ipso iure* and *ipso facto* effective expulsion or dismissal as the sanction for specified crimes.[21] It is to be noted that there are extant two

---

[17] Villien, *loc. cit.*

[18] Pius X, const. *Sapienti consilio*, 29 iun. 1908, I, 5o, 2—*AAS*, I (1909), 12.

[19] Cf. Vermeersch, "art. cit.," Annotatio III, I, b)—*Periodica,* VI (1912), 51.

[20] Vermeersch, "art. cit.," Annotatio III, 1, a),—*Periodica,* VI (1912), 51; Wernz-Vidal, *Ius Canonicum,* III, p. 473, nota 10.

[21] Cf. the text of the law on this point—*supra,* p. 61, note 11.

preparatory copies of the decree *Quum singulae,* and that in the first (considered by the Sacred Congregation of Religious on January 13, 1911) not the least mention of this type of dismissal was made. The text of the second copy (for the plenary session of March 3, 1911) proposed a sentence of expulsion inflicted as it were by law, against those committing certain delicts.

The delicts under consideration were: public apostasy from the Catholic faith; civil marriage; and public concubinage. In these cases, the general council of the institute was to be authorized to proceed when it was assured of the truth of the matter.[22] This was further revised and extended to the form in which it ultimately appeared in the decree *Quum singulae* of May 16, 1911.[23]

In the course of their respective commentaries on the decree *Quum singulae* Villien [24] and Tamayo [25] devoted considerable discussion to the interpretation of this particular norm.

The use of the phrase "*veluti lata a iure*" to characterize the "*poena expulsionis vel dimissionis*" was readily understood to signify a penalty incurred *ipso iure* [26] or as a *latae sententiae* punishment.[27] The term *latae sententiae* did not connote the idea that the delinquent was bound to inflict the penal sanction on himself. Rather it signified simply that the application of the

---

22 "2. In committentes quaedam delicta censetur veluti lata a iure sententia expulsionis. Quae delicta sunt: publica apostasia a fide catholica, matrimonium civile, publicus concubinatus. 3. Sufficit in casu, ut Consilium Generale Ordinis vel Instituti procedat, sola facti veritate inspecta." —Tabera, "De Dimissione Religiosorum"—*CpR,* XI (1930), 412, nota 5.

23 Cf. *supra,* p. 61, note 11.

24 "La Procédure Canonique pour l'Expulsion des Religieux"—*Le Canoniste Contemporain,* XXXVI (1913), 135–142; 211–221. It is noteworthy that the post-Code authors consulted in this dissertation do not make reference to this article. Nevertheless, the present writer deems it the clearest expression of the juridic thought that pervades both pre-Code and present legislation.

25 *Procedimientos de Derecho Penal Canónico* (Manila: Tip. del Colegio de Sto. Tomás, 1913), nn. 300 and 301.

26 Tamayo, *loc. cit.*

27 Villien, "art. cit."—*Le Canoniste Contemporain,* XXXVI (1913), 136; Vermeersch, "Forma Expellendi vel Dimittendi Religiosos et Moniales," Annotatio II, A, 1, a)—*Periodica,* VI (1912), 47.

penalty would not be the result of an ordinary procedure; that it would not depend on a sentence which a judge has a right to moderate or augment; that the competent judge was not free to mitigate the sentence or to admit extenuating circumstances; for it was not the judge who prepared, pronounced, or inflicted this sentence, it was the law itself. The judge was only the authorized spokesman who declared, on the one hand, what the law had determined, and, on the other, that the act committed contained all the conditions required by the law, and that from the union of these two elements—an express law and a real fault—there resulted an automatic effect—the penalty.

By way of illustration Villien drew an analogy from chemistry, likening this penalty to a precipitate. The declaration that followed did not bring about the precipitate or penalty, but only testified to its presence. However, the difference between the two fields was apparent in that in the case of automatic expulsion the proof and declaration made by any witness, even a jurist, no matter how certain and authoritative it might be in point of legal doctrine, did not produce any juridic effect: whereas the proof and declaration made by the competent judge produced a juridic effect, namely, the official expulsion.[28]

The law in number 18 of the decree in question specifically determined and clearly limited the cases, and hence was subject to a strict interpretation. Thus Villien noted that, even if a religious would commit graver faults than those mentioned in the text, he would not be subject to this expulsion, for then there would be invoked a sanction that was not in the law. It would be useless to argue *a pari* or *a fortiori,* for the law did not allow of an extension by way of deductive reasoning. The law and it alone established the faults which were visited with this penalty. Superiors were completely incompetent in this matter, and any contrary act on their part was invalid and implied an encroachment on the authority of the Holy See.[29] Moreover, the law not only

---

[28] Villien, *ibid.,* pp. 136–137.

[29] "Il serait vain d'argumenter ici *a pari* ou *a fortiori.* La loi présente ne prévoit pas ces extensions de peine par déduction. Il faut prendre la peine telle qu'elle est portée par le législateur. et par lui seul. Même le Supérieur Général serait, dans l'espèce, incompétent. La loi est portée par

enumerated the faults which lent themselves to the incurring of this *latae sententiae* penalty, but also did so as excluding all others. In no part did it employ a formula that permitted any extension or even hinted at the possibility of it. It enumerated the delicts one after the other, and then stopped without any *etc.* or similar expression. The list presented was then an exhaustive list.[30]

Villien summed up the guiding juridic purpose of the law as follows:

> If one looks for the reason of the peculiar treatment accorded to these faults and to them alone, while others which are more grave are less seriously punished, one will soon perceive that the motive is very clear: it is that, by this act, the guilty person has himself expressly, equivalently, in an unquestionable manner, broken the bond that attaches him to the Order or Institute, and, furthermore, he has placed himself in a situation which would with difficulty permit him to return: the declaration of dismissal then only takes account of the ruptured bond, and inflicts on him the logical juridical sanction.[31]

In reference to the first listed delict, namely apostasy from the Catholic Faith, Villien pointed out that it was not the same as apostasy from the Christian Faith.[32] Apostasy from the Catholic Faith was a more restricted species of apostasy than apostasy

---

une autorité plus haute, le Saint Siège, qui y fait son *appositio manus;* tout effort de l'Ordre ou de l'Institut religieux serait un empiètement sans valeur."—Villien, *ibid.*, p. 137.

30 Villien, *ibid.*, pp. 137–138.

31 " Si on demande la raison du traitement si particulier fait à ces fautes, et à celles-là, seulement, alors que d'autres plus graves sont punies moins sévèrement, on s'apercevra bientôt que ce motif est très clair: c'est que, par cet acte, le coupable a rompu lui-même expressément, équivalemment, d'une manière indubitable, le lien qui l'attachait à l'Ordre ou à l'Institut, et il s'est mis, de plus, dans une situation qui lui permettrait malaisément de revenir: la déclaration de renvoi ne fait donc que prendre acte de la rupture et lui infliger la sanction juridiquement logique."—Villien, *ibid.*, p. 138.

32 " Il faut signaler d'abord qu'il ne s'agit pas ici de l'apostasie pure et simple, de l'apostasie de la foi chrétienne, qui est frappée d'excommunication par la constitution *Apostolicae Sedis*. . . . "—Villien, *ibid.*, p. 138.

from the Christian Faith. Thus, one who passed over to Mohammedanism, to Judaism, to Buddhism, to a well-defined paganism, apostatized from the Catholic and the Christian Faith; whereas one who passed over to Protestantism apostatized from the Catholic Faith only, and not from the Christian Faith.[33] It was not necessary to enroll oneself in the lists of a precise cult or of a society positively excluding Catholicism or every other religion in order to be juridically considered as an apostate; one was commonly deemed to be such from the day that he abandoned the Catholic Faith.[34]

However, pre-Code authors were not in agreement as to the extent of the application of this latter concept in the realm of penalty. The majority affirmed that, also from the viewpoint of penalty, apostasy was constituted by the *recessus a fide,* with or without *accessus* to another cult or organized society. Others, nevertheless, thought that enrollment on the registers of another religious or anti-religious society was required to constitute juridic apostasy.[35] Villien [36] and Tamayo [37] espoused the latter view.

Villien explained that the law seemed to envision the case of a religious who, not only withdrew from the Catholic Faith, but

[33] " Sans doute, l'apostasie de la foi chrétienne contient comme une espèce plus restreinte l'apostasie de la foi catholique, et qui passe au mahométisme, au judaïsme, au bouddhisme, à un paganisme bien défini, apostasie de la foi catholique. Mais on apostasie aussi de la foi catholique en passant au protestantisme."—Villien, *ibid.*, p. 138.

[34] " Que l'on soit apostat, en réalité, du jour où l'on abandonne la foi catholique, même si on ne lui substitue pas la profession d'une autre religion ou l'accession à un autre culte, c'est ce qui paraît admis par tous . . ." —Villien, *ibid.*, pp. 138–139.

[35] " La plupart des auteurs affirment que, au point de vue pénal aussi, l'apostasie est constituée par le *recessus a fide,* avec ou sans *accessus* à un autre culte ou à une autre societe organisée. D'autres pensent, au contraire, Santi-Leitner par example, que 'l'adscripto' sur les registres d'une autre société cultuelle ou anticultuelle est nécessaire pour constituer juridiquement l'apostasie."—Villien, *ibid.*, p. 139; Tamayo, *op. cit.*, n. 300, 1o.

[36] *Loc. cit.*

[37] " Para los efectos del decreto, que venimas comentando, creemos que no bastaría abandonar la fe catolica solo para caer en el indiferentismo religioso; sino que sería necessaria la afilíacion á alguna secto ó sociedad anticatolica, como una secta protestante, ó sociedad de librepensadores etc."— Tamayo, *loc. cit.*

also went over to a cult, to a sect, to a religious anti-Catholic society, such as a Protestant sect or a league of freethinkers.[38] On the contrary, the simple withdrawal from Catholicism by falling into practical indifferentism, but without adopting new obligations in exchange, did not appear to constitute apostasy in a measure clearly enough opposed to the earlier religious profession, or to create an irreconcilable breach.[39] Accordingly, this same author stated that it was necessary, from the viewpoint of the penal sanction, that the act of apostasy leave no room for doubt as to its existence and import. The law was primarily concerned with the manifestation of the anti-Catholic attitude in thought and action, and not with the moral culpability of the religious.[40]

Both Villien[41] and Tamayo[42] spoke at length concerning apostasy from an Order or Institute. For the present work it suffices to note that for the first time the term " apostasy " was officially used in reference to the unlawful desertion of the institute by religious of simple vows.[43]

Flight from the monastery as subject to the *latae sententiae* penalty of this passage was not flight pure and simple, but a flight

---

[38] " Il semble bien que l'hypothèse prévue est celle du Religieux qui, non seulement s'éloigne de la foi catholique, mais fait accession à un culte, à une secte, à une societe religieuse anticatholique, comme serait une secte protestante ou une ligue de libre-pensée."—Villien, *loc. cit.*

[39] " Le simple éloignement du catholicisme pour tomber dans l'indifférentisme pratique et sans prendre aucun engagement ne paraît pas affirmer suffisamment l'apostasie, l'opposer assez nettement à la profession religieuse antérieure, ni creuser un fossé infranchissable."—Villien, *ibid.*, p. 139.

[40] " Il faut, au point de vue de la sanction pénale, que l'acte d'apostasie ne laisse aucun doute sur son existence et sa signification. La culpabilité morale n'est pas precisement ce qui est ici en cause, mais la manifestation anticatholique."—Villien, *ibid.*, p. 139.

[41] *Ibid.*, pp. 139–142.

[42] *Ibid.*, n. 300, 2o.

[43] " Notons cette formule nouvelle: ' L'apostasie de l'Ordre ou de l'Institut '; elle est caractéristique. En effet, la législation antérieure ne parlait que d'apostasie de l'Ordre, ne visant que les Réguliers à voeux solennels; elle ne connaissait pas le terme d'apostasie pour les Religieux à voeux simples. C'est donc désormais une assimilation des uns aux autres."—Villien, *ibid.*, p. 139; Tamayo, *loc. cit.*

"qualified" by association with a woman companion. Hence, it was not flight in itself that the law contemplated, but a flight attended with the aggravating circumstances just mentioned.[44] Automatic expulsion in this case was resorted to, not only because of the scandal that such conduct engendered, but also because of the fact that such an action indicated that one wished to preclude the possibility of return to the institute, and that in the person of the woman companion whom he took along with him he gave adequate assurance that he would not return to his obligations as a religious.[45]

In order to understand fully the sense of this phrase, Villien introduced a question. Was it necessary that the woman be associated with the religious in the initial stage of his departure, or was it sufficient that she join with him at any later time? The latter supposition could be realized if a religious left the monastery alone for the purpose of taking a few weeks' liberty, and then during this time succumbed to the temptations of a woman who attached herself to him.[46] But this author observed that the obvious sense of the text seemed to be that it wished to punish directly the culpable flight of a religious who abandoned his monastery for the love of a woman whom he joined in his departure and whom he took away with him.[47] He realized that the sense of the text could be extended still further, so that it

---

[44] "Mais ce n'est pas la fuite pure et simple qui est visée dans le présent passage du décret. Ce que l'on vise, c'est une fuite 'qualifiée,' la fuite avec une femme. La fuite sera constituée par le fait matériel de quitter le couvent. La peine est encourue si le religieux quitte en compagnie d'une femme."—Villien, *ibid.*, p. 211; Tamayo, *ibid.*, n. 300, 3o; ". . . fuga a Monasterio, non omnis tamen, sed suscepta secum muliere; . . ."—Vermeersch, "art. cit.," *Annotatio* II, A, 1, a.)—*Periodica*, V (1912), 48.

[45] "Et cela non seulement à cause du scandale qui pourrait, dans telles séries de circonstances données, être évité, mais parce que le fait d'associer ainsi une femme à sa vie montre que l'on veut se fermer la possibilité du retour et prendre pour ainsi dire avec sa compagne des garanties contre un retour à ses obligations de religieux."—Villien, *ibid.*, pp. 211–212.

[46] Villien, *ibid.*, p. 212.

[47] "Le sens obvie du texte paraît bien être que l'on veut directement punir la fuite coupable du religieux que abandonne son couvent pour l'amour d'une femme avec laquelle il a combiné son départ et qu'il emmène."—Villien, *loc. cit.*

would apply to every case in which a religious should flee from his monastery in the company of a woman. In this sense it would matter little whether the association was foreseen and willed, or whether it was an unforeseen consequence of the flight.[48]

Villien noted that there was an important difference between these two cases: in the first the religious was more culpable, for he desired the added evil; in the second he manifested more weakness than passion. The author then stated that one cannot demand of a penalty that it be always and exactly molded to cover the slightest shade or hint of the punishable act.[49] Moreover, in the light of a literal consideration of the matter, what the law adverted to was not the fact that a religious lived *in actu praesenti* with a woman, but that he had joined her and led her away as his companion in the flight. This initial association of their lives was sufficient to entail the incurring of the penalty, and hence subsequent cohabitation or abandonment of their relationship did not enter into consideration.[50]

Tamayo likewise required that the association take place in the very act of the flight, and that it be with a woman with whom there was a previous agreement or understanding;[51] otherwise there would not be present the case envisioned by the law.[52]

Relative to the fourth delict, that of attempted or contracted marriage, the decree likewise introduced an innovation.[53] The Constitution *Apostolicae Sedis* had enacted a *latae sententiae* excommunication reserved to the ordinary as befalling clerics in

---

[48] Villien, *loc. cit.*

[49] ". . . mais on ne peut exiger d'une peine qu'elle soit moulée toujours exactement sur les moindres nuances de l'acte puni."—Villien, *loc. cit.*

[50] Villien, *loc. cit.*

[51] ". . . la circumstancia de ser fuga *cualificada,* es decir, que en el acto de la fuga se asocie una mujer, con la cual se supone estaba ya en combinación ó inteligencia."—Tamayo, *loc. cit.*

[52] "Si incurriría ó no en la pena de expulsion *ipso facto* un religioso que, al fugarse, no fuese en campañia de una mujer, sino que se la asociase hallandose ya fuera, sin haber estado antes en inteligencia con ella, no se puede asegurar, pues el texto del decreto dice terminantemente *suscepta secum muliere,* lo cual no es aplicable exactamente al caso supuesto."—Tamayo, *loc. cit.*

[53] Villien, *ibid.*, p. 213.

sacred orders, Regulars, and nuns, who after thc profession of the solemn vow of chastity presumed to contract marriage.[54] Hence, members of congregations or institutes of simple vows, if not in sacred orders, did not incur any *ipso facto* established penalty by contracting a civil or church marriage. The decree *Quum singulae* remedied this inequality by introducing the *ipso iure* effective penalty of expulsion, binding upon religious of solemn and of simple vows alike. Religious in solemn vows and clerics in sacred orders were moreover bound by the excommunication.[55] The new enactment was readily understandable, since the fault committed by the one or the other was in itself the same, occasioned the same scandal, and above all denoted a similar break with the order or institute.[56]

The civil contract of marriage was that entered upon before a civil magistrate in accordance with the norms of the civil law and from which there resulted a purely civil bond.[57] The *attempt* or *celebration* of marriage, on the other hand, was understood as referring to a canonical marriage. The authors assumed that an attempt at contracting marriage before the Church would be made chiefly in those regions where civil marriage did not exist.[58] Except in the case of religious in simple vows, it was a marriage only in appearance, for in reality it was null by reason of the impediment either of vows or of orders. Villien stated that, considered in itself and in relation to the order or institute, the fault of the religious was the same whether the marriage was valid or invalid; and so the penalty of expulsion or dismissal was the same.[59]

Furthermore, Villien considered the possibility that such a marriage might be entered upon under the influence of error, of coercion, or in conditions wherein the agent did not perform a

[54] Pius IX, const. *Apostolicae Sedis,* 12 oct. 1869, III, n. 1—*Fontes,* n. 552.

[55] Villien, *loc. cit.;* Tamayo, *op. cit.,* n. 300, 4o.

[56] Villien, *loc. cit.*

[57] Villien, *loc. cit.;* Tamayo, *loc. cit.*

[58] Villien, *loc. cit.;* Tamayo, *loc. cit.*

[59] ". . . en soi, et vis-à-vis de l'Ordre ou de l'Institut, la faute est la même, qui le mariage soit valide ou non: la peine sera la même. Ce qui parait plus logique encore quand le mariage contracté est valide."—Villien, *ibid.,* pp. 213–214.

human act. It was certain that in such circumstances one would not incur the excommunication enacted in the Constitution *Apostolicae Sedis,* since that document in its penal law employed the word *praesumentes.* Although the decree *Quum singulae* did not contain this added qualification, Villien judged that the same principles could apply.[60] Nevertheless, he noted that the same argument could not be urged in the matter of ignorance. The law of the decree did not envision the case in which a guilty religious was unaware of the prohibition to contract marriage. He deemed this ignorance unlikely.[61] He stressed again that it was not the precise intention of the law to punish the attempt at or the contraction of marriage; rather the law sought to punish the effected break with the institute, whenever that breach manifested itself in this particular form.[62]

In the last part of n. 18 the decree stated that the Superior General or Provincial with his respective council was to make a declaratory sentence regarding the fact of the automatic dismissal.[63] This obligation rested upon both superior and council, but the law appointed the superior to collect the votes and to execute the decision of the majority.[64] Since there was question of a declaratory sentence, the authors deemed it necessary that there be instituted a summary process with the intervention of the promoter of justice and the citation of the delinquent.[65] The

[60] "Si toutefois le mariage apparent avait été contracté sous l'empire de l'erreur, de la contrainte, bref, dans des conditions où l'agent ne faisait pas un acte humain, la peine ne serait pas encourue. L'excommunication portée par la Constitution *Apostolicae Sedis* contre les clercs et les Religieux n'est pas encourue quand l'attentat de mariage n'a pas été fait avec pleine liberté; il en serait de même sans doute dans l'espèce présente."—Villien, *ibid.,* p. 214.

[61] "On notera toutefois que le décret ne prévoit pas l'hypothèse où le religieux coupable ignorerait que le mariage lui est interdit: cette ignorance, en effet, ne serait guère, aujourd'hui, vraisemblable; . . ."—Villien, *loc. cit.*

[62] ". . . d'autre part, l'intention de la loi n'est pas precisément de punir l'attentat ou le contrat de mariage pour lui-même, elle est plutôt de punir la scission faite sous cette forme particulière avec l'Institut."—Villien, *loc. cit.*

[63] Cf. text of law *supra,* p. 61, note 11.

[64] "C'est Supérieur et Conseil qui émettent la déclaration par la voix du seul Supérieur."—Villien, *ibid.,* p. 214.

[65] "Aun cuando el decreto no lo dice, se supone que para dictar una

council was to declare its competence, and then the promoter of justice was to lay before it the results of his investigations, set forth his proofs, and present his witnesses.[66] The council was to proceed with a deliberative vote.[67] Villien noted that the decree did not treat these particular points, but deemed that they were to be employed, since there was no reason to depart from the common law on the establishment of proofs.[68]

During the course of the process the accused religious was to be allowed to defend himself with all the guarantees that the Church had instituted in his favor; nevertheless, if his culpability appeared certain, the superiors were to recognize that they had the right and the duty to dismiss him. After the sentence of expulsion, the delinquent was despoiled of his insignia, and cast out into the world. All was over between him and his Order.[69] The expelled member was no longer considered as a religious. This was the most notable innovation of the decree.[70]

The constant care of the ancient legislation had been the return of the religious to the monastery of his profession.[71] It was with this intent that the law imposed on superiors the strict obligation to search every year for the fugitive and expelled religious and force them, if necessary, by means of ecclesiastical censures, to

---

sentencia declaratoria se verifica un proceso sumario, con intervención del Promotor de Justicia ó Fiscal, y citando al reo en la forma que fuere posible."—Tamayo, *ibid.*, n. 301.

[66] Villien, *loc. cit.*

[67] Tamayo, *loc. cit.*

[68] "Le décret *Quum singulae* ne marque rien de particulier sur tous ces points: il n'y a donc aucun motif de s'écarter cette fois de la loi commune sur l'établissement des preuves."—Villien, *ibid.*, p. 215.

[69] "Le Religieux inculpé a pu se protéger de toutes les garanties que l'Eglise avait instituées en sa faveur; néammoins, sa culpabilité a paru assez certaine pour que les supérieurs se soient reconnu le droit et le devoir de le chasser. L'expulsion prononcée, le coupable a été dépouillé de ses insignes, du costume de son Ordre ou de sa Congrégation, et rejeté dans le siècle. Entre lui et son Ordre tout est fini."—Villien, *ibid.*, p. 215; "Terminado el proceso y dictada la sentencia de expulsión contra un religioso, este queda completamente separado de la Orden ó Instituto á que pertenecía, . . ."—Tamayo, *ibid.*, n. 302.

[70] Villien, *ibid.*, p. 221; cf. *infra*, p. 75, note 77.

[71] Villien, *ibid.*, p. 220.

return to their monastery.[72] Expulsion was only a provisory measure, a sort of excommunication which was of the nature of a censure rather than a vindicative penalty. The Church could not persuade herself to leave in the world those who had professed the religious life.[73] This discipline was restored and renewed by the decree *Sacra Congregatio,* with the one exception concerning the case in which an expelled member did not give evident hopes of amendment.[74] The decree *Auctis admodum* passed over this obligation in silence, and simply declared that the expelled religious remained suspended until the Holy See decided concerning him.[75]

In the decree *Quum singulae,* however, expulsion or dismissal became a strict vindicative penalty and a permanent measure. With this action the member ceased to be a religious.[76]

A new law appeared also in the third part of n. 20,[77] in which a general rule [78] stated that one who was expelled or dismissed

---

[72] C. 24, X, *de regularibus et transeuntibus ad religionem,* III, 31; cf. *supra,* p. 28.

[73] "L'((ejectio)) n'était qu'une mesure provisoire, une sorte d'excommunication qui acait nature de censure plus que de peine. L'Eglise ne pouvait se résoudre à laisser dans le monde ceux qui avaient professé la vie religieuse."—Villien, *loc. cit.*

[74] Cf. *supra,* p. 42.

[75] S. C. Ep. et Reg., decr. *Auctis Admodum,* 4 nov. 1892, 4—*Fontes,* n. 2020.

[76] "Bref, l'expulsion du religieux, dans la nouvelle discipline, au lieu d'être une mesure provisoire, devient une mesure définitive. L'expulsé n'est plus considéré comme religieux. Il ne peut le redevenir que grâce à une permission spéciale du Saint-Siège.

C'est l'innovation la plus considérable du présent décret."—Villien, *ibid.,* p. 221.

[77] S. C. de Rel., decr. *Quum singulae,* 16 maii, 1911, n. 20: "Omnes Religiosi, de quibus agitur, in sacris constituti, qui expulsi vel dimissi fuerint, perpetuo suspensi manent, donec a competente Auctoritate, post emendationem vitae, dispensationem obtinuerint. Religiosi vel clerici, non in sacris, expulsi vel dimissi, prohibentur, quominus ad superiores ordines adscendant sine venia Sanctae Sedis. Omnes autem expulsi vel dimissi, etiamsi sese vere emendaverint, ad suum vel ad alium Ordinem vel Congregationem admitti non poterunt absque speciali licentia Sedis Apostolicae."—*AAS,* III (1911), 238; *Fontes,* 4409.

[78] "La troisième partie est d'ordre général. Elle concerne tous les re-

could not be *admitted* to his own or to another institute without the special permission of the Holy See. By implication this denoted that there was a dispensation from the vows in the act of expulsion or dismissal.

Accordingly, the decree did not contain any other enactment regarding the effects of expulsion or dismissal. There was only one effect, and that was common to all. What might appear as effects [79] in numbers 19 and 20 of the decree were rather, as Villien [80] and Tamayo [81] pointed out, complementary measures in the interest of the clerical state.

In quitting his congregation and the religious life, the delinquent did not fall into an unorganized world. Above all, the religious cleric who had received sacred orders could not be returned to the anonymous body of the laity. For besides his personal status resulting from his religious profession, he had been admitted to a higher class of Christian society with powers, rights, and obligations which did not permit one to treat him as a layman. On the other hand, the grave faults which had brought on his rejection from his religious family could not but have a repercussion also on the exercise of certain rights that he had received in ordination. In short, a cleric, particularly a cleric in major orders, could not be left acephalous.

He necessarily fell under the surveillance of an ordinary who would watch over him either with the purpose of rendering an account that he had not violated his obligations as a cleric *in sacris,* or to prevent him from scandalizing the faithful as he had scandalized his brethren in religion.[82] Hence the decree in n.

---

ligieux expulsés de n'importe quelle catégorie, et elle porte une loi nouvelle." —Villien, *ibid.,* p. 220.

[79] Vermeersch, "Forma Expellendi vel Dimittendi Religiosos et Moniales," Annotatio II, A, 2—*Periodica,* VI (1912), 49–50.

[80] *Ibid.,* p. 215.

[81] *Op. cit.,* n. 302.

[82] "En quittant sa Congrégation et la vie religieuse, le coupable ne tombe pas dans un monde inorganisé. Surtout le religieux clerc, qui a reçu les Ordres sacrés, ne peut rentrer dans la foule anonyme des simples chrétiens. Outre sa condition personnelle résultant de sa profession religieuse, il a été agrégé à la classe supérieure de la société chrétienne, avec des pouvoirs, des droits et des obligations qui ne permettent pas de le traiter

19[83] imposed on religious superiors the obligation to communicate the sentence of expulsion or dismissal of a cleric in major orders to the ordinary of this cleric's place of origin and to the ordinary of the place where the expelled member resided or intended to reside. In this manner these respective ordinaries immediately were made aware of their duty of surveillance, and were enabled the more readily to observe and enforce the sanctions enacted in n. 20 of the decree.[84]

The sanctions delineated in n. 20[85] were primarily enacted with a view to upholding and safeguarding the purity of the clerical state. Thus, a religious in major orders, when expelled or dismissed, was under a perpetual suspension until he was dispensed from it by the competent authority. The only authority competent to grant the dispensation was the Holy See.[86] This dispensation was granted only after the expelled or dismissed religious had effected a proper amendment of life. The decree did not indicate what proofs would suffice for establishing the fact of this amendment. This was a matter that the Holy See would have to investigate and determine in each case. Naturally the ordinary of the place where the expelled member resided would be the first one consulted.[87] Villien stated that the competent authority would, as a condition for absolving the expelled religious from the sus-

---

comme un fidèle quelconque. D'autre part, les fautes graves qui l'ont fait rejeter de sa famille religieuse ne peuvent pas ne pas avoir aussi leur répercussion sur l'exercice de certains des droits qu'il avait reçus de l'ordination. Enfin, un clerc, particulièrement un clerc *in sacris,* ne peut être *nullius.* Il tombe nécessairement sous la surveillance d'un Ordinaire qui veillera sur lui, soit afin de se rendre compte s'il n'enfreint pas ses obligations de clerc *in sacris,* soit afin de l'empêcher de scandaliser les fidèles comme il a scandalisé ses frères en religion."—Villien, *ibid.,* p. 215.

[83] S. C. de Rel., decr. *Quum singulae,* 16 maii 1911, n. 19: "Sententia expulsionis vel dimissionis, quocumque modo lata, si agatur de Religioso in sacris, illico communicanda erit Ordinario originis et Ordinario loci, ubi ille moratur, aut sedem suam statuere velle dignoscatur."—*AAS,* III (1911), 238; *Fontes,* n. 4409.

[84] Villien, *ibid.,* p. 217; Tamayo, *ibid.,* n. 302.

[85] Cf. *supra,* p. 75, note 77.

[86] Villien, *ibid.,* p. 219; Tamayo, *ibid.,* n. 303.

[87] Villien, *loc. cit.*

pension, demand that the latter had found an ordinary willing to receive him.[88]

Moreover, expelled or dismissed members not in sacred orders were forbidden to receive higher orders without the permission of the Holy See. Tamayo[89] considered the prohibition as applying only to sacred orders, but Villien[90] and Vermeersch[91] maintained that it was in force for any order higher than the one previously received by the expelled religious. Villien deemed this disposition of the law a logical consequence of the whole discipline. For, on the one hand, the Holy See had reserved to itself exclusive competence in these matters; and, on the other, such an expelled or dismissed person could scarcely be ordinarily deemed a fit subject for ordination.[92]

Finally, as has been noted above,[93] all expelled or dismissed members ceased to be religious, and could not become religious again except in consequence of a special permission of the Holy See.[94]

---

88 "Le décret *Auctis* ajoutait comme condition supplémentaire que la suspense durerait jusqu'à ce que l'expulsé eût trouvé un Ordinaire qui voulût bien le recevoir. Cette condition n'est pas exprimée ici: non pas qu'elle soit abrogée: rien ne l'indique, mais sans doute parce que ce n'était pas dans la perspective immédiate du législateur. D'ailleurs, l'autorité compétente en absolvant de la suspense précisera ses conditions."—Villien, *loc. cit.*

89 *Ibid.*, n. 304.

90 *Ibid.*, p. 220.

91 "Art. cit.," Annotatio II, A, 2, b)—*Periodica,* VI (1912), 50.

92 Cette disposition est une conséquence logique de toute cette discipline. L'*Appositio manus* du Saint-Siège s'oppose à ce qu'une autorité quelconque vienne modifier l'état de fait existant quand le religieux a été expulsé. Le Saint-Siège se réserve l'avenir en ce qui concerne le sujet. D'autre part, l'expulsion de l'Ordre ou de l'Institut, qui suppose nécessairement une série de fautes graves, n'est pas une préparation à la réception pieuse des saints ordres. Il y aurait quelque scandale a voir s'élever dans la hiérarchie ecclésiastique des hommes que l'on a dû expulser de l'état religieux, à voir destiner au commandement ceux qui se sont refusés à obéir."—Villien, *loc. cit.*

93 Cf. *supra*, pp. 75–76.

94 "L'expulsé n'est plus considéré comme religieux. Il ne peut le redevenir que grâce a une permission spéciale du Saint-Siège."—Villien, *ibid.*, p. 221: "Por último, el decreto *Quum singulae* ha introducido una modifi-

Vermeersch stated that, in accordance with n. 3 of the decree, Institutes might still use privileges contrary to the present decree. Nevertheless, he maintained that in reference to n. 18 a Superior general, even though using his privileged form, was bound to issue the declaratory sentence of expulsion or dismissal.[95] The same author was of the opinion that the *ipso facto* effected expulsion or dismissal did not apply to women who were professed with solemn vows, since the law was silent on the point, and since these did not have a tribunal that could pass a declaratory sentence with reference to the perpetrated crime.[96] Perhaps a stronger reason for such a contention lay in the fact that the part of the decree which contained this enactment was legislated for men in solemn or perpetual vows.

The norms for the expulsion or dismissal of religious as set forth in the decree *Quum singulae* remained in force as general legislation until the operative enactment of the Code. A comparison of the decree with Book II, Part II, Title XVI, of the Code renders quite obvious its contribution to the present law. In particular, the new institute of *ipso facto* effected dismissal was wholly incorporated into the schemata of the Code in 1914 and 1916; but in the edition of the Code one of the earlier specified elements which likewise had implied the effect of such a dismissal was no longer mentioned, namely, the apostasy from an

---

cación muy notable respecto á los religiosos expulsados ó despedidos, y es que la Orden ó Instituto, á que pertenecian, no sólo quodan relevados de la obligación de procurar el regresso de tales religiosos, ó de volverlos á admitir, aun cuando se hubiesen enmendado, sino que terminantemente se les prohibe admitirlos, sin licencia especial de la Sta. Sede, no sólo en la Orden ó Instituto de donde fueron expulsado ó despedidos, pero ni tampoco en ninguna otra Orden ó Congregación Religiosa."—Tamayo, *ibid.*, n. 304.

95 "3. Num contraria privilegia praesenti decreto supprimuntur?

De *forma* expellendi vel dimittendi sua cuique Instituto privilegia manent. Tertio enim decreti articulo reservantur. Quae autem art. 18 instar poenae ipso iure latae expulsio inducitur de omnibus valere videtur, ita ut Generalis privilegiata forma utens, sententiam declaratoriam dare debeat."—Vermeersch, "De Forma Expellendi vel Dimittendi Religiosos et Moniales," Annotatio III, 3—*Periodica*, VI (1912), 51-52.

96 Vermeersch, "art. cit.," Annotatio III, 9, c)—*Periodica*, VI (1912), 53.

order or from a religious institute.[97] The other changes that entered into the new law will be noted later in the course of the canonical commentary.

[97] Tabera, "De Dimissione Religiosorum"—*CpR,* XI (1930), 412; Larraona, "Quaestio Canonica"—*CpR,* IV (1923), 174, nota 1.

PART II
CANONICAL COMMENTARY

CHAPTER VII

THE *IPSO FACTO* EFFECTED DISMISSAL

Canon 646, § 1. *Ipso facto habendi sunt tanquam legitime dimissi religiosi:*

1°. *Publici apostatae a fide catholica;*

2°. *Religiosus, qui fugam arripuerit cum muliere; aut religiosa quae cum viro;*

3°. *Attentantes aut contrahentes matrimonium aut etiam vinculum, ut aiunt, civile.*

§ 2. *In his casibus sufficit ut Superior maior cum suo Capitulo vel Consilio ad normam constitutionum emittat declarationem facti; curet autem probationes facti collectas in domus regestis asservare.*[1]

Article 1. The Position of the Canon

At the very outset of a commentary on this canon, it is proper to note the setting of this canon in the Code. A glance will reveal that it is placed in Title XVI of the Second Book; but the surprising thing is its position immediately after the general rubric "*De dimissione religiosorum,*" before any division of the title itself into chapters. The recognition of this peculiar material position will be of great service in properly understanding the canon, both in itself and in its relation to others.[2]

[1] § 1. The following religious are *ipso facto* regarded as lawfully dismissed:

1°. Religious who have publicly apostatized from the Catholic faith;

2°. A religious who will have run away with a person of the opposite sex;

3°. Religious who attempt or contract marriage, even the so called civil marriage.

§ 2. In these cases it suffices that the higher Superior with his Chapter or Council according to the prescriptions of the Constitutions make a declaration of fact; but he must take care to preserve in the register of the house the collected evidence of the fact.—*Canonical Legislation Concerning Religious* (Authorized English Translation, Rome: Vatican Printing Office, 1918), pp. 57–58.

[2] Palombo, *De Dimissione Religiosorum,* n. 196.

Larraona, in the introductory article to his commentary on the Second Book, devotes one section to "preliminary canons."[3] With these words he denotes the canons which immediately follow the designation of the various divisions of the Code, i.e., book, part, section, title, chapter. In presenting the varied meanings or purposes that such canons may have, he enumerates lastly that they may be resorted to as a means for gathering together in some way things that cannot readily be reduced to any of the received divisions, and yet are not sufficient to constitute a new division. In the enumeration of examples he does not explicitly mention the present canon, but he seems to imply it in a later reference.[4] Indeed, there are authors who term this a "general or preliminary" canon.[5]

Palombo is explicit in maintaining that its very location has the effect of establishing its relation to the remainder of the title.[6] Hippolytus a S. Familia states that the legislator was very logical in assigning the first place to canon 646, since it applies to all

---

[3] Larraona, "Commentarium Codicis," *CpR,* I (1920), 214, n. 28, a; II (1921), 134.

[4] "In Titulo *De Dimissione* (cc. 646–668) prae primis sermo fit de dimissione quae *ipso iure* incurritur (c. 646), de delictis ob quae ipsa imponitur (§ 1) et de modo quo facti declaratio facienda est (§ 2). Dimissioni *ab homine* tria capita consecrantur."—Larraona, "Commentarium Codicis"—*CpR,* I (1920), 347.

[5] "Per modum proemii . . ."—Claeys Bouuaert-Simenon, *Manuale Juris Canonici* (Gandae et Leodii: prostat apud Auctores, 1924), p. 384; Beste, *Introductio in Codicem,* p. 438; Cocchi, *Commentarium in Codicem Iuris Canonici* (8 vols. in 5, Lib. II, pars II–III, *De Religiosis et Laicis,* Taurinorum Augustae: Marietti, 1922), IV, p. 249 (hereafter cited *Commentarium,* IV); Aleixo, "De Religiosis Ipso Iure Dimissis"—*Revista Eclesiastica Brasileira* (Petrópolis, Estado do Rio: Editora Vozes Ltda., 1941—), VI (1946), 387 (hereafter this periodical is cited *Rev. Ecl. Bras.*); ". . . per modum introductionis . . ."—Hippolytus a S. Familia, "De Dimissione Religiosorum"—*Analecta O. C. D.,* IV (1930), 157; ". . . canonem praeliminarem . . ."—Oesterle, *Praelectiones Iuris Canonici,* p. 367; ". . . canonem praeliminarem . . ."—Prümmer, *Manuale Iuris Canonici* (6. ed., Friburgi Brisgoviae: Herder, 1933), p. 346; "Die Vorbemerkung . . ."—Leitner, *Handbuch des katholischen Kirchenrechts auf Grund des neuen Kodex* (5 vols., Vol. III, *Das Ordensrecht,* 2. ed., Regensburg: Pustet, 1922), III, 487 (hereafter cited *Das Ordensrecht*).

[6] Palombo, *loc. cit.*

religious and its process is the simplest of all.[7] This observation finds confirmation in the words "*salvo praescripto can. 646*" of canon 654. The latter canon prescribes that a judicial process be employed in the dismissal of members in perpetual vows of clerical exempt institutes.[8] Nevertheless, in formulating this general norm, the law affirms that such religious are still subject to the provisions of the present canon.[9]

Accordingly, canon 646, without any preliminaries, proceeds to state its manner of operation. In this it brings forth how it differs from the other forms of dismissal to follow, what its relations are to them, and hence why it rightly stands alone and ahead of the rest.

Article 2. The Introductory Words of the Canon

A. *Ipso facto habendi sunt* . . .

In the article on the bond of religious profession it has been shown that even an imperfect society has a natural right to use means morally necessary for its welfare, which in certain instances requires that a delinquent religious be dismissed from the institute.[10] However, such a society must proceed according to rules prescribed for it by the perfect society. In the case of a religious institute it is the higher authority in the Church that has in Title XVI of Book Two of its Code laid down the rules for the dismissal of members. Canons 647–668 provide the ordinary and usual means for the subordinate society to protect its well-being. These have the characteristic mark that they require the *action* of the superiors designated as representatives of the Church in this matter—whether it be in an administrative or in a judicial capacity.

However, there are cases which by reason of their very enor-

---

[7] "*Ratio ordinis.* Recte proposuit legislator can. 646, in quo de dimissione ipso iure incurrenda, in vestibulo tituli *de dimissione* et hoc ex duplici ratione: 1º quia genericus, utpote comprehendens quoslibet professos cuiuslibet instituti; 2º quia procedura in casu adhibenda omnium simplicissima."—Hippolytus a S. Familia, *loc. cit.*

[8] Can. 654.

[9] Palombo, *loc. cit.*

[10] Cf. *supra*, p. 8.

mity cannot brook the delay that always accompanies the regular course of dismissal, without very great scandal to the faithful and very grave harm to the religious institute and even to religion itself. In these cases the Church anticipates the power ordinarily possessed by religious superiors, and in canon 646 directly decrees the dismissal of such a member by the very operation of law.[11]

While it is true that the authors do not treat of this form at great length, yet from their brief expressions a fairly accurate description can be gleaned. Thus, this form of dismissal is inflicted by the law,[12] not in the sense that there are not other forms of dismissal provided in the law,[13] but that this manner of dismissal takes place solely through the ministry of the law [14] without any intervention of a judge or religious superior.[15] The law takes the place of the superiors,[16] and hence there is no judicial process,[17] nor are there any other formalities.[18] The dismissal is automatic,[19] so that upon the very commission [20] of

---

[11] Wernz-Vidal, *Ius Canonicum,* III, n. 438; Hippolytus a S. Familia, "art. cit."—*Analecta O. C. D.,* IV (1930), 157-158; Creusen-Vermeersch, *Summa Novi Iuris Canonici Commentariis Aucta* (ed. 4., Mechliniae: Dessain, 1921), n. 237.

[12] ". . . tamquam inflicta a iure . . ."—Oesterle, *op. cit.,* p. 370; ". . . a iure lata . . ."—Schaefer, *De Religiosis,* n. 575.

[13] Cf. *supra,* p. 13, where consideration is given to the divisions *a iure* and *ab homine* usually made by the authors.

[14] ". . . per ministerium iuris . . ."—Beste, *op. cit.,* p. 439; Aleixo, "art. cit."—*Rev. Ecl. Bras.,* VI (1946), 387.

[15] ". . . sine ministerio iudicis vel Superioris religiosi . . ."—Schaefer, *De Religiosis,* n. 575; Goyeneche, *De Religiosis,* n. 105.

[16] ". . . lex locum Superioris tenet."—Tabera, "De Dimissione Religiosorum"—*CpR,* XI (1930), 413.

[17] ". . . quin processus iudicialis praecedat . . ."—Gerster a Zeil, *Ius Religiosorum in Compendium Redactum pro Iuvenibus Religiosis* (Taurini: Marietti, 1935), p. 146 (hereafter cited *Ius Religiosorum*); ". . . quin necessarius sit aliquis processus iudicialis."—Fanfani, *De Iure Religiosorum,* p. 493; "The few exceptional cases not demanding judicial action are specified in canons 646 and 668."—O'Brien, *The Exemption of Religious in Church Law* (Milwaukee: Bruce, 1943), p. 40.

[18] ". . . sine ullis aliis formalitatibus . . ."—Prümmer, *loc. cit.*

[19] Lydon, *Ready Answers in Canon Law* (2. ed., New York: Benziger,

the specified acts, the juridical status consequent upon an effected dismissal is present. The words "*ipso facto,*"[21] then, refer to the ominous act of the religious, while the words "*habendi sunt*" relate to the fixed judgment of the legislator. Taken together the force of these words is that, under the circumstances enumerated in the canon, a religious is immediately, both in the eyes of the Church and of the respective institute,[22] considered as having effected by his own act the dismissal established by law.[23]

B. . . . *tanquam legitime dimissi* . . .

In these words the Code states the effects of this dismissal. The phrase is general, it is true, and somewhat indefinite. Nevertheless, it is important at present to determine its meaning, in order to facilitate the discussion of particular effects in a separate and subsequent chapter.[24]

While most of the authors consulted are content with a mere repetition of the wording of the canon, Blat,[25] Tabera,[26] De Meester,[27] Hippolytus a S. Familia,[28] Mayer,[29] O'Neill,[30] and Aleixo[31] expressly and briefly indicate the sense in which these words are to be understood. Blat interprets the words

---

1937), p. 210; O'Leary, *Religious Dismissed After Perpetual Profession,* p. 44.

20 ". . . a momento patrati delicti . . ."—Sipos, *Enchiridion,* p. 409; ". . . posito facto . . ."—Coronata, *Institutiones,* I, n. 646; ". . . ideoque illico factum consequitur . . ."—Chelodi, *Ius de Personis,* n. 289.

21 Cf. *infra,* pp. 97, 161.

22 ". . . coram Ecclesia et respectiva religione . . ."—Blat, *Ius de Religiosis,* n. 658.

23 O'Neill, *The Dismissal of Religious in Temporary Vows,* p. 126; Schönsteiner, *Grundriss des Ordensrechtes* (Wien: Ludwig Auer, 1930), p. 624; Chelodi, *loc. cit.*

24 Cf. *infra,* Chapter X, pp. 183–191.

25 *Loc. cit.*

26 "Art. cit."—*CpR,* XI (1930), 413.

27 *Juris Canonici et Juris Canonico-Civilis Compendium* (nova ed. 3 vols. in 4, Brugis: Desclée, 1921–1928), II, n. 1057, 3o.

28 "Art. cit."—*Analecta O. C. D.,* IV (1930), 163.

29 *Benediktinisches Ordensrecht in der Beuroner Kongregation* (4 vols., Beuron: Kunstverlag, 1929–1936), III, 359 (hereafter cited *Benediktinisches Ordensrecht*).

30 *Loc. cit.*

31 "Art. cit."—*Rev. Ecl. Bras.,* VI (1946), 393.

"*tanquam legitime*" as indicating that the religious is in the same condition as he would have been had the dismissal taken place according to the norms of the canons.[32] Tabera[33] and Mayer[34] affirm that one dismissed according to canon 646 is truly dismissed, and hence subject to all the effects that the law has established for the dismissed. Hippolytus, furthermore, states that the juridic condition of a religious dismissed by the law is the same as that of a religious dismissed by the act of a superior, and hence that the same canons apply to both.[35] Finally, in presenting the same view, Aleixo points out that the canons having application will be determined by the type of vows involved.[36]

Since it is evident that canon 646 gives only a guiding rule, but does not enumerate specific effects, one must consult the canons in which the law presents the effects of dismissal. For religious in perpetual vows, whether simple or solemn, these effects are listed in canons 669–672. Hence these latter canons will necessarily enter into a discussion of the effects of canon 646.[37] Moreover, religious in temporary vows are also subject to this canon,[38] but the effects in their dismissal are those of canon 648.[39] Sweeney[40] and McGrath,[41] relying on the words "*ad normam*

[32] ". . . *tamquam legitime* scilicet: ad normam sacror. can. ideoque cum iuris effectibus *dimissi* . . ."—Blat, *loc. cit.;* cf. Palombo, *op. cit.,* n. 198.

[33] ". . . revera ut dimissi, cum omnibus effectibus quos pro dimissis ius statuit, habendi sunt . . ."—Tabera, *loc. cit.*

[34] *Loc. cit.*

[35] "Religiosi iure ita dimissi eandem conditionem iuridicam sortiuntur ac qui per actus Superioris dimittuntur; applicentur ergo eis quae de re in subsequentibus capitibus exponemus."—Hippolytus a S. Familia, *loc. cit.*

[36] "Quod statum iuridicum religiosi ipso iure dimissi attinet, ipsi applicandi sunt canones qui de dimissione religiosorum agunt iuxta diversitatem casuum, prout agitur de simpliciter professo vel perpetuo ac solemniter professo."—Aleixo, *loc. cit.*

[37] De Meester, *loc. cit.;* Aleixo, *loc. cit.*

[38] Cf. *infra,* p. 89.

[39] De Meester, *loc. cit.;* Vermeersch-Creusen, *Epitome,* I, n. 821; O'Neill, *loc. cit.;* Aleixo, *loc. cit.*

[40] *The Reduction of Clerics to the Lay State,* The Catholic University of America Canon Law Studies, n. 223 (Washington, D. C.: The Catholic University of America Press, 1945), pp. 74–75.

[41] *The Privilege of the Canon,* The Catholic University of America Canon

can. 647" contained in canon 648, discount the view of the authors who apply canon 648 to canon 646. If their contention were true, there would be no way to determine the effects of this dismissal for those in temporary vows. However, they do not take cognizance of the words "*tanquam legitime dimissi*" as contained in canon 646, which furnish the basis of the contention that canon 648 applies, and which offer the compelling reason for this conclusion.

The phrase "*tanquam legitime dimissi,*" then, indicates that this dismissal is to have the same force and effects that it would have had if, apart from the intervention of the perfect society, the subordinate society had acted according to the procedure prescribed in law.

C. . . . *religiosi:*

In the unrestricted use of this term the Code speaks of religious in the sense of canon 488, 7°.[42] This marks a departure from the former law,[43] since it includes women religious[44] and also religious who are professed with temporary vows.[45]

Canon 646, therefore, applies to all professed religious, whether their vows are temporary or perpetual, simple or solemn, and of whatever Order, Congregation, or Institute—be it exempt or non-exempt, clerical or lay, of pontifical or of diocesan approval.[46]

Law Studies, n. 242 (Washington, D. C.: The Catholic University of America Press, 1946), pp. 76–77.

42 ". . . qui vota nuncuparunt in aliqua religione; . . ." Cf. Palombo, *op. cit.*, n. 196; Blat, *op. cit.*, n. 658; Tabera, "art. cit."—*CpR*, XI (1930), 413; Hippolytus a S. Familia, "art. cit."—*Analecta* O. C. D., IV (1930), 157.

43 Cf. *supra*, p. 63.

44 Canon 490. Cf. Tabera, *loc. cit.;* Smith, *The Penal Law for Religious,* The Catholic University of America Canon Law Studies, n. 98 (Washington, D. C.: The Catholic University of America, 1935), p. 39; Geser, *The Canon Law Governing Communities of Sisters* (St. Louis: Herder, 1939), n. 1152; and others.

45 Tabera, *loc. cit.;* Schaefer, *De Religiosis,* n. 576; Geser, *loc. cit.;* O'Neill, *The Dismissal of Religious in Temporary Vows,* p. 126; Pejška, *Ius Canonicum Religiosorum,* p. 189; and others.

46 Woywod, *A Practical Commentary on the Code of Canon Law,* I, 289; Mayer, *Benediktinisches Ordensrecht,* III, 359; Beste, *Introductio in Codicem,* p. 438; Chelodi, *Ius de Personis,* n. 289; Palombo, *loc. cit.;* Michalicka, *Judicial Procedure in Dismissal of Clerical Exempt Religious,* p. 12; Smith,

Furthermore, in consequence of an authentic interpretation of law,[47] this canon also extends to religious professed with the so-called conditional vows *"as long as I live in the Congregation,"* which are equivalent to temporary vows.[48] Finally, in virtue of canon 681 [49] members of societies of men or women living in common without vows are subject to this canon. In the case of these quasi-religious [50] the effects of this dismissal will depend on whether the bond that links them to their society is temporal or perpetual.[51] If there is no bond with the society, this canon does not apply; but recourse must be had to the constitutions or to the use of canon 571, § 1, by analogy.[52]

Moreover, those excluded in article 1 of the first chapter [53] as not being religious, such as those with private vows, novices,[54] postulants, etc., are by that fact excluded from the provisions of this canon. On the other hand, apostates and fugitives,[55] those who while bound by perpetual vows are dismissed in consequence of the action taken by their superior, the exclaustrated,[56] and those

---

op. cit., pp. 39, 104, 119; Toso, *Commentaria Minora,* Lib. II, pars II, p. 246; and others.

[47] P. C. I., 1 mart. 1921—*AAS,* XIII (1921), 177.

[48] Schaefer, *De Religiosis,* n. 581, 7; cf. *supra,* p. 3, note 18.

[49] " Praeter proprias cuiusque societatis constitutiones, . . . serventur, congrua congruis referendo, . . . circa eorum dimissionem, praescripta can. 646–672." Cf. Berutti, *Institutiones Iuris Canonici* (6 vols. in 7, Vol. III, *De Religiosis,* Taurini, Romae; Marietti, 1936), III, n. 188 (hereafter cited *De Religiosis*).

[50] Cf. *supra,* pp. 4–5.

[51] P. C. I., 1 mart. 1921—*AAS,* XIII (1921), 177. Cf. Maroto, " Annotationes"—*CpR,* II (1921), 133; Vermeersch, " Annotationes "—*Periodica,* X (1922), 326; Beste, *Introductio in Codicem,* p. 456.

[52] Maroto, *loc. cit.;* Vermeersch, *loc. cit.;* Wernz-Vidal, *Ius Canonicum,* III, n. 458.

[53] Cf. *supra,* pp. 1–3.

[54] Tabera ("art. cit."—*CpR,* XI [1930], 413, nota 7) states that, though novices are not subject to this dismissal, such an action on their part would either interrupt the novitiate (can. 556, § 1) or certainly offer causes for the dismissal treated by the law in canon 571, § 1.

[55] Cf. Schaefer, *De Religiosis,* n. 571; Larraona, " Quaestio Canonica "—*CpR,* IV (1923), 175, nota 2.

[56] Cf. Piontek, *De Indulto Exclaustrationis necnon Saecularizationis,* The Catholic University of America Canon Law Studies, n. 29 (Washington, D. C.: The Catholic University of America, 1925), p. 135.

who have been promoted to dignities [57] are still religious, and as such are subject to this enacted form of dismissal.

Though the term "*religiosi*" which designates the subjects of this canon seems to comprise all those who come under this nomenclature as described in the preliminary notions,[58] an exception must be noted here. Oriental religious in their own disciplines are not liable to this form of dismissal.[59] While some form of dismissal is necessary in order that Oriental communities may also exercise their natural right to protect their well-being by removing a delinquent member, it is not required by the very nature of things that it be this *ipso facto* effected dismissal. Nevertheless, this norm can have application in these groups if it is so stated in their constitutions, for then it becomes particular law.[60] In this manner an Oriental in a Latin religious community is subject to canon 646.

In conclusion, then, the following religious are subject to the provisions of this canon:

(a) all Latins and some of the Orientals,
(b) men and women,
(c) clerical or lay,
(d) of pontifical or diocesan institutes,
(e) with solemn or simple vows,
(f) with perpetual or temporary vows,
(g) apostates, fugitives, and dismissed,
(h) the exclaustrated, and those promoted to dignities,
(i) members of societies living in common without vows.

Article 3. The Body of the Canon

After the general statement, in the opening words of the first paragraph, concerning the manner of operation, concerning the effects, and concerning the subjects, the Code proceeds to enumerate the cases that come under this law. In these the Code has

---

[57] Cf. *infra*, pp. 105–106.

[58] Cf. *supra*, Chapter I, Article 1, pp. 1–5.

[59] "Nemo delinquens ipso facto dimissus habetur, licet delicta de quibus in can. 646 sufficentia iudicentur ad dimittendum monachum."—Coussa, *Epitome*, n. 162.

[60] "Recentissimae constitutiones praescripta praesentis canonis referunt." —Coussa, *loc. cit.*

preserved almost intact the description of the cases in the decree *Quum singulae.*[61] Apostasy from a religious institute, however, is no longer listed under the present law.[62] The cases that now bring about the *ipso facto* effected dismissal are: apostasy from the Catholic Faith, flight with a person of the other sex, attempted marriage, contracted marriage, and civil marriage.[63]

Since the three last mentioned are variations of the same case, authors follow the divisions of the Code in stating that the cases contained in canon 646 are three in number.[64] Furthermore, the authors use various terms, such as cases,[65] crimes,[66] and delicts,[67] to designate the causes of this dismissal as listed in the canon. The term "case" is used by the canon itself in § 2,[68] while the term "delict" is used in canon 670 in its reference to canon 646,[69] and constituted also the term used in the decree *Quum singulae.*[70]

The delicts that prompted the legislator to proceed so rigorously [71] are of their very nature so grave [72] that it was no longer deemed expedient to employ the ordinary process of dismissal

[61] Cf. *supra,* p. 61, note 11.

[62] Berutti, *De Religiosis,* n. 158.

[63] Aleixo, "De Religiosis Ipso Iure Dimissis"—*Rev. Ecl. Bras.,* VI (1946), 393; cf. *infra,* Chapter VIII, pp. 107-158.

[64] Tabera, "art. cit."—*CpR,* XI (1930), 413; Hippolytus a S. Familia, "art. cit."—*Analecta O. C. D.,* IV (1930), 158; Sipos, *Enchiridion,* p. 409; Schaefer, *De Religiosis,* n. 576; Brandys, *Kirchliches Rechtsbuch für die religiösen Laiengenossenschaften der Brüder und Schwestern nach dem neuen Gesetzbuch der hl. Kirche* (2. ed., Paderborn: Schöningh, 1920), n. 109 (hereafter cited *Kirchliches Rechtsbuch*); Bouscaren-Ellis, *Canon Law* (Milwaukee: Bruce, 1946), p. 310; and others. Aleixo (*loc. cit*), on the other hand, counts each of the marriage cases separately and so gives the number as five.

[65] Brandys, *loc. cit.;* Schaefer, *loc. cit.;* and others.

[66] Tabera, *loc. cit.;* Bouscaren-Ellis, *loc. cit.;* O'Leary, *op. cit.,* p. 52; and others.

[67] Hippolytus a S. Familia, *loc. cit.;* Sipos, *loc. cit.;* Mayer, *Benediktinisches Ordensrecht,* III, 359; and others.

[68] "In his casibus, . . ."

[69] ". . . qui aliquod delictum commisit de quo in can. 646, . . ."

[70] Cf. *supra,* p. 61, note 11.

[71] Hippolytus a S. Familia, *loc. cit.*

[72] Tabera, *loc. cit.;* Toso, *Commentaria Minora,* Lib. II, pars II, p. 246; Creusen-Garesché-Ellis, *Religious Men and Women in the Code,* n. 345.

when they were committed.[73] The perpetration of any one of these acts denotes an implicit desertion of the institute,[74] an evident intention to destroy the bond with the community,[75] and an extreme and incurable incorrigibility on the part of the delinquent.[76] Hence, it is taken for granted that it would be useless to attempt his amendment by means of the usual warnings and admonitions, and since his action brings with it a certain and imminent danger of grave scandal and harm, dismissal must be decided at once.

Moreover, since these delicts are for the most part notorious, or of such a nature that proof of them is presumed to be at hand, there is no need of a probative process.[77] Finally, as Villien had already noted under the law of the decree *Quum singulae,*[78] the canon speaks only of specified and determined delicts,[79] and hence the enumeration of the delicts as mentioned in canon 646 points to an all-inclusive listing.[80]

In § 2 of the canon the Code outlines the rôle which the superior and the minor society are to assume after the dismissal has taken place.[81]

Article 4. The Nature of This Dismissal

Although canon 646, § 1, indicates in general the manner of operation, the relevancy of the subjects, and the effects of this dismissal, it does not state just what its nature is. Thus, is it a penalty, a quasi-penalty, a sanction, a remedy, an administrative

---

[73] Coronata, *Institutiones,* I, n. 645.

[74] Cocchi, *Commentarium,* IV, n. 144; Fanfani, *De Iure Religiosorum,* p. 493.

[75] Villien, "La Procédure Canonique pour L'Expulsion des Religieux"—*Le Canoniste Contemporain,* XXXVI (1913), 138; cf. *supra,* p. 67.

[76] Hippolytus a S. Familia, *loc. cit.*

[77] Hippolytus a S. Familia, *loc. cit.*

[78] Cf. *supra,* pp. 66–67.

[79] Schönsteiner, *Grundriss des Ordensrechtes,* p. 624; Palombo, *De Dimissione Religiosorum,* n. 197.

[80] Falco, *Corso di Diritto Ecclesiastico* (Padova: Casa Editrice Dott. A. Milani Cedam, 1930), p. 86; Aleixo, "art. cit."—*Rev. Ecl. Bras.,* VI (1946), 387.

[81] Blat, *Ius de Religiosis,* n. 657; cf. *infra,* Chapter IX, pp. 159–182.

act, or what? It is on this very point that the post-Code authors either make definite statements without further explanation or justification, or remain uncertain, indefinite, or even silent. Nevertheless, it is most important to determine the exact nature of this law at the very outset, for then only can one rightly interpret the canon, and present clear notions in doing so.

Accordingly, it is deemed advisable to consider the question at this point, and to endeavor to arrive at some definite conclusion. Perhaps this can best be done by means of a brief survey of the law as it existed before the Code, through a consideration of the authors who comment on the law of the Code, and ultimately with the aid of an analysis of the canon in the light of these reflections.

As regards the law enacted in the decree *Quum singulae,* it is quite definite that the dismissal was a penalty. The very wording of the law stated that those who committed the delicts in question were subject to the *penalty* of expulsion or dismissal,[82] and that this was to be attested to by means of a *declaratory sentence* regarding the fact.[83] Pre-Code authors who commented on this law treated it as a penalty.[84] The post-Code authors who make reference to this earlier law likewise state that it was introduced as a penalty.[85] While the nature of the former law is easily ascertainable, the same cannot be said of the new. For the very words that made the law of the decree clear have been changed in the Code.

In speaking of the law as it is now in the Code, some authors consider it substantially the same as the former with only minor changes in the direction of a more polished form of expression.[86]

---

[82] Cf. *supra,* p. 61, note 11.

[83] *Loc. cit.*

[84] Vermeersch, "Forma Expellendi vel Dimittendi Religiosos et Moniales," Annotatio I, A, 1.—*Periodica,* VI (1912), 47; Villien, "*La Procédure* Canonique pour l'Expulsion des Religieux"—*Le Canoniste Contemporain,* XXXVI (1913), 136 sqq.; Tamayo, *Procedimientos de Derecho Penal Canónico,* n. 300; cf. *supra,* Chapter VI, Article 2, pp. 64–80.

[85] ". . . haec dimissio *ut poena* reapse fuerit inducta . . ."—Tabera, "De Dimissione Religiosorum," *CpR,* XI (1930), 412; Smith, *The Penal Law for Religious,* p. 34; Goyeneche, *De Religiosis,* n. 105.

[86] "Haec eadem disciplina, aliquantulum perpolita quoad formam, fuit recepta in schematibus an. 1914 et 1916. In editione tamen Codicis omis-

Perhaps it is in view of this opinion of the continuance of the former law [87] that certain authors [88] regard this dismissal as a penalty, for they offer no reasoning for their classification. Thus, though Palombo,[89] Coronata,[90] and Mayer [91] state that it is a *latae sententiae* penalty, Berutti allows only a similarity to such a penalty.[92]

Tabera [93] and Goyeneche,[94] while terming this dismissal a penalty and stating that as such it was introduced and as such it should be considered, are quick to add that it is not a penalty in the strict juridic sense current throughout the Fifth Book of the Code, and so seem to imply that it is only a quasi-penalty at most. However, they do state as certain that it is a remedy given to the religious institute to free itself from a member who by his act does grave harm to the Christian life, stains the honor of Religion, or even directly makes an onslaught upon the moral fiber and vital existence of the institute. Schaefer,[95] also, adopts this last presented view.

While Tabera, Goyeneche and Schaefer apply two ideas to this dismissal, namely that of a penalty and that of a remedy, Wernz-Vidal [96] and Hippolytus a S. Familia [97] call it simply and purely

---

sus fuit numerus 2us, . . ."—Tabera, *loc. cit.;* "In c. 646 alii tres casus dimissionis ipso iure incurrendae, quos decretum *Quum singulae* introduxit, aliquantulum expoliti quoad formam, recepti sunt, . . ."—Larraona, "Quaestio Canonica"—*CpR,* IV (1923), 174.

[87] Cf. canon 6, 2o.

[88] Smith, *op. cit.,* pp. 39, 104, 120; Coronata, *Institutiones,* I, n. 645; Palombo, *De Dimissione Religiosorum,* n. 196; Schaefer, *De Religiosis,* n. 575; Blat, *Ius de Religiosis,* n. 659; Creusen-Garesché-Ellis, *Religious Men and Women in the Code,* n. 345; Bouscaren-Ellis, *Canon Law,* p. 310; Aleixo, "De Religiosis Ipso Iure Dimissis"—*Rev. Ecl. Bras.,* VI (1946), 388; Larraona, "Quaestio Canonica"—*CpR,* III (1922), 326; and others.

[89] *Loc. cit.*

[90] *Loc. cit.*

[91] *Benediktinisches Ordensrecht,* III, 359.

[92] "Si dimisso fit ipso iure, similitudinem habet cum poena latae sententiae; . . ."—Berutti, *De Religiosis,* p. 338.

[93] *Loc. cit.*

[94] *Loc. cit.*

[95] *Loc. cit.*

[96] *Ius Canonicum,* III, nn. 438, 452.

[97] "De Dimissione Religiosorum"—*Analecta O. C. D.,* IV (1930), 158, 162.

a sanction of the law, without any further differentiation. Finally, a great number of authors either deem the answer to be self-evident, or propose not to commit themselves in their view, or fail to advert to the problem, for they make no statement as to the nature of this dismissal.[98]

This examination of the authors reveals among them a general lack of proffered reasons, a variety of divergent views, and withal a character of indefiniteness, so that the accumulation of these factors serves little to beget the desired assurance. However, the canon itself offers several points for further study that may lead to the solution. To the present writer it seems that the crux lies in the change made in the law as it now appears in the Code. Thus recourse must be had to the norms of canon 6.

Tabera and Larraona consider this law simply as a re-enactment of the pre-Code law in a more polished form; yet they seem to say this only of the *cases* that come under this law.[99] In the same manner Berutti states that the enumeration of the causes of this dismissal constitutes a verbatim repetition of the earlier listing of these causes in the decree.[100] However, they do not make any specific mention of the changes made in the introductory clause, concerning which one would expect a comment. The heading of the law as first promulgated was:

> *Item contra quaedam delicta censetur veluti lata a iure poena expulsionis vel dimissionis,*[101]

which in the law of the Code has been changed to:

> *Ipso facto habendi sunt tanquam legitime dimissi religiosi.*[102]

This is not a complete change, for "*ipso facto habendi sunt*" can

[98] Beste, *Introductio in Codicem,* p. 438; Sipos, *Enchiridion,* p. 409; Woywod, *A Practical Commentary on the Code of Canon Law,* I, 289; and others.

[99] Cf. *supra,* p. 94, note 86.

[100] Berutti, *De Religiosis,* n. 158.

[101] S. C. de Rel., decr. *Quum singulae,* 16 maii 1911, n. 18—*AAS,* III (1911), 237.

[102] Canon 646, § 1.

be considered as a rewording of "*censetur veluti lata a iure,*" "*dimissi*" incorporates the notions of "*expulsionis vel dimissionis,*"[103] "*tanquam legitime*" appears to be an addition of the present law,[104] "*religiosi*" supplants "*item contra quaedam delicta*" as the focal point of the canon, and "*poena*" is used only in the earlier law. Thus the very word that made the old law clear has been omitted in the new. It seems certain that if the law had meant to retain the nature of the former law, it would at least have kept the word "*poena*" which delineated that nature. The authors make no reference to this conspicuous change. Perhaps it may be urged that the change is only in the manner of expression, and not in the substance of the law; and that "*poena expulsionis vel dimissionis*" and "*ipso facto . . . dimissi*" are two ways of saying one and the same thing. With regard to the earlier used wording in the law it is definite that the word "*poena*" determined the nature of the act of expulsion or dismissal. Whether the same can be said of the present terminology in the law is a matter that must be considered further.

From the language of the Code it is certain that the words "*ipso facto*" in themselves neither affirm nor deny the presence of a penalty, but simply designate the manner of operation.[105] In this uniform sense they are found throughout the Code.[106] They appear most frequently in Part II of the Fifth Book, but even there they denote only how the penalty is incurred. The penalty itself is made clear by some other word, such as excommunication, suspension, etc. Thus it is readily seen that the words "*ipso facto*" characterize the action, and as such can be applied to a variety of subjects. The nature of the latter must be evident from some other word in the text.

Accordingly, it may be urged that in canon 646 "*ipso facto*" is predicated of a penalty expressed in the word "*dimissi,*" just

---

[103] Cf. *supra*, pp. 9–10.

[104] Cf. *infra*, p. 184.

[105] Cf. *supra*, p. 87.

[106] Maroto, "Annotationes"—*CpR,* XV (1934), 355. For a listing of the canons in which the words "*ipso facto*" occur, cf. Laver, *Index Verborum Codicis Iuris Canonici* (Civitate Vaticana: Typis Polyglottis Vaticanis, 1941), pp. 302–303.

as in other places it is predicated of suspension, etc. However, the argument cannot be invoked *a pari,* for one must first establish whether or not dismissal in general is a penalty. It is noteworthy that only with reference to canon 646 do the authors in general designate dismissal as a penalty; the authors who speak of the other types of dismissal as penalties are remarkably few.[107] In the latter case, also, the authors do not adduce reasons in support of their assertions, and so the problem remains the same.

The recourse to the word "*dimissi*" would have force, if there were evidence in the Code that it connotes a penalty. However, dismissal is not listed under any of the received types of penalties enacted by the Church.[108] The only reference made to dismissal in the Fifth Book of the Code appears in canon 2385,[109] and there it is evident that a distinction is being made between the enacted or threatened penalty on the one hand, and the *ipso facto* effected dismissal on the other.[110]

Nowhere does the Code speak of any dismissal as a penalty. Moreover, the Code limits the treatment of dismissal to title XVI of the Second Book, and in this gives no statement as to its nature. Though it is readily admitted that dismissal was a penalty in the law of the decree,[111] that fact does not argue for its inclusion as such in the law of the Code. The present discipline differs considerably in some instances from that which was in force under the decree *Quum singulae.*[112] Notable among these changes is the difference of terminology.

[107] Palombo, *De Dimissione Religiosorum,* n. 2; Smith, *The Penal Law for Religious,* p. 87; Schaefer, *De Religiosis,* n. 591; Fuchs, "Von der gerichtlichen oder gerichtsähnlichen Gewalt der Ordensoberinnen und ihrer Assistentinnen"—*Theologisch-praktische Quartalschrift* (Linz, 1832—), LXXXVII (1934), 813; Tabera, "De Dimissione Religiosorum," *CpR,* XIV (1933), 267; and others. O'Leary (*op. cit.,* p. 8) terms it a quasi-penalty.

[108] Cf. canons 2216, 2241, 2255, 2286, 2291, 2298, 2306, 2313.

[109] "Firmo praescripto can. 646 . . ."

[110] By analogy this reasoning is adopted from McDevitt, *The Renunciation of an Ecclesiastical Office,* The Catholic University of America Canon Law Studies, n. 218 (Washington, D. C.: The Catholic University of America Press, 1946), p. 116.

[111] Cf. *supra,* p. 61, note 11.

[112] Prümmer, *Manuale Iuris Canonici,* p. 346.

Reference has already been made to the sole use of the term "dismissal" in the present law, and to its consequent extension of meaning.[113] Certainly dismissal cannot be considered a penalty for some of the actions or factors listed in canon 647 as potential causes for dismissal, since they can exist apart from any connotation of fault on the part of the religious and still offer ground for dismissal.[114] Hence the term "dismissal" in itself does not necessarily denote a penalty. Dismissal is indeed mentioned in the Code. But since it is not designated as a penalty, it follows according to canon 6, 5°, that the notion of penalty must be excluded. For the present, then, it suffices to say that with reference to the supposed penal character of dismissal as mentioned in canon 646 no confirmation is obtained by appealing to the notion of dismissal in general, for the entire question hinges on whether dismissal is a penalty at all. Hence, it will suffice to restrict the consideration of this point to canon 646, and to refer to the other forms of dismissal only for the sake of corroboratory arguments. On the other hand, the arguments adduced for the conclusion which is reached will for the most part apply also to dismissal as a whole.

Even though cognizance is taken of the omission of the word "*poena*" in the present law, some may still urge that all justified departure from the sense of the pre-Code law remains in doubt, and that accordingly one must abide by the import of the earlier law.[115] In this manner canon 646 would still be considered as treating of a strict penalty. However, such a doubt seems unreasonable, since it does not account for the change in text from words indicating a clear intent to the absence of words indicating such an intent, which words however should be present if the lawgiver wished to retain the idea of a penalty in the act of dismissal. Moreover, whereas the former law required a "declaratory sentence of the fact" in these cases,[116] the present law

---

[113] Cf. *supra,* Chapter I, Article 3, pp. 9–15.

[114] Palombo, *De Dimissione Religiosorum,* n. 2; Schaefer, *De Religiosis,* n. 579.

[115] Canon 6, 4°.

[116] Cf. *supra,* p. 61, note 11.

speaks only of a "declaration of fact." [117] This may well serve as a further argument that the Code wished to abolish the idea of a penalty in connection with the act of dismissal.

In view of these facts it seems certain that there is a change in the text, and that this change was made for the definite purpose of altering the nature of the pre-Code law the while some of the matters incidental to it were retained in force. It is necessary to note that, even though these incidental matters, i.e., the circumstances that bring on the dismissal, are worded the same or nearly the same in both laws,[118] they are to be judged in the light of their proper relevancy in the present law.[119]

Thus the earlier law can be viewed with profit for an understanding of what is meant by an incidental aspect of canon 646, i.e., for determining just what cases the present law intends to include under these terms, for in this respect it still agrees with the earlier law. However, in considering these cases in connection with the rest of the canon, as to its nature, its manner of operation, and its effects, one must follow the present law exclusively, since it involves a discrepancy from the earlier law.[120]

Aside from this consideration of the law in itself, there is another element that could seem to constitute dismissal as a true penalty, or at least lend support to that view. It is the fact that the three cases mentioned in canon 646 are termed delicts in canon 670.[121] As such, according to canon 2195, they postulate the inherence of some canonical sanction.[122]

First of all, it must be granted that these cases do constitute true delicts, since canon 2195 sets up the definition of a delict as it is to be understood in ecclesiastical law.[123] Thus the properly defined sense of the word seems applicable not only in the Fifth

---

[117] Canon 646, § 2.

[118] Cf. *supra,* p. 96.

[119] Cf. Neuberger, *Canon 6 of the Relation of the Codex Juris Canonici to Preceding Legislation,* The Catholic University of America Canon Law Studies, n. 44 (Washington, D. C.: The Catholic University of America, 1927), p. 80.

[120] Canon 6, 3º.

[121] Cf. *supra,* p. 92.

[122] ". . . cui addita sit sanctio canonica saltem indeterminata."

[123] ". . . iure ecclesiastico. . . ."

Book of the Code, but also in any and every canon throughout the whole Code. It may be questioned, however, whether the *canonical* sanction which receives mention in canon 2195 must necessarily be understood as a *penal* sanction. Though the authors in general [124] consider these two terms as signifying the same thing, Tummolo-Iorio in presenting the same view mention the possibility of making a distinction between them.[125]

Canon 2195 itself seems to insinuate a distinction through the juxtaposition of the *sanctio canonica* in § 1 with the *sanctio poenalis* in § 2. However, even if both of these terms signify a penalty in the strict sense, it does not follow that the effected dismissal must be acknowledged as the penalty for the delicts in question. The delicts listed in canon 646 are punished with their proper penalty in the Fifth Book of the Code.[126] Hence their rôle in the present canon is simply that of conditions postulated for the automatically effected dismissal.[127]

The delicts postulated in canons 649 and 656 for other forms of dismissal are also cited as indications that dismissal is a penalty.[128] However, the fact that the perpetration of three delicts is postulated in these canons for the imminence of a dismissal readily shows that these must be delicts in their own right, i.e., external and morally imputable violations of a law to which from some

---

[124] Roberti, *De Delictis et Poenis* (Vol. I, Partes I & II, ed. altera, Romae: Apud Custodiam Librariam pontificii Instituti Utriusque Iuris, 1944), Vol. I, Pars I, n. 38; Chelodi, *Ius Canonicum de Delictis et Poenis* (5. ed. recognita et aucta a Pio Ciprotti, Trento: Libreria Moderna Editrice, 1943), n. 2; Michiels, *De Delictis et Poenis* (Vol. I, Lublin: Universitas Catholica, 1934), p. 77; Beste, *Introductio in Codicem,* p. 874; and others.

[125] "Nisi quis velit admittere distinctionem inter sanctionem *canonicam* et sanctionem *poenalem,* applicabiles: *hanc* quidem ob patratum delictum *grave, illam* vero ob delictum sive *grave* sive *leve, sive* patratum sive ad periculum avertendum ne *grave* deinde patretur neve scandalum aliudve detrimentum ordinis publici sequatur, ad normam can. 2306–2311 (de remediis poenalibus)."—Tummolo-Iorio, *Compendium Theologiae Moralis* (2 vols. in 4, Vol. II, *Supplementum,* 5. ed., Neapoli: M. D'Auria, 1936), II, 705, nota 2.

[126] Cf. *infra,* p. 185.

[127] Tabera, "art. cit."—*CpR,* XI (1930), 413.

[128] Fuchs, "art. cit."—*Theologisch-praktische Quartalschrift,* LXXXVII (1934), 813.

other source there attaches some canonical sanction. Thus the delicts in question must be delicts in fact, regardless of whether dismissal follows, and so they are to be considered simply as conditions postulated as necessarily present previous to any proceedings for dismissal.[129]

This exclusion of dismissal from the realm of penalty is better understood when viewed in connection with the profession-contract and the purpose of the law.

In the article on the bond of profession reference was made to the general acceptance of the teaching that the bond which unites a religious with his community is to be sought in a contract.[130] With this contract there enter corresponding rights and duties. By accepting a profession a community is bound to keep a religious and to furnish him a living, provided that he on his part fulfills the obligations consequent upon his profession. On the other hand, a professed member can, on account of the non-fulfillment of this agreement, be dismissed.[131] A grave imputable violation of this contract by a religious constitutes a breach of contract, and gives the institute the right to sever relations with the offending member.[132] A similar view was advanced by Villien in reference to the pre-Code law.[133]

Dismissal, then, is the sanction for this breach of contract. It is a sanction, and not a penalty,[134] for it is the withholding of

---

[129] Tabera, "art. cit."—*CpR,* XIV (1933), 267–268; Larraona, "Consultationes"—*CpR,* III (1922), 15–16; Michalicka, *Judicial Procedure in Dismissal of Clerical Exempt Religious,* pp. 17–18.

[130] Cf. *supra,* Chapter I, Article 2, pp. 5–8.

[131] Eichmann, *Lehrbuch des Kirchenrechts,* (2. ed., Paderborn: Schöningh, 1926), p. 257; Michalicka, *ibid.,* p. 5; cf. *supra,* p. 8.

[132] ". . . eiici debet praevaricator voti et pacti sui, cum iam Institutus non teneatur ei de promisso eum secum tenendi, qui promissum suum praevaricando pluries violavit."—Palombo, *De Dimissione Religiosorum,* n. 6.

[133] Cf. *supra,* p. 67.

[134] "Insuper non sunt poenae . . . sanctiones conventionales in contractibus . . ."—Roberti, *De Delictis et Poenis,* Vol. I. pars II, n. 235.

In American Law it is firmly established that the right to rescind a contract for non-performance is a remedy as old as the law of contract itself. When the contract is whole and entire or indivisible this right is unquestioned. Norrington v. Wright, 115 U. S. 188. When the agreement is rights which one has already forfeited by his action. In some cases this sanction severs the bond with the institute, in others it leaves the bond intact but shorn of its rights. In the latter case there is a "bare" contract, i.e., one bound to duties but deprived of rights. The contract remains as long as the vows remain. The effects of this sanction vary as a greater or lesser bond is involved,[135] and hence there are different types of dismissal depending on the degrees of firmness in the contract. Moreover, the

mutual and dependent, and one party fails to perform his part, the other party may treat it as rescinded. South Texas Telephone Co. v. Huntington (Tex.) 121 S. W. 242.

If this remedy were in any way considered by the civil law courts as penal in nature, the state would of necessity have to be the party instituting the criminal process. In the cases cited the remedy was effected between the parties to the contract themselves. Furthermore, the misconduct of a partner of such character and degree as materially to interfere with the conduct of the business is a cause for dissolution by decree on petition of the injured, but not of the guilty partner. Gerard v. Gateau, 84 Ill. 121. In such case, for example, the desertion or absconding of a partner has been held to work a dissolution *ipso facto;* Whitman v. Leonard, 3 Pic. (Mass.) 177; Ayer v. Ayer, 41 Vt. 346; Beaver v. Lewis, 14 Ark. 138; Potter v. Moses, 1 R. I. 430; but generally it is usually treated as a ground of suit; Burgess v. Badger, 124 Ill. 288; Arnold v. Brown, 24 Picl. (Mass.) 80; Denver v. Roane, 99 U. S. 355; Ambler v. Whipple, 20 Wall (U. S.) 546.

A court of equity may dissolve a partnership on the occurrence of events or changes of circumstances which render the continuance of the relation impossible or unprofitable.—Crane, *Handbook of the Law of Partnership* (St. Paul, Minn.: West Publishing Co., 1938), p. 335. Equity will not act on slight grounds; Appeal of Slemmer, 58 Pa. 168; it requires a strong case; Gerard v. Gateau, 84 Ill. 121. What are slight or grave causes is sometimes difficult to determine, and must depend on the circumstances of the case as bearing on the question whether the acts complained of would prevent a profitable continuance of the business upon the terms of the articles; Page v. Van Kirk, 1 Brewst. (Pa.) 282.

The effects of such a dissolution, as between the immediate partners is to terminate all transactions between them as partners, except for the purpose of the winding up of the business and of a general accounting. Petrikin v. Collier, 1 Pa. 247. While the dissolution of a partnership under American Law in certain circumstances affords an apt example of the principle of contract law as just enunciated, it is not without unfortunate intendments for our purposes.

[135] Michalicka, *ibid.*, p. 10.

Church legislates here only for the bond with the community; it does not take cognizance of the violations of contract in the matter of the vows made to God, except in so far as such violations disturb also the public order of the Church.[136]

As regards the purpose of the law, authors state that a dismissal provides the society with the means necessary to protect its interests.[137] Thus Toso[138] and Mayer[139] maintain that, as in Title XV of the Second Book of the Code the legislator has provided for egress from religion undertaken unilaterally by the religious, so in Title XVI there is provision for the dismissal or forced separation of a religious from religion through the unilateral action of the institute, which uses its right against a member who has become harmful.[140] In this manner the society is enabled to safeguard the common good, and to shield itself and its members from scandal, from the weakening of discipline, from the diminution of the good name, etc., by authorizing the removal of such an offender.[141] Hence, it appears that the main purpose of dismissal is to offer protection to the religious state, so that it may continue to be held in honor by all.[142]

Canon 646 contemplates the crimes of a religious which are so alien to the religious state that it is imperative to remove him immediately from the state to which his continued presence is only a cause of further harm. Consequently the law itself anticipates the religious superior's power to discharge the guilty religious, and decrees that the dismissal is effected at the very moment of the commission of the delictual act.[143] In many ways the purpose of this law resembles that which establishes an irregularity *ex delicto* in the case of those who are in sacred orders, for as the latter was primarily instituted for the protection of the sacred

136 Chelodi, *Ius Canonicum de Delictis et Poenis*, n. 101.

137 Palombo, *loc. cit.;* Coronata, *Institutiones*, I, n. 645; Augustine, *A Commentary*, III, 385; cf. *supra*, p. 8.

138 *Commentaria Minora*, Lib. II, pars II, p. 242.

139 *Benediktinisches Ordensrecht*, III, 358.

140 Cf. *supra*, p. 11.

141 Wernz-Vidal, *Ius Canonicum*, III, n. 438.

142 Canon 487.

143 Tabera, "De Dimissione Religiosorum."—*CpR*, XI (1930), 413.

ministry,[144] so the former was invoked for the protection of the religious state.

For these reasons the present writer is of the opinion that dismissal is not to be classified as a penalty. Though for the religious his dismissal bears a great similarity to a penalty, its main purpose is to provide a remedy for society.[145] As such it is not a penalty, but rather a sanction,[146] for its aim is that of procuring the public good, and not that of directly punishing the action of the religious, whether for the sake of expiating the crime, or for the sake of amending the delinquent. The latter point will become clearer from a consideration of the effects of this dismissal.[147] Dismissal, then, though it be conditioned on the presence of criminal act, takes place not in punishment of a crime, but as a necessary means to forestall greater evil. It is, as Villien termed it,[148] the logical juridic sanction. Further, it is a canonical sanction, for it is established and regulated by the canons, proceeds from the competent authority, and begets its juridic effects. Roberti states that there are many sanctions in the Code which are not penalties.[149] Though he makes no mention of dismissal in this regard, what is said of sanctions introduced for the preservation of the public good, and of sanctions for the due honoring of contracts,[150] can well be applied here. It is in this sense that Tummulo-Iorio [151] speak of the possibility of distinguishing between a penal and a canonical sanction.

While cardinals are not subject to any penal law unless they

---

[144] Hickey, *Irregularities and Simple Impediments in the New Code of Canon Law,* The Catholic University of America Canon Law Studies, n. 7 (Washington, D. C.: The Catholic University of America, 1920), p. 10.

[145] Schaefer, *De Religiosis,* n. 575; Goyeneche, *De Religiosis,* p. 208, nota 15; Tabera, "art. cit."—*CpR,* XI (1930), 412.

[146] Wernz-Vidal, *Ius Canonicum,* III, n. 438; Hippolytus a S. Familia, "De Dimissione Religiosorum"—*Analecta O. C. D.,* IV (1930), 158.

[147] Cf. *infra,* Chapter X, pp. 183–191.

[148] Cf. *supra,* p. 67, note 31.

[149] "Aliae sanctiones plures inveniuntur in Codice, quae tamen naturam poenae minime assequuntur."—Roberti, *De Delictis et Poenis,* Vol I, pars II, n. 235.

[150] Roberti, *loc. cit.*

[151] Cf. *supra,* p. 101, note 125.

receive express mention in the law,[152] the writer believes that they are subject to the prescriptions of canon 646 without any such special mention, since in his opinion this canon is not of the nature of a penal canon. *A fortiori* bishops are subject to this canon, since it is certain that the canon does not enact a *latae sententiae* suspension or interdict. Hence, religious promoted to dignities are listed as subjects of this canon.[153] However, the same kind of reasoning cannot be invoked in favor of other forms of dismissal, for in those cases the religious tribunal is not competent.[154] The dismissal, on the other hand, which canon 646 envisions, is an act of the law, and so binds all religious, irrespective of their dignity.

Finally, since in profession a religious acquires a vested right,[155] and since his dismissal deprives him of the exercise of the rights thus acquired, the dismissal which is sanctioned in canon 646 is subject to a strict interpretation.[156]

---

[152] Canon 2227, § 2.

[153] Cf. *supra*, p. 91.

[154] Cf. canon 627, § 2.

[155] Cocchi, *Commentarium,* IV, n. 144, d).

[156] Canon 19.

CHAPTER VIII

THE THREE CRIMES

The three causes which precipitate the *ipso facto* effected dismissal are properly styled delicts,[1] and the norms of Book Five in regard to delicts [2] are to be applied to them. Since the dismissal of which canon 646 treats has been shown to be a juridical remedy or sanction provided by the legislator to protect a religious institute when one of its members flagrantly violates the profession-contract,[3] the problem of imputability will arise only in regard to the crimes. Since canon 646 is operative only upon the commission of a specified delict, circumstances [4] which preclude the delict by one and the same token raise an effective barrier to the dismissal. Thus, for example, if a sufficient degree of ignorance is present to excuse from a delict,[5] the dismissal is not effected. If there intervenes, on the other hand, a knowledge which proves sufficient for the perpetration of a delict, then the dismissal will accompany the perpetration of that act.

Unlike the case of penalties which are incurred *ipso facto*,[6] this dismissal is incurred even if the religious is entirely ignorant of the law regarding it and on that particular point exists in good faith, for the incurrence of this juridic effect is not conditioned by any degree of knowledge. This view receives support from the comments of Cardinal La Puma (1874–1943) on the statutes for extern sisters issued by the Sacred Congregation of Religious [7]

---

[1] Cf. *supra*, pp. 92, 100.

[2] Canons 2195–2213.

[3] Cf. *supra*, Chapter VII, Article 4, pp. 93–106.

[4] Cf. canons 2201–2209.

[5] Cf. canon 2202.

[6] Cf. canon 2229.

[7] S. C. de Rel., decr. *Statuta pro Sororibus externis monasteriorum Monialium cuiusque Ordinis servanda*, 16 iul. 1931—*AAS*, XXIII (1931), 380; cf. La Puma, "Statuta a Sororibus Externis Servanda"—*CpR*, XII (1931), 409–425, for the text.

while he was Secretary of the Congregation. The statutes speak of procedural dismissal in articles 118 and 119, but are silent on canon 646. In commenting on article 116,[8] however, the Cardinal noted that canon 646 was omitted lest offense be given to pious souls.[9] In this manner he equivalently states that in a given case this dismissal will also have application for these religious, in spite of the very probable ignorance of the sanction.

Hence, if there is sufficient imputability for the commission of the qualified delicts postulated in canon 646,[10] even though this imputability is insufficient to allow also for the incurring of the penalty attached to the crime, the dismissal is nevertheless effected. For the dismissal is attached to the commission of the delicts and not to the penalties which ensue from the commission of the delicts. The mercy of the Church may free a culprit from criminal action for his crime, but the effect of his misdemeanor as regards his civil relation with the institute is not thereby prevented.

In the ordinary case, however, the imputability of these acts is intensified, for, on the one hand, the religious has an obligation to know and to observe the duties of his station in life,[11] and, on the other hand, his transgressions assume special gravity [12] because of the ever present danger of scandal and of harm to the social order. Moreover, in the external forum, the external violation creates a presumption of the presence of a delict,[13] and therefore

---

[8] S. C. de Rel., decr. *Statuta pro Sororibus externis monasteriorum Monialium cuiusque Ordinis servanda,* art. 116: "Si qua Soror externa sine Superiorissae licentia monasterium deserat, nec ad illud redeat eo animo ut religiosae obedientiae se subtrahat, certior reddatur quamprimum Ordinarius loci, qui pro gravitate culpae eam puniat; ac si casus ferat, ad eius quoque dimissionem procedatur ad normam articulorum 118 et 119 praesentium Statutorum."—*CpR,* XII (1931), 422.

[9] "I. Omissis *iure meritoque* casibus *dimissionis a iure* in can. 646 recensitis, quia satis rari sunt et pias Sororum externarum aures offenderet, mentio fit de casu apostasiae (can. 644, 1, 2)."—La Puma, "Statuta a Sororibus Externis Servanda"—*CpR,* XV (1934), 16.

[10] Cf. *infra,* pp. 110–158, for discussion of what constitutes the delicts in question.

[11] Canon 593.

[12] Cf. canon 2207, 1°.

[13] Cf. canon 2200, § 2.

also of the dismissal. Nevertheless this presumption yields to proof which succeeds to establish the fact to the contrary. Hence, if the religious (on whom the burden of proof would then rest) establishes his innocence of the delict—not merely his ignorance of any of the penalties which may be attached to the delict—he likewise proves the non-application of this canon.

Furthermore, other religious who co-operate in any way in the perpetration of the acts enumerated in canon 646 incur some imputability of the delict,[14] and necessary co-operators [15] are, according to canon 2231, liable to the penalty as stated in the pertinent canon.[16] However, since the dismissal which canon 646 enacts is not the penalty for these delicts, but rather an added sanction, co-operators are not *ipso facto* dismissed unless in their act of co-operation they actually commit the specified delict involved. In the latter case the *ipso facto* effected dismissal enters in, not by reason of the act of co-operation, but by reason of the properly specific act of the religious.

It is necessary, then, to determine the extent and exact meaning of each of the delicts listed in canon 646, § 1, as postulated conditions for this dismissal. Smith gives a fairly full account of these in his dissertation,[17] and hence his general plan will be followed here, reference to his work being made only when one of his own conclusions is cited, or when expression is given to some divergency of view in relation to them. While it is true that he treats these cases as the basis for a penalty, whereas that view has been excluded in this dissertation, in this section both Smith and the present writer are primarily concerned with them as delicts.

---

[14] Cf. canon 2209.

[15] Canon 2209, §§ 1–3.

[16] Cf. Eltz, *Cooperation in Crime,* The Catholic University of America Canon Law Studies, n. 156 (Washington, D. C.: The Catholic University of America Press, 1942), p. 101; Riesner, *Apostates and Fugitives from Religious Institutes,* The Catholic University of America Canon Law Studies, n. 168 (Washington, D. C.: The Catholic University of America Press, 1942), pp. 96–97.

[17] Smith, *The Penal Law for Religious,* pp. 39–47, 104–107, 119–120.

Article 1. The Apostasy from the Catholic Faith

Canon 646, § 1. *Ipso facto habendi sunt tanquam legitime dimissi religiosi:*
1°. *Publici apostatae a fide catholica.*

Religious, though they have embraced a public and juridic state in the Church for the observance of the evangelical counsels, are still primarily bound to the common precepts.[18] The latter are to be observed by all as members of the necessary society, the Church; the former, by those who seek greater perfection in a subordinate and free society within the Church.[19] It is altogether incongruous that one should remain in good standing and in full possession of his rights in the lesser society when he strikes at the very roots of his adherence to the necessary society.[20] Accordingly, the Code provides for an automatic dismissal from the religious institute of those religious who publicly apostatize from the Catholic Faith.

This portion of the canon is almost identical with its source as found in number 18 of the decree *Quum singulae;* [21] the only difference is in the form of the words used. Thus the decree spoke directly of the delict—"*publica apostasia a fide Catholica,*" while the Code speaks of the religious who commit this delict—"*publicae apostatae a fide catholica*"—to conform to other changes made in the heading of the canon. It is evident, then, that both the decree and the present Code are dealing with the very same crime. There is only a variation of terminology for the very same concept.

The delict must be public. Leitner (1862–1929)[22] explained this in the sense of canon 1037; [23] but Coronata [24] rightly notes that the term "public" must be understood as defined in canon

[18] Canon 487.

[19] Beste, *Introductio in Codicem,* p. 305.

[20] Wernz-Vidal, *Ius Canonicum,* III, n. 438; Regatillo, *Institutiones Iuris Canonici* (2 vols., Santander: Sal Terrae, 1941–1942), I, n. 759.

[21] Cf. *supra,* p. 61, note 11.

[22] *Das Ordensrecht,* p. 488.

[23] "Publicum . . . quod probari in foro externo potest: . . ."

[24] *Institutiones,* I, 866, nota 5.

2197, 1°, since canon 646 is subject to a strict interpretation.[25] Moreover, the possibility of proving a delict in the external forum establishes that the act is external, but not necessarily that it is a matter of public knowledge.[26] The apostasy, then, must be public according to the definition of publicity which is given in canon 2197, 1°:

> *Delictum est publicum, si iam divulgatum est aut talibus contigit aut versatur in adiunctis ut prudenter iudicari possit et debeat facile divulgatum iri.*

The authors are in quite general agreement that this is the type of publicity required for this delict.[27] Thus it may be public by reason of the fact that it is already known to a notable part of the people of the locality. The law does not prescribe any special number as being necessary to constitute a notable part of these persons. Determination of this point is left to man's prudent judgment. Besides being public by reason of actual divulgation, the delict may be public also because of the fact that the circumstances force one to conclude that it will easily be divulged in the future.[28]

Hippolytus a S. Familia [29] judges that this danger is present if the apostasy of the religious is known to the entire religious community. *A fortiori,* apostasy notorious according to canon 2197, 2° or 3°, is subject to this sanction.[30] On the other hand, if the delict, though external and externally manifested, is not public

[25] Cf. *supra,* p. 106.

[26] Cocchi, *Commentarium,* IV, n. 154; Schaefer, *De Religiosis,* n. 576.

[27] Tabera, "De Dimissione Religiosorum"—*CpR,* XI (1930), 415; Goyeneche, *De Religiosis,* n. 106; Fanfani, *De Iure Religiosorum,* n. 496; Schönsteiner, *Grundriss des Ordensrechtes,* p. 624; Cocchi, *Commentarium,* IV, n. 145; Palombo, *De Dimissione Religiosorum,* n. 197; Schaefer, *loc. cit.;* Hippolytus a S. Familia, "De Dimissione Religiosorum,"—*Analecta O. C. D.,* IV (1930), 159; Aleixo, "De Religiosis Ipso Iure Dimissis"—*Rev. Ecl. Bras.,* VI (1946), 388; and others.

[28] Cf. Michiels, *De Delictis et Poenis,* I, 117–118; McDevitt, *The Renunciation of an Ecclesiastical Office,* p. 139.

[29] "Art. cit."—*Analecta O. C. D.,* IV (1930), 159–160.

[30] Tabera, *loc. cit.;* Aleixo, *loc. cit.;* Mayer, *Benediktinisches Ordensrecht,* III, 360.

as expressed above, it is occult[31] and as such is excluded from the purview of canon 646.[32] Moreover, it is to be noted immediately that adherence to or inscription in a non-Catholic sect is not required to constitute this apostasy. Pre-Code authors were divided on this point,[33] but post-Code authors are unanimous in stating that this is not required.[34]

Though the authors are in general agreement as to the publicity required for this delict as envisioned in canon 646, they differ sharply as to the nature of the very delict in question. The divergence of interpretation is directly attributable to the words "*apostatae a fide catholica.*"[35]

Since three specific crimes, namely, apostasy, heresy, and schism, will enter into this discussion, it is necessary to give the definitions of them as found in the Code. These definitions are contained in canon 1325, § 2, which reads as follows:

> *Post receptum baptismum si quis, nomen retinens christianum, pertinaciter aliquam ex veritatibus fide divina et catholica credendis denegat aut de ea dubitat, haereticus; si a fide christiana totaliter recedit, apostata; si denique subesse renuit Summo Pontifici aut cum membris Ecclesiae ei subiectis communicare recusat, schismaticus est.*

These definitions are quite clear. Apostasy is a total defection from the faith, while heresy is only a partial defection, but as Mackenzie remarks,[36] they are essentially the same, since rejec-

---

[31] Canon 2197, 4o.

[32] Cocchi, *Commentarium,* IV, n. 145; Prümmer, *Manuale Iuris Canonici,* p. 346; Schaefer, *loc. cit.;* Beste, *Introductio in Codicem,* p. 438; Toso, *Commentaria Minora,* Lib. II, pars II, p. 247; and others.

[33] Cf. *supra,* pp. 67–69.

[34] Fanfani, *De Iure Religiosorum,* n. 496; Blat, *Ius de Religiosis,* n. 658; Schaefer, *De Religiosis,* n. 576; Bastien, *Directoire Canonique a L'usage des Congregations a voeux simples* (3. ed., Bruges: Beyaert, 1923), p. 128 (hereafter cited *Directoire Canonique*); Brandys, *Kirchliches Rechtsbuch,* n. 109; and others.

[35] Hippolytus a S. Familia, "art. cit."—*Analecta O. C. D.,* IV (1930), 158; Aleixo, "art. cit."—*Rev. Ecl. Bras.,* VI (1946), 387; Mayer, *Benediktinisches Ordensrecht,* III, 360.

[36] Mackenzie, *The Delict of Heresy in its Commission, Penalization,*

tion of any one truth involves the same blasphemous attitude towards God that is involved in a denial of all truths. Schism, on the other hand, is rather an offense against obedience and charity than against faith, although heresy is almost always joined with it.[37] In canon 646 the authors employ these concepts in determining just who commits this crime, that is, who is classified as having *apostatized from the Catholic Faith.*

One group[38] insists that the term *apostatized* be taken here strictly as defined in canon 1325, § 2, that is, having *totally abandoned the Christian Faith.* The other group[39] contends that the inclusion of the word *Catholic* before *Faith* indicates that it is to be taken in a wider sense than that delineated in canon 1325, § 2.

Absolution, The Catholic University of America Canon Law Studies, n. 77 (Washington, D. C.: The Catholic University of America Press, 1932), p. 19.

[37] MacKenzie, *ibid.,* pp. 16–17; cf. McDevitt, *The Renunciation of an Ecclesiastical Office,* p. 137.

[38] Fanfani, *loc. cit.;* Biederlach-Führich, *De Religiosis* (Oeniponte: Typis Feliciani Rauch, 1919), n. 171; Bastien, *Directoire Canonique,* pp. 127–128; Cocchi, *Commentarium,* IV, n. 145; Tabera, "De Dimissione Religiosorum"—*CpR,* XI (1930), 413–415; Schönsteiner, *Grundriss des Ordensrechtes,* p. 624; Hippolytus a S. Familia, "De Dimissione Religiosorum" —*Analecta O. C. D.,* IV (1930), 158–160; Blat, *Ius de Religiosis,* III, n. 658; Claeys Bouuaert-Simenon, *Manuale Juris Canonici,* n. 691; Geser, *The Canon Law Governing Communities of Sisters,* n. 1153; Goyeneche, *De Religiosis,* n. 106.

[39] Smith, *The Penal Law for Religious,* p. 46; Schaefer, *De Religiosis,* n. 576; Leitner, *Das Ordensrecht,* p. 488; Mayer, *loc. cit.;* Coronata, *Institutiones,* I, n. 646; Coronata, *Manuale Practicum Iuris Disciplinaris et Criminalis Regularium* (Taurini: Marietti, 1938), n. 235 (hereafter cited *Manuale Practicum*); Toso, *Commentaria Minora,* Lib. II, pars II, pp. 246–247; Chelodi, *Ius de Personis,* p. 547, nota 3; Sipos, *Enchiridion,* p. 409; Regatillo, *Institutiones Iuris Canonici,* I, n. 759; Oesterle, *Praelectiones Iuris Canonici,* I, 370; Augustine, *A Commentary,* III, 386; Berutti, *De Religiosis,* n. 158; Cappello, *Summa Iuris Canonici* (3 vols., Vol. II, ed. 4, Romae: Apud Aedes Pontificiae Universitatis Gregorianae, 1945), II, n. 70; Eichmann, *Lehrbuch des Kirchenrechts,* p. 257; Wernz-Vidal, *Ius Canonicum,* III, n. 438; Palombo, *De Dimissione Religiosorum,* n. 197; Aleixo, "art. cit."—*Rev. Ecl. Bras.,* VI (1946), 387–388; Bouscaren-Ellis, *Canon Law,* p. 310. Roberti ("Respectus sociales in Codice iuris canonici" —*Apollinaris* [Romae, 1928—], X [1937], 362) seems to imply the same.

In the latter group all maintain that it includes heretics, and a number extend it to include schismatics also.[40]

The arguments for the first group have been succinctly set forth by Hippolytus a S. Familia,[41] Tabera[42] and Goyeneche.[43] In the first place, so these authors maintain, canon 646 deals with unfavorable issues ("*in odiosis*"),[44] and since these invite a restrictive interpretation,[45] especially when the law itself is not altogether clear, the minimum is to be held.[46] Furthermore, they have recourse to parallel places in the Code,[47] and cite canons 985, 1065, 1240, 1453, 1470, 2314, 2339, and 2372 as parallel places where the term "apostasy" is used strictly according to the definition afforded in canon 1325 § 2. They appeal to the constant canonical tradition as distinguishing *apostasy* from *heresy* and *schism*, and as restricting the former to the total abandonment of the Christian Faith. They argue further that nowhere in the law is there to be found any distinction between apostasy from the Christian Faith and apostasy from the Catholic Faith.[48]

These arguments, as presented, do not rest on an unshakable foundation. Though some are valid in themselves, they are not so in their application to the question at hand. Thus, granted that "*res odiosa restringenda est*" and that the term *apostate* when standing alone and unqualified should be interpreted according to the definition of canon 1325, § 2, it does not follow therefore that this term is still to be so interpreted in every possible

---

[40] Mayer, *loc. cit.;* Eichmann, *loc. cit.;* Berutti, *loc. cit.;* Cappello, *loc. cit.;* Oesterle, *loc. cit.;* Regatillo, *loc. cit.;* Toso, *loc. cit.;* Bouscaren-Ellis, *loc. cit.* Smith (*loc. cit.*) lists Coronata as favoring this view, and Schaefer as opposed; but the reverse seems to be true, for Coronata makes no reference to schism, whereas Schaefer's statement could be construed to include it.

[41] *Loc. cit.*

[42] *Loc. cit.*

[43] *Loc. cit.*

[44] Tabera, *ibid.,* p. 414; Goyeneche, *ibid.,* p. 208, nota 18.

[45] Canon 19; Reg. 15, R. J. in VI°: "Odia restringi et favores convenit ampliari."

[46] Tabera, *loc. cit.;* Goyeneche, *loc. cit.;* Hippolytus a S. Familia, *ibid.,* p. 159.

[47] Cf. canon 18.

[48] Smith, *The Penal Law for Religious,* pp. 40–41.

text and context.[49] There is but one passage in the Code where the phrase *apostate from the Catholic Faith* is used,[50] and so in determining the meaning of apostate here one should not disregard the qualifying adjective *Catholic*. Only in giving due consideration to "*apostatae*" and to "*a fide catholica*" will there appear what is meant in this text and context. The authors cited rule out the possibility of understanding this concept in its proper text and context, and immediately have recourse to what appear to be parallel places in the Code. A careful scrutiny will show that this parallelism is not evident, and will force a return to a consideration of the text and context. Other norms of interpretation as indicated in canon 18 can claim legitimate attention in only such cases in which an interpretation according to the text and context cannot obtain.

The canons that would appear to be parallel places are of two kinds; namely, those that contain the words "*apostate*" or "*apostasy*" and, to a lesser degree, those that contain the words "*fides catholica*." The canons that contain the word "*apostate*" are canons 985, 1240, 1453, 1470, 2314, 2339, 2372. Smith strives to show that in these canons the term "*apostasy*" may at times have a wider sense than that which is warranted in canon 1325, § 2.[51] The present writer, on the other hand, grants the validity of the contention that in these canons *apostasy* is used according to canon 1325, § 2, for this is evident from its proper signification in text and context. Though there is some variation of use, such as "apostate," "apostate from the faith," and "apostate from the christian faith," it is clear that all are in conformity with canon 1325, § 2, for they are all followed in the continuance of the enumeration by words indicating "*heresy*" and "*schism*." [52]

---

[49] Cf. Neuberger, *Canon 6 or the Relation of the Codex Juris Canonici to the Preceding Legislation,* p. 82.

[50] Smith, *ibid.*, p. 41; Mayer, *Benediktinisches Ordensrecht,* III, 360, note 4.

[51] Smith, *The Penal Laws for Religious,* pp. 43–45.

[52] Canon 985, 1o *Apostatae a fide, haeretici, schismatici:* . . .

Canon 1240, § 1. 1o. *Notorii apostatae a christiana fide, aut sectae haereticae vel schismaticae . . . notorie addicti;* . . .

Canon 1453, § 1 . . . *publice apostatas, haereticos, schismaticos* . . .

Canon 1470, § 1, 6o . . . *lapsus in apostasiam, haeresim, aut schisma* . . .

The same is true of canons 751, 1470, § 1, 6°, and 2318, § 1. The agreement, uniformity, and evident meaning of these canons are in marked contrast to what is encountered in canon 646. The latter canon speaks of *apostasy from the Catholic Faith*—a phrase found nowhere else in the Code—and in doing so makes no reference to heresy or schism as is done in other parts of the Code when apostasy is mentioned. Though canons 188, 4°, and 1065, § 1, do not have direct bearing on this canon, since they speak of defection and lapse from the Catholic Faith and not of apostasy, they can still be viewed with profit as to the extent of the meaning of the phrase "Catholic Faith." In speaking of a lapse or a defection from the Catholic Faith, the authors grant that it may be total or partial, and as such may signify apostasy, or heresy and schism. It is in this sense that McDevitt [53] understands canon 188, 4°, and that Heneghan [54] interprets canon 1065, § 1. Moreover, canon 1325, § 2, itself, as Coronata [55] notes, marks a distinction between the Catholic and the Christian Faith. Hence it seems certain that there are in the Code no parallel passages to which recourse can be had.

As regards the argument of those who in their restrictive interpretation appeal to the constant canonical teaching and tradition, Smith [56] shows that they employ the theological rather than the canonical sense of the term "*apostasy*." However, granted that the word "apostasy" in itself is understood as a total *recessus a fide* in contradistinction to heresy and schism, it is not thereby established that "*apostasia a fide christiana*" and "*apostasia a fide catholica*" are identical. Tabera [57] reaches the conclusion that these two phrases are identical in meaning, since he

Canon 2314, § 1. *Omnes a christiana fide apostatae, et omnes et singuli haeretici aut schismatici:*

Canon 2339 . . . *apostatas a fide, vel haereticos, schismaticos,* . . .

Canon 2372 . . . *a notorio apostata, haeretico, schismatico:* . . .

[53] *The Renunciation of an Ecclesiastical Office*, pp. 136–138.

[54] *The Marriages of Unworthy Catholics: Canons 1065 and 1066*, The Catholic University of America Canon Law Studies, n. 188 (Washington, D. C.: The Catholic University of America Press, 1944), pp. 58 and 69.

[55] *Institutiones*, I, n. 646.

[56] *Ibid.*, pp. 41 and 46.

[57] "Art. cit."—*CpR*, XI (1930), 414–415.

notes that there is no word among canonists and theologians that would indicate a difference in these concepts. Toso takes exception to this view, and maintains that there is a difference.[58] Indeed, Villien, in commenting on the decree *Quum singulae,* stated that there was no doubt on this point.[59] Accordingly, it will suffice to return to a consideration of canon 646 in itself and in relation to the other norms of canon 18.

The text "*apostatae a fide catholica*" of canon 646 is a verbatim repetition of its source, the decree *Quum singulae.*[60] In reference to this earlier law Villien already pointed out that the apostasy spoken of there was not the same as apostasy from the Christian Faith as treated in the Constitution *Apostolicae Sedis.*[61] Thus the observation of Hippolytus a S. Familia that the difference of the sources of the laws is at times accountable for the difference of terminology in the Code finds application here.[62]

However, his further reasoning that the discrepancy found in canon 646 may easily be attributed to the fact that many collaborators were employed in codifying the law [63] cannot be sustained. For the phraseology of the law of the decree *Quum singulae* remained unchanged in the preparatory schemata, and was wholly incorporated into the Code. This consistent acceptance of the term, in spite of the fact that it is not in agreement with the usage of other passages in the Code, and in spite of the fact that it could easily have been brought into conformity with the rest of the Code, seems to show conclusively that the legislator intended to retain the special sense given to *apostate* by the qualifying term *from the Catholic Faith.* As the common adage has it: "*Quidquid legislator voluit, expressit; . . .*" In the law of the decree *Quum singulae* apostasy from the Catholic Faith was considered as a more extensive species of apostasy than the usually accepted one,[64] and as including any abandonment of the Catholic

[58] Toso, *Commentaria Minora,* Lib. II, pars II, pp. 246–247.

[59] Cf. *supra,* p. 68, note 33.

[60] Hippolytus a S. Familia, "art. cit."—*Analecta O. C. D.,* IV (1930), 158.

[61] Cf. *supra,* p. 67, note 32.

[62] Hippolytus a S. Familia, *ibid.,* p. 159.

[63] Hippolytus a S. Familia, *loc. cit.*

[64] Cf. *supra,* p. 68, note 33.

Faith.[65] Hence, in accordance with canon 6, 3°, it is to be understood in the same way in the present law.

This conclusion is further evidenced by a consideration of the context. Canon 646, as is well known, is in Book II, Part II, of the Code where the law for religious is given. Now, in this section, canon 538 demands as a *conditio sine qua non* for admission into religion that one be a Catholic;[66] hence the same basis should be required for his continuance therein,[67] and so a religious who ceases to be a Catholic, who bids farewell to the Catholic Church, is rightly considered as legitimately dismissed from the religious institute.[68]

Moreover, the purpose of the law lends support to this view. Already in reference to the pre-Code law Villien stated that the manifest existence of an anti-Catholic status on the part of the religious occasioned this measure.[69] Not only passing over to Judaism, Mohammedanism or paganism, but also joining a Protestant sect, a group of freethinkers, etc., were deemed manifestations of this spirit.[70] This reasoning can be urged also in the present law. Since canon 646 as a whole is considered as a means for preserving and protecting the welfare and reputation of the institute,[71] it is equally as applicable to cases involving heresy and schism as it is applicable to cases involving apostasy in the strict sense.[72]

In this sense, then, a public apostate from the Catholic Faith is one who publicly renounces the Catholic Church.[73] Thus the religious would renounce the Catholic Faith in passing over to a non-Christian group, such as Buddhism, Mohammedanism,[74] some

---

[65] Cf. *supra*, p. 68, note 34.

[66] Eichmann, *Lehrbuch des Kirchenrechts*, p. 257; Smith, *The Penal Law for Religious*, p. 42; Aleixo, "art. cit."—*Rev. Ecl. Bras.*, VI (1946), 387; Mayer, *Benediktinisches Ordensrecht*, III, 360.

[67] Smith, *loc. cit.*

[68] Aleixo, *ibid.*, pp. 387–388.

[69] Cf. *supra*, p. 69, note 40.

[70] Cf. *supra*, pp. 68–69.

[71] Cf. *supra*, p. 85.

[72] Toso, *Commentaria Minora*, Lib. II, pars II, p. 247.

[73] Aleixo, *ibid.*, p. 387.

[74] Villien, "La Procédure Canonique pour l'Expulsion des Religieux"—

well-defined cult of paganism, Judaism, etc.; [75] or in joining a Protestant,[76] heretical, non-Catholic Christian sect or a schismatic church; [77] or in joining any professedly and manifestly anti-Catholic group, such as a league of freethinkers; [78] or, finally, in openly denying even one article of the Catholic Faith.[79] Since the act must be one that manifests the anti-Catholic spirit of the religious, a scandalous neglect of duty or a practical religious indifferentism is not comprehended by this law.[80]

As stated earlier, the defection must be public, i.e., either by way of public profession, or by way of evidence obtained from official sources.[81] Hence, the act must leave no doubt as to its existence and significance,[82] and is subject to strict interpretation by reason of the vested right of the religious.[83] By strict interpretation is meant, not the arbitrary limiting of the scope of the canon, but an understanding of the latter's proper signification and the subsequent use of the strict application.

Thus, by following the meaning of the words embodied in the text and context, by consulting the source of the law in the previous legislation, the purpose, the circumstances, and the intention of the lawgiver,[84] the present writer comes to the conclusion that the law is clear in itself, and so is to be understood according to its own proper signification. By no means is canon 646, § 1, 1°, to be classified as a doubtful law, as it is by Smith; [85] rather it must be said that those who deem it doubtful can at most

---

Le Canoniste Contemporain, XXXVI (1913), 138; Augustine, *A Commentary*, III, 386.

[75] Villien, *loc. cit.*

[76] Villien, *ibid.*, p. 139; Tamayo, *Procedimientos de Derecho Penal Canónico*, n. 300, 1°; cf. *supra*, pp. 67–69, for the text of these authors; Brandys, *Kirchliches Rechtsbuch*, p. 104.

[77] Bouscaren-Ellis, *Canon Law*, p. 310; and others; cf. *supra*, p. 68.

[78] Villien, *loc. cit.*; Tamayo, *loc. cit.*; Augustine, *loc. cit.*

[79] Coronata, *Institutiones*, I, n. 646; Augustine, *loc. cit.*; Oesterle, *Praelectiones Iuris Canonici*, I, 370; cf. canon 1323.

[80] Villien, *loc. cit.*; Tamayo, *loc. cit.*; cf. *supra*, pp. 68–69.

[81] Augustine, *loc. cit.*

[82] Villien, *loc. cit.*; cf. *supra*, p. 69, note 40.

[83] Cf. *supra*, p. 106.

[84] Cf. canon 18.

[85] *Op. cit.*, p. 46.

rest their view on extrinsic authority, but without intrinsic reasons.

It is to be noted further that a religious may be subject to the penalties of canon 2314 and still not come effectively under the sanction invoked in canon 646,[86] for the latter postulates the additional element of publicity. Likewise the apostasy contemplated in canon 646 is not identical with apostasy from religion;[87] the latter may indeed, but does not necessarily, accompany the former, for one could be an apostate from the Catholic Faith while living in his own institute.[88]

Finally, since matters relating to faith are reserved to the Holy Office,[89] and since all superiors are forbidden to interfere in cases thus reserved,[90] the question arises as to the application of these norms to canon 646, § 1, 1°. Among the authors consulted, Coronata alone takes cognizance of this point. He states that the apostasy treated in canon 646 is a matter pertaining to the Holy Office, which alone is competent to investigate the matter and to issue the declaration of dismissal.[91] Since no reasons are advanced by him in support of this view, it is imperative to consider the matter independently of his views. The decree of the Holy Office of 1901, which is still in force,[92] declares what superiors may not do in matters reserved to that Congregation. To the extent that he is permitted to act, a superior may not interfere on his own authority, but only as a delegate of the Holy Office.[93] He is not forbidden, indeed, to do what he can without using his jurisdictional power; in fact, he can do all that which does not pertain properly to a canonical judgment of the case.[94]

---

[86] Mayer, *Benediktinisches Ordensrecht,* III, 360; Toso, *Commentaria Minora,* Lib. II, pars II, p. 247.

[87] Canon 644, § 1.

[88] Coronata, *Institutiones,* I, n. 646.

[89] Canon 247, § 1.

[90] Canon 501, § 2.

[91] Coronata, *Manuale Practicum,* n. 238.

[92] S. C. S. Off., decr. *In congregatione,* 15 maii 1901—*ASS,* XXXIV (1901-1902), 383; cf. Schaefer, *De Religiosis,* n. 106; Mayer, *Benediktinisches Ordensrecht,* II, 182.

[93] Schaefer, *loc. cit.;* O'Leary, *The Dismissal of Religious in Temporary Vows,* p. 124.

[94] Larraona, "Commentarium Codicis—Canon 501"—*CpR,* VII (1926), 96; Schaefer, *loc. cit.;* O'Leary, *ibid.,* pp. 125-126.

However, these norms are in no way infringed upon by the law of canon 646. Thus, since this dismissal is effected upon the very commission of the delict, there is never question of a judicial process.[95] The subsequent intervention of superiors in gathering proofs and issuing the declaration of fact are not required for the validity of the dismissal.[96] Furthermore, they are acts of dominative power rather than of jurisdiction.[97] Moreover, these actions are not undertaken on the superior's own authority, but at the behest of the law itself through its commission of power.[98] Hence, it is the opinion of the present writer that a superior who would proceed to the issuing of a declaration of fact in this matter would not be acting in contravention of canons 247, § 1, and 501, § 2.

Article 2. Flight with a Person of the Other Sex

> Canon 646, § 1. *Ipso facto habendi sunt tanquam legitime dimissi religiosi:*
> 2°. *Religiosus, qui fugam arripuerit cum muliere; aut religiosa quae cum viro.*

The present law is a restatement and extension of the law as first promulgated in the decree *Quum singulae.*[99] It is a restatement, for, though its wording differs from that of the decree, it will be found to convey the same concepts. It is an extension, for it applies also to women religious; [100] but since this is true of the whole canon by force of the word "*religiosi,*" the words "*religiosus*" and "*religiosa*" must serve another purpose here. It seems that the present form is an emphatic manner of expressing the species of the flight as one with a person of the other sex.

It is not easy to define the nature of this delict.[101] The dif-

[95] Cf. *supra*, p. 86.

[96] P.C.I., 30 iul. 1934, ad I—*AAS*, XXVI (1934), 494; cf. *infra*, pp. 160–161.

[97] Mayer, *op. cit.*, III, 364.

[98] Cf. canon 646, § 2.

[99] Cf. *supra*, p. 61, note 11.

[100] Cf. *supra*, pp. 63, 89.

[101] Toso, *Commentaria Minora*, Lib. II, pars II, p. 247; Aleixo, "De Religiosis Ipso Iure Dimissis"—*Rev. Ecl. Bras.*, VI (1946), 388.

ficulty centers largely in the proper signification of the words "*fugam*" and "*cum muliere . . . cum viro.*" Toso [102] notes that two things are required by the text of the canon: namely, that the religious take flight, and that this flight be with a person of the other sex. These two points, then, with their various ramifications form the burden of this article.

First of all, in reference to the word "*fugam*" authors are not in agreement as to the sense in which it is to be understood.[103] In order to avoid all difficulties in this matter, Toso deems it necessary to interpret the phrase "flight with a person of the other sex" in the commonly accepted sense.[104] Tabera,[105] Schaefer,[106] Mayer,[107] Goyeneche [108] and Regatillo [109] share the same view. Goyeneche states that authors generally require flight only in this sense, and that this suffices.[110]

Thus, some authors define the word flight in canon 646 as "the hasty desertion of a given place for the sake of going to some other place," [111] while others simply mention that it is flight in the sense in which that word is commonly used by the people.[112] In the latter case it closely approximates the English expressions "elopement," as used by Smith,[113] or "run away," as employed

[102] *Loc. cit.*

[103] ". . . alii auctores requirunt, ut delinquens in casu fugitivus sit ad normam can. 644; alii e contra sufficere dicunt fugam in sensu vulgari, . . ." —Aleixo, *ibid.*, p. 391.

[104] ". . . locutio *fugam arripere cum muliere* sensu vulgari, quo populus, accipiatur."—Toso, *loc. cit.*

[105] "De Dimissione Religiosorum"—*CpR,* XI (1930), 415.

[106] *De Religiosis,* n. 576.

[107] *Benediktinisches Ordensrecht,* III, 361.

[108] "Consultationes"—*CpRM,* XVII (1936), 343; *De Religiosis,* n. 106.

[109] *Institutiones Iuris Canonici,* I, n. 759.

[110] ". . . auctores communiter requirunt fugam saltem sensu vulgari intellectam. Et haec revera sufficeret."—Goyeneche, "Consultationes"—*CpRM,* XVII (1936), 344.

[111] ". . . derelictio nempe unius loci cum festinatione, ut ad alium quis se conferat."—Tabera, *loc. cit.;* cf. Goyeneche, "Consultationes," *CpRM,* XVII (1936), 343; Goyeneche, *De Religiosis,* n. 106; Regatillo, *loc. cit.*

[112] Toso, *loc. cit.;* Mayer, *loc. cit.*

[113] *The Penal Law for Religious,* p. 104.

in the Authorized English Translation [114] and by Bouscaren-Ellis.[115]

It is to be noted that most of these authors resort to the foregoing explanation of the word " fugam " in canon 646, inasmuch as they judge that the word is not used in exactly the same sense as " fugitivus " in canon 644, § 3.[116] Tabera advances what appears to be the main objection of this group; namely, that the flight spoken of in canon 646 is effected immediately,[117] and so is minus the factor of the time element of two or three days as commonly required by the authors for constituting the flight which receives mention in canon 644, § 3.[118] Bastien [119] and Palombo [120] likewise are opposed to accepting flight here in the sense employed in canon 644, § 3, but mainly because they observe that the flight mentioned in canon 646 is usually undertaken with the intention not to return, whereas the intention to return is required by the former canon.

On the other hand, Blat,[121] Fanfani,[122] Vermeersch,[123] Hippolytus a S. Familia,[124] Coronata,[125] Beste,[126] Smith,[127] and others, though adducing no reasons, state that the element inherent in flight as mentioned in canon 646, § 1, 2°, is identical with that of flight as defined in canon 644, § 3. However, the differences

---

[114] Cf. *supra*, p. 83, note 1. As stated in the Foreword of this translation, it has not the official character of the Latin text, although it has been specially authorized by the Holy See.

[115] *Canon Law*, p. 310.

[116] Tabera, *loc. cit.;* Schaefer, *loc. cit.;* Mayer, *loc. cit.;* Goyeneche, " Consultationes "—*CpRM*, XVII (1936), 343; Goyeneche, *De Religiosis*, n. 106.

[117] Tabera, *ibid.*, p. 415, nota 19.

[118] Cf. Riesner, *Apostates and Fugitives from Religious Institutes*, pp. 75-76.

[119] *Directoire Canonique*, p. 128, nota 4.

[120] *De Dimissione Religiosorum*, n. 197.

[121] *Ius de Religiosis*, n. 658.

[122] *De Iure Religiosorum*, n. 496.

[123] " De fuga cum persona alterius sexus, in casu can. 646, § 1, n. 2."—*Periodica*, XIX (1923), 121*-122*.

[124] " De Dimissione Religiosorum "—*Analecta O. C. D.*, IV (1930), 160.

[125] *Institutiones*, I, n. 646; *Manuale Practicum*, n. 236.

[126] *Introductio in Codicem*, p. 438.

[127] *Loc. cit.*

of opinion between these two groups are not as great as would at first appear; and hence, from a consideration of the points in which they agree, one can arrive at a truer sense of flight as contemplated in canon 646, § 1, 2°.

The word "*fugam*" in canon 646 denotes an illegitimate egress from the religious house,[128] whether with or without the intention of returning.[129] While it is certain that the canon does not require apostasy from the institute,[130] it does not follow that the latter is to be excluded. In fact, Villien,[131] Palombo[132] and Fanfani[133] deem that apostasy is ordinarily involved in the case of this flight. Thus, by putting aside the intention of the delinquent,[134] they assign a wider sense to the word "fugam" used in canon 646 than that which inheres in the word "fugitivus" used in canon 644, § 3, but still remain within the scope of canon 644. Moreover, the dismissal is effected by the very fact of this flight and at its very beginning.[135]

In this manner the canon itself eliminates the element of time in relation to it. Yet, it is this very fact that prompts Tabera to lodge his objection to accepting the term flight in the sense of canon 644, § 3. He does not intend to exclude the latter kind of flight from the ambit of canon 646 if it should actually be present,

---

128 Toso, *loc. cit.;* Tabera, *ibid.*, p. 416; Vermeersch, *ibid.*, p. 122*; Mayer, *loc. cit.;* Goyeneche, "Consultationes"—*CpRM,* XVII (1936), 343; and others.

129 Toso, *loc. cit.;* Goyeneche, *De Religiosis,* n. 106; Mayer, *loc. cit.;* Palombo, *loc. cit.;* Vermeersch, *loc. cit.;* Geser, *The Canon Law Governing Communities of Sisters,* n. 1155; Bouscaren-Ellis, *loc. cit.*

130 Fanfani, *loc. cit.;* Tabera, *ibid.*, p. 415; Schaefer, *De Religiosis,* n. 576; Palombo, *loc. cit.;* Schönsteiner, *Grundriss des Ordensrechtes,* p. 625; Sipos, *Enchiridion,* p. 409.

131 Cf. *supra,* p. 70, note 45.

132 *Loc. cit.*

133 *Ibid.*, p. 128, nota 4.

134 ". . . abstrahendo a delinquentis intentione . . ."—Palombo, *loc. cit.*

135 Beste, *loc. cit.;* Coronata, *Manuale Practicum,* n. 236; Geser, *loc. cit.;* Goyeneche, "Consultationes"—*CpR,* IX (1928), 428; Schaefer, *loc. cit.;* Gerster a Zeil, *Ius Religiosorum,* p. 146; Tabera, *ibid.*, pp. 415–416; "Generatim auctores affirmant dimissionem effectum producere ipso fugae initio."—Aleixo, "art. cit."—*Rev. Ecl. Bras.,* VI (1946), 391; cf. *supra,* pp. 86–87.

but, since authors usually speak of it in terms of an absence of two or three days, he judges that the word flight in canon 646 must, in consequence of the very element of instantaneousness which attaches to it, have a wider sense in its own right.[136]

For the present it suffices to note that even in canon 644, § 3, the absence of two or three days is not of the essence of the flight, for it is not so stated in the law. This requirement is rather an interpretation of the authors in favor of the religious should there be a doubt as to his intention, and a presumption for the external forum, much like that given by the law itself in § 2 of the canon for apostates. However, if a religious leaves with the intention of deserting the institute perpetually or the religious house for a time, he is an apostate or a fugitive from that moment on.[137]

Riesner states further that in committing one of the three crimes in canon 646 a religious manifests the malicious intent of not returning, and that upon such evidence in the external forum the religious may immediately be presumed to be an apostate from his institute.[138] Hence, as regards the time element, canon 646, § 1, 2°, may coincide with either § 1 or § 3 of canon 644. In his opposition to accepting an identical meaning for the word flight in canon 644, § 3, and canon 646, § 1, 2°, Tabera seems to assign too comprehensive a meaning to the term as used in the latter of these canons. His definition, as Aleixo points out,[139] could be urged in almost every illegitimate egress from the religious house. The same observation applies to other authors who support the view of Tabera or advance similar views of their own. It seems rather that the sense of the word flight in canon 646 must be kept within the scope of canon 644 as a whole.[140] Tabera himself indicates this view when he states that the actions which draw upon them-

---

[136] Tabera, *ibid.*, p. 415, nota 19.

[137] Riesner, *Apostates and Fugitives from Religious Institutes*, pp. 61–62, 72, 78 and 100.

[138] Riesner, *ibid.*, pp. 66–67.

[139] Aleixo, "art. cit."—*Rev. Ecl. Bras.*, VI (1946), 391.

[140] "Certo constare debet quod proprie de apostasia a Religione vel de fuga e domo religiosa agitur, quae reapse simul coniunctum habeat contubernium cum persona alterius sexus; . . ."—Berutti, *De Religiosis*, n. 158.

selves the sanction enacted in canon 646 are almost always acts of apostasy or flight.[141]

Accordingly, the present writer is of the opinion that the solution as regards the meaning of the word "*fugam*" in canon 646 is not to be sought in canon 644, § 3, but beyond it. Although the term "*fugitivus*" receives a defined meaning in the Code,[142] the term "*fuga*" is not defined by it. However, this does not rule out the more fundamental concept of flight which is common to an apostate as well as to a fugitive. "*Fuga*" is the material element of the delict on the side of the "*apostata*" and the "*fugitivus*" alike: the formal element on the side of an apostate is his intention not to return in connection with his illegitimate absence, while on the side of a fugitive it is the illegitimate absence despite the presence of the intention to return. Yet both perform the same material act, namely, that of deserting the state they have professed.[143] It is this material element which seems to constitute the basis of the delict considered in canon 646, § 1, 2°.

Hence it seems that the term flight in canon 646 should at least be understood according to the elements of flight as delineated in canon 644, that is, in the light of the factors which are common to the delict of both apostates and fugitives, inclusive of,

1. the leaving of the religious house without the permission of the proper superior; [144] and
2. the removing of oneself from religious obedience and the regular observance.[145]

These two elements readily coalesce to form the one concept of desertion of the institute.[146]

It was exactly in this sense that the pre-Code authors, Villien, Tamayo, and Vermeersch, characterized the word "*fuga*" as used

---

141 "Casus in c. 646 contemplatus semper, vel fere, cum apostasia aut saltem cum fuga coincidet; . . ."—Tabera, *ibid.*, p. 415, nota 19.

142 Canon 644, § 3.

143 Riesner, *Apostates and Fugitives from Religious Institutes*, pp. 4–5.

144 Cf. *supra*, p. 124.

145 Prümmer, *Manuale Iuris Canonici*, p. 345; Coronata, *Institutiones*, I, n. 642; Riesner, *ibid.*, pp. 62–63 and 73–74; "Dicunt auctores . . . fugam includere voluntatem sese subtrahendi ad tempus regulari observantiae et obedientiae."—Aleixo, "art. cit."—*Rev. Ecl. Bras.*, VI (1946), 392.

146 Cf. Riesner, *loc. cit.*

in the source of the present law.[147] It is evident, then, that post-Code authors in their views on the meaning of the term flight in canon 646 all present an element of truth, but it appears also that many of them have interpreted the term too restrictively. It is unfortunate that they should deadlock on the significance of canon 644, § 3, in this matter, but with these attendant differences equalized they would indeed be in substantial agreement.

Thus, though admitting that the term flight in canon 646 is not exactly or strictly to be identified with the notion of flight as connoted in canon 644, § 3, one must maintain that there inhere in it the basic elements which serve to constitute the notion of flight as dealt with in canon 644. In this manner the notion of flight in canon 646 is connoted by:

1. the departure which in itself is lawful, but which becomes protracted into an illegitimately continued absence;

2. the departure which is unlawful, but which nevertheless has inherent in it the intention of returning; and

3. the desertion which connotes at the same time the intention of not returning.[148]

It is postulated in these cases that the desertion, the unlawful departure, as also the illegitimately continued absence, be motivated with the desire of withdrawing oneself, at least for a time, from the regular discipline and religious obedience.[149]

It is not postulated that the religious have made his final profession of vows, for canon 646 speaks simply of religious, which manner of expression comprises also such religious whose vows are of a temporary character.[150]

In the law of the decree *Quum singulae,* the starting point of this flight was designated as the monastery,[151] but this limitation

---

[147] Cf. *supra,* p. 70, note 44.

[148] ". . . a) Fuga domum religiosam deserentis, sine vel cum animo redeundi; . . ."—Vermeersch, "art. cit."—*Periodica,* XIX (1923), 122*.

[149] "Religiosus cum muliere, vel religiosa cum viro fugam arripere dicitur, si domum Religionis illegitime deserat, aut si post legitimum egressum ad eam non redeat, ut ad aliquod tempus eius contubernalis sit, et obedientiae religiosae interim se subtrahat."—Berutti, *De Religiosis,* n. 158.

[150] Cf. *supra,* pp. 89–91.

[151] "fuga e monasterio . . ."—decr. *Quum singulae,* 16 maii 1911, n. 18 c—*AAS,* III (1911), 237.

of concept is lacking in the present law. The starting point is now commonly given as a religious house.[152] However, the omission of the former restricting phrase seems to extend the ambit implied in the notion of this flight, so that its starting point is not only the religious house, but also any place or scene of activity assigned by obedience.[153] For one who dwells outside the religious house, as long as one does it legitimately, is in the law considered alike with the one who dwells in the religious house.[154]

To leave one of these places illegitimately, then, is the first source of the flight. On the other hand, if a religious would leave any one of these places with the proper permission, one could not say that he had taken flight, and so he would not be subject to the sanction enacted in canon 646.[155] However, even in a legitimate egress the religious could act illegitimately and against the permission as granted. Thus, a legitimately absent religious who would join company with a person of the other sex with a view to withdrawing himself from religious obedience, or who for the sake of remaining in the company of this person would refuse to return, surely would furnish one of the elements constitutive of the flight contemplated in canon 646.[156] Hence the starting point of the flight (*terminus a quo*) can be any place where the religious has up to that moment resided in due subjection and obedience to his superiors.

Further, this flight must be with a person of the other sex. This element or factor is clearly expressed both in the pre-Code law[157] and in the law of the Code.[158] In view of this requirement over and above the simple fact of flight, the expression "*qualified* flight" gained currency among both the pre-Code

---

[152] Tabera, *ibid.*, p. 416; Bouscaren-Ellis, *Canon Law*, p. 310; Riesner, *ibid.*, p. 72; and others.

[153] Brandys, *Kirchliches Rechtsbuch*, n. 109.

[154] Toso, *Commentaria Minora*, Lib. II, pars II, p. 247.

[155] Smith, *op. cit.*, p. 106; Goyeneche, "Consultationes"—*CpR*, IX (1928), 429.

[156] Toso, *loc. cit.*; Berutti, *loc. cit.*

[157] ". . . suscepta secum muliere."—Decr. *Quum singulae*, 16 maii 1911, n. 18 c—*AAS*, III (1911), 237.

[158] ". . . cum muliere, . . . viro."—Canon 646, § 1, 2o.

authors [159] and the post-Code authors.[160] For some authors this expression simply means a flight qualified by the aggravating circumstance of the association in it of a person of the other sex,[161] while for others it connotes likewise the elements of complicity and libidinous intent.[162]

Though the words in canon 646, § 1, 2°, could be construed to imply any associated presence of a person of the other sex in the flight of a religious, the authors [163] ordinarily require a formal complicity. Hippolytus a S. Familia,[164] arguing from the word "*suscepta*" in the law of the decree, states that the flight must involve an associated presence sought by the religious, and that such a presence is in no way effected through a purely material and simple coincidence. This view was already expounded by Villien in reference to the pre-Code law.[165]

The presence or absence of the complicity must be gauged from the union that exists in the flight. Only from the degree of the union can one establish in how far the parties are accomplices. Since the crime is committed at the beginning of the flight,[166] it is at that point that the union must exist. In kind this union can be physical or moral, and either of these can be related to the matter under consideration.[167]

---

[159] Cf. *supra*, pp. 69–70.

[160] Tabera, *loc. cit.;* Goyeneche, *De Religiosis*, n. 106; Hippolytus a S. Familia, "art. cit."—*Analecta O. C. D.*, IV (1930), 160; Schönsteiner, *op. cit.*, p. 625; Schaefer, *loc. cit.*

[161] Villien, "La Procédure Canonique pour l'Expulsion des Religieux"—*Le Canoniste Contemporain,* XXXVI (1913), 211; Schaefer, *loc. cit.;* Schönsteiner, *loc. cit.*

[162] Tamayo, *Procedimientos de Derecho Penal Canonico,* n. 300, 3°; Tabera, *loc. cit.;* Hippolytus a S. Familia, *loc. cit.;* Goyeneche, *De Religiosis*, n. 106.

[163] Tabera, *loc. cit.;* Hippolytus a S. Familia, *loc. cit.;* Vermeersch, "art. cit."—*Periodica,* XIX (1923), 122*; "Alii [auctores] . . . statuunt ad fugam requiri, ut religiosus et mulier simul proficiscantur: alii ad crimen inducendum satis esse dicunt, ut alter cum altero fugam, libidinis explendae causa, pactus sit vel composuerit."—Aleixo, "art. cit."—*Rev. Ecl. Bras.,* VI (1946), 391.

[164] *Loc. cit.*

[165] Cf. *supra,* pp. 70–71.

[166] Cf. *supra,* p. 124.

[167] Schaefer, *loc. cit.;* Sipos, *Enchiridion,* p. 408; Creusen-Garesché-Ellis,

The union is a physical one if both of the accomplices leave the religious house at the same time.[168] However, in view of the fact that ordinarily such a union is highly improbable,[169] a moral union in the case suffices.[170] In order that there be a moral union it is necessary that a motivating cause, namely, an earlier agreement and a subsequent union, link the egress of the religious with the associated presence of a person of the other sex.[171] It was in this sense that Tamayo understood the former law.[172]

Flight undertaken with a prior agreement is designated as undertaken *ex condicto.*[173] When this pre-existing agreement is not conclusive, the associated presence of another party in the flight is regarded as existing *de facto.*[174] In the latter instance the moral union is presumed if the parties knew each other before (i.e., in a way which would denote a "*prava consuetudo*" in their relations), and joined company soon after the beginning of the flight.[175] Regatillo seems to postulate that the flight be continued after the union.[176] It matters little how long the parties are together, where they part soon after or repent later,[177] for these elements do not alter the juridic status induced by the fact of flight.

In this regard the question arises: "Must there always be an agreement between the parties?" It is evident that this agree-

Religious Men and Women in the Code, n. 345; Goyeneche, "Consultationes"—*CpRM,* XVII (1936), 344.

[168] Creusen-Garesché-Ellis, *loc. cit.*

[169] Wernz-Vidal, *Ius Canonicum,* III, n. 438; Regatillo, *Institutiones Iuris Canonici,* I, n. 759; Bouscaren-Ellis, *Canon Law,* p. 310.

[170] Palombo, *De Dimissione Religiosorum,* n. 197; Wernz-Vidal, *loc. cit.;* Regatillo, *loc. cit.*

[171] Vermeersch-Creusen, *Epitome,* I, 595, nota 1; Schaefer, *loc. cit.;* Palombo, *loc. cit.;* Goyeneche, "Consultationes"—*CpRM,* XVII (1936), 344 sq.; Goyeneche, *De Religiosis,* p. 209, nota 21.

[172] Cf. *supra,* p. 71, note 51.

[173] Blat, *Ius de Religiosis,* n. 658; Fanfani, *De Iure Religiosorum,* n. 496.

[174] Blat, *loc. cit.;* Fanfani, *loc. cit.*

[175] Palombo, *loc. cit.;* Schaefer, *loc. cit.;* Goyeneche, "Consultationes"—*CpRM,* XVII (1936), 344–345.

[176] ". . . alteri uniatur et fugiant . . ."—Regatillo, *loc. cit.*

[177] Leitner, *Das Ordensrecht,* p. 488; Sipos, *loc. cit.;* Goyeneche, "Consultationes"—*CpR,* IX (1928), 428–429; cf. *supra,* p. 71.

ment is present in the flight undertaken *ex condicto,* but its presence is not similarly evident in the case which transpires simply *de facto.* In the latter, it is true, the religious must have the forbidden purpose in mind from the beginning of the flight, but must the other party consent when they meet? Thus, if the other person were a mere material accomplice, would the requisite element of a union still attach to the flight?

Creusen-Garesché-Ellis state that the flight must presuppose a mutual and a previous agreement, otherwise the crime mentioned in the canon would not exist.[178] Toso, on the other hand, maintains that such a previous agreement is not a requirement for constituting the case envisioned in the law.[179] Ordinarily there must be some agreement. However, this agreement is not necessarily that meeting of minds which would require that both elicit the act for the same end. Thus the person of the other sex may well lack the same motivation that prompts the religious, and yet may agree to accompany the religious.

In this matter, as Eltz notes,[180] the law does not seem to consider the other party beyond his (her) presence, and considers the crime only as it is verified on the part of the religious.[181] Accordingly, Toso states that it is not necessary that the other party consent to the delict of the religious; [182] and Tabera and Aleixo do not require a formal complicity, but deem a material complicity to be sufficient, inasmuch as they point to a case of

---

178 Creusen-Garesché-Ellis, *loc. cit.*

179 ". . . non requiritur . . . ut fuga cum dissimilis sexus persona ex condicto facta fuerit, quamvis conspiratio praevia, si adsit, multum conferat ad figuram delicti definiendam, praesertim in casu apostasiae vel fugae de quibus in can. 644: siquidem Legislator de turpi *facto* decernit, sed de origine non quaerit; . . ."—Toso, *Commentaria Minora,* Lib. II, pars II, p. 248.

180 "Canon 646, § 1, n. 2, punitively singles out, to the exclusion of the guilty partner, those religious who take flight with a member of the opposite sex."—Eltz, *Cooperation in Crime,* p. 101.

181 Blat, *loc. cit.;* Fanfani, *loc. cit.;* Gerster a Zeil, *Ius Religiosorum,* p. 146.

182 ". . . imo nec requiritur, ut eadem persona in delictum consentiat: nam is etiam, qui ex. c., domo religiosa relicta, mulierem in malum finem rapuerit, recte dicitur cum muliere profugisse; . . ."—Toso, *loc. cit.*

abduction as potentially exemplifying the flight of a religious with the abducted woman.[183]

As regards the number of persons involved, it is evident that two persons are required, one of each sex. Moreover, two with one or one with two, or several with one or one with several, could likewise constitute a "flight with a person of the other sex," if the other postulated elements are present.[184] Though the presence of a person of the other sex is postulated as an element of the flight which canon 646, § 1, 2°, treats of, the phraseology employed is such that the law takes cognizance only of the action of the religious, with no reference to the mutually requisite action of the partner. Hence, Eltz lists this canon as pointing to a simple crime which does not juridically postulate necessary co-operators.[185]

Hippolytus a S. Familia raises a further question whether the associated presence of a person of the other sex in the flight of a religious—provided it is intended, sought, or consented to by the religious—suffices for his incurring of the dismissal, even when no evil is intended on his part.[186] Tabera,[187] Aleixo,[188] Goyeneche,[189] Hippolytus a S. Familia,[190] Vermeersch,[191] Toso, [192] Regatillo [193] and Smith [194] reply in the negative, and require that the flight be motivated by a libidinous intent.

---

183 Tabera, "art. cit."—*CpR,* XI (1930), 416, nota 20; "Sufficit etiam materialis complicitas, i.e. certe adest hoc crimen 'fugam cum muliere arripere,' si religiosus mulierem rapuerit."—Aleixo, "art. cit."—*Rev. Ecl. Bras.,* VI (1946), 388.

184 Goyeneche, "Consultationes"—*CpR,* IX (1928), 429.

185 Eltz, *loc. cit.*

186 Hippolytus a S. Familia, "art cit."—*Analecta O. C. D.,* IV (1930), 160.

187 *Ibid.,* p. 416.

188 "Deinde requiritur ad hoc delictum patrandum, ut habeatur complicitas materialis vel formalis personae alterius sexus, et etiam ut haec fuga sit *libidinis explendae causa,* prout ex spiritu legis, imo ex ipsis verbis clare deducitur."—Aleixo, *loc. cit.;* cf. Tabera, *loc. cit.*

189 *De Religiosis,* n. 106.

190 *Loc. cit.*

191 "Art. cit."—*Periodica,* XIX (1923), 122*.

192 *Ibid.,* p. 247.

193 *Institutiones Iuris Canonici,* I, n. 759.

194 *Op. cit.,* p. 107.

Hippolytus a S. Familia, referring back to the decree *Quum singulae* from which this canon is taken, deduces that the close connection in the text between this qualified flight and an attempted marriage [195] indicates that the flight must be undertaken for an evil end; otherwise nothing more criminal would be had than a simple flight.[196] Villien likewise seems to have implied this in reference to the old law by stating that the obvious sense of the text was that the religious abandoned the religious house for the love of a woman.[197]

This libidinous intent does not entail the intention to contract marriage,[198] nor does it necessarily point to a desire of cohabitation.[199] It rather evinces the intention to satisfy the desires of lust,[200] and thus connotes about the same as the words "*explendae libidinis causa*" which occur in canon 2353. It is not necessary that this intention be carried to completion; it suffices that the religious perpetrated the flight and that it furnished evidence of this purpose.[201] Mayer, though noting that most of the authors espouse this view,[202] takes exception to it. He deems that there can be a case in which canon 646, § 1, 2°, applies even though no libidinous intent is present.[203] However, from what has been said above in keeping with the strict interpretation of canon 646, it seems that this opinion cannot be sustained.

Upon consideration of the various elements that enter into the concept of the flight as here treated, there still remains the task of determining how extensive the terms "cum muliere" and

---

195 "2. fuga . . .
3. et multo magis, contractus . . ."—cf. *supra*, p. 61, note 11.

196 Hippolytus a S. Familia, *loc. cit.*

197 Cf. *supra*, p. 70, note 47.

198 Augustine, *A Commentary*, III, 386; Michalicka, *Judicial Procedure in Dismissal of Clerical Exempt Religious*, p. 13.

199 Beste, *Introductio in Codicem*, p. 438; cf. *supra*, p. 71.

200 ". . . ut ea fruatur . . ."—Vermeersch, *loc. cit.*; Toso, *loc. cit.*; Berutti, *De Religiosis*, n. 158.

201 Toso, *loc cit.*

202 "Fast alle Autoren verlangen, dass die Flucht wenigstens von seiten des (der) Religiosen geschehe *libidinis explendae causa.*"—Mayer, *Benediktinisches Ordensrecht*, III, 362.

203 Mayer, *loc. cit.*

"cum viro" are. Some authors[204] admit no distinction in that they maintain that all persons of the other sex, whether unmarried, married, or widowed, capable or incapable of marriage, seducing or seduced, of good or of ill repute, adult, minor or even below the age of puberty, are included under this term. Other authors[205] make an exception for persons related by consanguinity in the direct line or in the first degree of the collateral line. Finally, a number of authors[206] hold that both relatives and persons who have not attained the age of puberty are not contemplated in canon 646.

The argument of the first group is based solely on a strict and even on a literal interpretation of the law, while the arguments of the latter two groups are based on the reason of the law and the fitness of things.[207] Authors require that the flight be undertaken with a libidinous purpose. This ordinarily presupposes the presence of a person on whom suspicion can rest, otherwise there would not be grounds to presume any evil intention or purpose.[208] Now, traveling with a person under the age of puberty, with an old person, with a person of good character, or with a near rela-

---

[204] Blat, *Ius de Religiosis,* n. 658; Berutti, *loc. cit.;* Bastien, *Directoire Canonique,* p. 128; Cance, *Le Code de Droit Canonique* (6. ed., 3 vols., Paris: Librairie Lecoffre, J. Gabalda et fils, 1930), II, n. 88; Fanfani, *De Iure Religiosorum,* n. 496.

[205] Beste, *loc. cit.;* Coronata, *Manuale Practicum,* p. 110, nota 2; Tabera, "art. cit."—*CpR,* XI (1930), 416, nota 21; Gerster a Zeil, *loc. cit;* Wernz-Vidal, *Ius Canonicum,* III, n. 438; Palombo, *De Dimissione Religiosorum,* p. 236, nota 3; Bouscaren-Ellis, *Canon Law,* p. 310; "Communiter auctores excipiunt ab hac lege fugam cum consanguinea in linea recta vel in primo gradu lineae collateralis. Ratio quidem evidens est: nam in hoc casu necessario abesse debet, quod ius supponit, nempe fugam libidinis explendae causa."—Aleixo, "art. cit."—*Rev. Ecl. Bras.,* VI (1946), 338.

[206] Leitner, *Das Ordensrecht,* pp. 488–489; Chelodi, *De Personis,* p. 457, nota 4; Coronata, *Institutiones,* I, p. 866, nota 7; Geser, *The Canon Law Governing Communities of Sisters,* n. 1156; Goyeneche, *De Religiosis,* n. 106; Hippolytus a S. Familia, "art. cit."—*Analecta O. C. D.,* IV (1930), 160–161; Schaefer, *loc. cit.;* Schönsteiner, *Grundriss des Ordensrechtes,* pp. 625–626; Toso, *op. cit.,* Lib. II, pars II, pp. 247–248; Woywod, *A Practical Commentary on the Code of Canon Law,* I, 289.

[207] Smith, *The Penal Law for Religious,* pp. 105–106.

[208] Toso, *ibid.,* p. 247.

tive, does not ordinarily reflect any such evil intent.[209] Rather, it offers ground for a contrary presumption,[210] for in these cases the suspicion of any evil purpose recedes into the background,[211] and thus it lacks the character of a flight with a person of the other sex.

Of the authors who apply this line of reasoning to near relatives only, and not to persons under the age of puberty, only Palombo and Tabera adduce arguments for their stand. Palombo [212] states that as regards such youthful persons no distinction is to be admitted, since it is not beyond the malice of men or the perversity of the passions that evil designs envision also them as potential co-operators. However, the same observation could also have been made in reference to near relatives. Nevertheless, he states that a distinction can be made if the case warrants it.[213]

Tabera, on the other hand, does not seem primarily to deny validity to the presumption which calls into question the presence of any rightful suspicion when persons under the age of puberty are involved. Rather he takes issue with the reasons adduced by Leitner. He accordingly rules out the pertinent applicability of the canons cited by the latter author, and takes pains to show that there are cases when canon 646 can have application even though the other party has not reached the age of puberty. In this matter his contention is against the total and absolute exclusion from the ambit of canon 646 of the cases which involve such youthful persons.[214] It must be granted that the canons cited by Leitner [215] are unfortunately not to the point. Thus, while canon 88, §. 2, differentiates indeed between persons above and persons below the age of puberty, it does not establish who is to be considered as a "*mulier*" or as a "*vir*." Moreover, since in canon

---

209 Toso, *loc. cit.;* Woywod, *loc. cit.*

210 Toso, *loc. cit.*

211 Leitner, *loc. cit.;* Schönsteiner, *loc. cit.*

212 *Loc. cit.*

213 "Quare, nisi in casu aliter constet, nulla distinctio admittenda videtur: . . ."—Palombo, *loc. cit.*

214 Tabera, "art. cit."—*CpR,* XI (1930), 416-417.

215 *Ibid.,* p. 488.

646 the crime is considered as attaching to the religious, and not to the other person involved, canon 2230 likewise remains devoid of proper application to the point in hand.[216]

Far better are the arguments presented by Schönsteiner in support of the view which regards the joining of company with persons below the age of puberty as presumptively free from all suspicion of libidinous intent.[217] First, this author notes that the common acceptance of the terms "man" and "woman" points to persons who have reached the age of puberty.[218] Secondly, he cites canons 600[219] and 2342, 2°,[220] as evidence of the fact that when the Code wishes to include all members of a sex without exception it states so specifically. Canon 598[221] offers another example of this observation. Hence, it seems that the use of the term "*mulier*" without further specification implies the designation of a person who has reached the age of puberty.[222] Thirdly, he judges that in the company of a person who has not attained the age of puberty the characteristic of a "flight with a person of the other sex"—namely, the presence of a libidinous purpose[223]—is lacking.[224] And fourthly, he points out that this favorable view with relation to very youthful persons is in keeping with the rules of strict interpretation.[225] Moreover, Tabera admits the existence of a presumption which ordinarily excludes the notion of a libidinous intent from the association between a religious and a near relative or a person who is still below the age of puberty.[226]

Accordingly, it is safe to hold that near relatives and persons under the age of puberty are not usually comprehended in the

---

216 Tabera, *ibid.*, p. 416.

217 Schönsteiner, *op. cit.*, pp. 625–626.

218 Schönsteiner, *ibid.*, p. 625; Woywod, *loc. cit.*

219 ". . . nemo, cuiusvis . . . aetatis . . ."

220 "Mulier . . . cuius cunque aetatis . . ."

221 ". . . mulieres cuiusvis aetatis . . ."

222 Schönsteiner, *loc. cit.;* cf. canon 2353.

223 Hippolytus a S. Familia, "*art. cit.*"—*Analecta O. C. D.*, IV (1930), 161; and others.

224 Schönsteiner, *ibid.*, p. 626; Leitner, *op. cit.*, pp. 488–489.

225 Schönsteiner, *loc. cit.*

226 Tabera, *ibid.*, p. 417.

concept of a "flight with a person of the other sex." This view does not rest solely on extrinsic authority as Aleixo contends,[227] but is founded in the reasons advanced above. But this view is nevertheless not to be construed as excluding from the scope of canon 646 any and every possibility of the flight of a religious with a relative or with a person under the age of puberty. Rather it is to be considered as warranting a presumption that in such circumstances the flight is not such as is postulated in the law. This presumption is simply of such a character that in the face of contrary fact duly established by proof it yields its place to the truth which supplants it.[228] Hence, if it is evident or legitimately proved in any given case that there are present all the elements which the law postulates in canon 646 for a flight, then the dismissal automatically results even though the flight was undertaken with a relative [229] or with a person still below the age of puberty; otherwise the presumption of non-suspicion, and consequently also of the absence of any flight on the part of the religious, will favor all cases in which near relatives and persons under the age of puberty are involved.

A few authors require that the flight be a public matter. Schaefer states that if the flight is so occult that there is no evidence of it in the external forum, the religious is not dismissed through the operation of canon 646.[230] Smith [231] requires a flight that is public according to the concepts furnished in canons 1037 and 2197, 3°. He cites Schaefer and Leitner as authorities for this conclusion, but neither of them makes mention of these

---

[227] "Nonnulli auctores excipiunt etiam fugam cum impubere; nescimus quo iure; propter auctoritatem extrinsecam haec sententia probabilis dici potest; nobis tamen non arridet."—Aleixo, "*art. cit.*"—*Rev. Ecl. Bras.*, VI (1946), 388.

[228] ". . . haec tamen praesumptio veritati cedere debet."—Tabera, *loc. cit.*

[229] Since Goyeneche (*De Religiosis*, n. 106), Schaefer (*loc. cit.*), and others include those who are related by affinity under the term "near relatives," it is deemed necessary to comprise also these "relatives" under the presumption which yields to contrary proof.

[230] "Si fuga ita occulta sit, non publica, ut in foro externo de illa non constet, Religiosus non est ipso iure dimissus vi canonis 646."—Schaefer, *De Religiosis*, n. 576.

[231] *Op. cit.*, p. 104.

canons. In fact, Leitner makes no reference to publicity at all at this point.[232]

Goyeneche[233] judges that if the factor of being with a person of the other sex is occult, the dismissal is not effected.[234] In this he agrees substantially with the authors just cited. However, in the added statement that superiors are to proceed to the declaration of the fact if the matter should at any time become public,[235] Goyeneche creates further confusion. One would expect the authors to hold either that a public flight is postulated, or that also an occult flight suffices, and that, whichever is demanded, the effected dismissal will be conditioned on the secret or public character of the flight at the moment when the flight was perpetrated. Nevertheless, from the whole tenor of his article it is clear that Goyeneche labors under the impression that the declaration of the fact is necessary for the effecting of the dismissal[236]—an impression quite prevalent prior to the authentic interpretation of July 30, 1934.[237]

It is true that as long as the matter remains occult, the superior with his chapter or council cannot proceed to the declaration of the fact.[238] However, this declaration is not required for the effecting of the dismissal,[239] for the dismissal operates by law and is present as soon as the delict is committed,[240] i.e., at the begin-

---

232 Leitner, *Das Ordensrecht*, p. 488.

233 " Consultationes "—*CpR,* IX (1928), 428–429.

234 " Prout casus proponitur, videtur circumstantiam illam " *cum muliere* " fuisse occultam ita ut in foro externo de illa non constet. In casu ergo Titius neque dimissus est ipso iure, neque dimittendus ad normam can. 646, § 2."—Goyeneche, *ibid.*, p. 428. Cf. Smith, *loc. cit.*

235 " Si, e contra, res publica devenerit, Superior, statim ac de facto constet, emittat cum suo Capitulo vel Consilio declarationem facti, . . ."—Goyeneche, *loc. cit.*

236 ". . . neque dimittendus ad normam can. 646, § 2 . . . dimissio enim comminatur in actum ipsum arreptionis fugae cum muliere . . . locus erit dimissioni a iure . . ."—Goyeneche, " Consultationes "—*CpR,* IX (1928), 428–429.

237 P. C. I., 30 iul. 1934, ad III—*AAS,* XXVI (1934), 494; cf. *infra,* p. 160.

238 Aleixo, "art. cit."—*Rev. Ecl. Bras.,* VI (1946), 391.

239 Cf. *infra,* p. 161.

240 Aleixo, *loc. cit.;* cf. *supra,* pp. 86–87, 124.

ning of the flight with the person of the other sex. This initial act, though of its very nature always external, is in the majority of cases an occult act,[241] and it is to this normal fact that the law seems to apply. Aleixo observes that, since the canon itself expressly postulates that the apostasy from the Catholic Faith be public, and since marriage is *de se* public, the lawgiver may well have intended that all the delicts which effect an automatic dismissal must be of a public character.[242]

While this same author notes that flight with a person of the other sex is not public in the same manner as are the delicts in relation to marriage, he nevertheless deems that this flight, even though it may be kept occult easier, belongs of its very nature to the public forum.[243] As a consequence of the view that this flight is of its very nature a public matter, Aleixo prefers the opinion which holds that the dismissal is effected at the very moment of the flight with a person of the other sex even though that fact remains occult.[244] Mayer supports a similar view.[245] All this is in conformity with the sense of the canon and with the purpose of the law,[246] so that there seems to be no need to demand that the fact be public or publicly known.

Authors,[247] moreover, carefully note that a furtive egress is

---

[241] "Initium vero fugae plerumque occultum erit."—Aleixo, *loc. cit.*

[242] "Inde forse concludere nobis licet Ecclesiam exigere ut omnia haec delicta quae secumferunt dimissionem ipso iure, sint publica."—Aleixo, *loc. cit.*

[243] "Jamvero fugam cum muliere arripere non eodem modo ac matrimonium civile et matrimonii attentatio vel celebratio est publicum, nam de ultimis constat ex documentis publicis, de fuga cum muliere autem non habetur documentum publicum. Attamen, quamvis facilius sit occultam servare per aliquod saltem tempus fugam cum muliere, de se est etiam actus, qui ad forum publicum, ut ita dicam, pertinet."—Aleixo, *ibid.*, pp. 391–392.

[244] "Ideoque nobis magis placet sententiam quae affirmat fugam cum muliere, etsi occulta maneat, tamen producere primo momento fugae dimissionem ipso iure."—Aleixo, *ibid.*, p. 392.

[245] "Ist dieses Moment, dass der Religiose mit einer *Frauensperson* geflohen ist, geheim und *in foro externo* nicht bewiesen, dann ist er zwar auch van Rechts wegen entlassen, . . ."—Mayer, *Benediktinisches Ordensrecht*, III, 361.

[246] Cf. *supra*, p. 70, 86–87, 104, 124.

[247] Coronata, *Institutiones*, I, n. 646; Coronata, *Manuale Practicum*, n.

something distinct from the flight contemplated in canon 646, § 1, 2°, and accordingly is not to be considered in relation to the latter. The term and concept of a " furtive egress " is taken from the pre-Code authors.[248] It denotes primarily an illicit [249] and occult [250] egress from the religious house to do something outside without the superior's knowledge.[251] It is not considered to be a flight, since the offender ordinarily does not show the intention of withdrawing himself from obedience and from the common observance.[252] Furtive egress is rather a violation of obedience and of the Constitutions,[253] and an infraction of the law of canon 606, § 1.[254] In view of these points the authors hold that the element of flight is not present.[255]

This egress could be resorted to for the sake of committing sins of lust, or of doing so more freely or frequently,[256] even if the departure were protracted to one or two days.[257] It must be noted that the expression " furtive egress " was used by pre-Code and also by the post-Code authors in a sense opposed to the egress connoted in canon 644, § 3, namely, as an egress of less than three days in duration.[258]

It is evident that this distinction can have no bearing in the present consideration, for the act of flight is accomplished *in ipso actu.* Hence, Aleixo points out that if one deems flight in its common acceptance (i.e., a hasty departure from one place to

---

236; Schaefer, *De Religiosis,* n. 576; Hippolytus a S. Familia, "art. cit." —*Analecta O. C. D.,* IV (1930), 160; Goyeneche, "Consultationes"—*CpRM,* XVII (1936), 344; Smith, *op. cit.,* p. 106.

[248] Cf. Wernz, *Ius Decretalium,* III, n. 675.

[249] Schaefer, *ibid.,* n. 567.

[250] Hippolytus a S. Familia, *loc. cit.*

[251] Coronata, *Institutiones,* I, n. 642.

[252] Schaefer, *ibid.,* nn. 567 and 576; Hippolytus a S. Familia, *loc. cit.;* Riesner, *Apostates and Fugitives from Religious Institutes,* p. 76.

[253] Schaefer, *ibid.,* n. 567.

[254] Schaefer, *ibid.,* p. 977, nota 149; Chelodi, *Ius de Personis,* p. 457, nota 1.

[255] Goyeneche, "Consultationes"—*CpRM,* XVII (1936), 344–345.

[256] Schaefer, *ibid.,* n. 576; Coronata, *Institutiones,* I, n. 646; Coronata, *Manuale Practicum,* n. 236; Smith, *loc. cit.*

[257] Riesner, *ibid.,* pp. 76–77.

[258] Riesner, *loc. cit.*

another) sufficient, then one must logically include furtive egress within the scope of the law enacted in canon 646. For the very circumstances attending the egress—revealing the purpose to sin by lust—create a strong presumption that all the postulated elements for the flight as understood in canon 646 are present, especially if the religious sins often with the same person so that they join in each other's company. However, if one maintains, as has been done in the present work, that the flight contemplated in canon 646 implies a desertion of the religious house and a withdrawal from religious obedience and the regular observance, then a furtive egress is definitely not comprehended by canon 646 under the notion of the flight of a religious with a person of the other sex.[259]

In passing it has already been stated that cohabitation is not a requisite constituent element in the notion of flight on the part of the religious,[260] but now it remains to determine what significance is to be attached to it if it is actually present. Does concubinage constitute a form of flight with a person of the other sex?[261]

In consulting the authors one must advert to the fact that some consider concubinage only in connection with 3° of canon 646, § 1, while others touch upon it in both 2° and 3° of the canon. In the present work concubinage will be treated at this point as it applies to the notion of flight, and later as it applies with reference to an attempted marriage. First of all, concubinage *in se* and *per se* does not imply the notion of a flight.[262] It could exist

[259] "Jamvero, si ad fugam cum muliere requiratur, ut religiosus sit fugitivus in sensu can. 644, non comprehenditur sub lege qui furtive exiit ad peccandum cum muliere; si vero sufficiat fuga in sensu vulgari, videtur et comprehendi sub lege qui furtive domum religiosam relinquit, ex praevia complicitate, praecise ad peccandum cum muliere."—Aleixo, "art. cit."—*Rev. Ecl. Bras.*, VI (1946), 392.

[260] Cf. *supra*, p. 133.

[261] ". . . alii [auctores] affirmant ex solo concubinatu exsurgere jam hoc crimen; alii negant, affirmantes tunc tantum ex concubinatu oriri praefatum delictum, si adest causalitas inter apostasiam, fugam et respectivum concubinatum; aliis verbis dicunt 'fugam cum muliere arripere' adesse, quoties, ut quis in concubinatu vivat, ex condicto cum muliere apostasiam vel fugam admiserit, etsi non simul religiosus et mulier fugam arripuerint . . ."—Aleixo, *ibid.*, p. 391.

[262] Tabera, "art. cit."—*CpR*, XI (1930), 417; Goyeneche, *De Religiosis*, p. 209, nota 25.

on the part of a religious who is not a fugitive at the time, e.g., an exclaustrated religious;[263] or it could obtain after a religious had left the religious house for some other reason, and then only later, with the occasion presenting itself, rendered his condition worse by entering upon concubinage.[264] Thus, an apostate or a fugitive religious who originally did not intend such an action could not be said to have taken flight with a person of the other sex, for there is no relation of causality between their apostasy or flight and the concubinage.[265] Such as these, then, are outside the scope of the law as expressed in 2° of canon 646, § 1.[266]

However, there are circumstances under which concubinage falls within the scope of this law,[267] namely, when the religious, by acting on a prior agreement with the other party, becomes an apostate or a fugitive from his religious institute for the purpose of living in concubinage.[268] In this manner a concubinage following immediately upon the perpetrated desertion of or illegitimate departure from the religious house would create a presumption against the parties, granted that they knew each other before.[269] Hence, whether or not concubinage actually involves the elements of a flight with a person of the other sex depends on the circumstances that attend the established concubinage.

The present article has stressed the acts of the religious as the necessary conditions for the application of the law enacted in canon 646. Some of these elements are internal in character, e.g., intention, malicious intent, etc. The law does not scrutinize these, but looks to the facts, and from these presumes the presence of all the elements postulated in the law. Thus, one who in the act of flight is accompanied by a woman is presumed to flee with her in the sense of the canon.[270] If there is no circumstance

---

263 Tabera, *loc. cit.*

264 Palombo, *De Dimissione Religiosorum,* n. 197; Tabera, *ibid.,* p. 418; Vermeersch, "art. cit."—*Periodica,* XIX (1923), 122*; Toso, *Commentaria Minora,* Lib. II, pars II, p. 247; Smith, *op. cit.,* p. 106; cf. *supra,* p. 70.

265 Tabera, *loc. cit.;* Aleixo, *loc. cit.*

266 Wernz-Vidal, *Ius Canonicum,* III, n. 438.

267 Wernz-Vidal, *loc. cit.*

268 Tabera, *loc. cit.;* Vermeersch, *ibid.,* p. 121*; Aleixo, *loc. cit.*

269 Palombo, *loc. cit.;* Smith, *loc. cit.*

270 "Quivis autem fugitivus cum muliere dicendus est iuridice fugam cum muliere arripuisse."—Vermeersch, *loc. cit.*

which precludes the operation of this presumption, the superior proceeds to the declaration of the fact, and the burden of proof to the contrary falls upon the religious.[271]

Among the various adducible proofs are the following: that one left for a different motive and only later accompanied the person; that one desisted from the flight before any joining of company could take place; that one was frustrated in his attempt;[272] that the egress lacked the character of a flight; that the flight was undertaken with a person on whom suspicion does not ordinarily rest; that one did not know the person before; and so forth. In the lack of definite evidence and conclusive proof, presumptions can be employed both by the institute and by the religious, but such presumptions stand only as long as conclusive proof has not prevailed against them, for they must ever give way to the truth, with relation to which the proffered conclusive proof furnishes an incontestable pledge and token.[273]

Accordingly, " flight with a person of the other sex " is a flight qualified by complicity and motivated with libidinous intent. These elements must be evident or at least legitimately presumable from the very beginning of the flight. Though not all the authors agree in postulating these conditions, it seems certain that abstraction from them would lift the flight in question out of the class of the flight with a person of the other sex as contemplated in the norm of canon 646, § 1, 2°.[274]

In consequence of the element of flight as postulated for the delict according to the norm of canon 646, § 1, 2°,[275] the religious would ordinarily also incur the penalties enacted in canons 2385 or 2386.[276] Those religious, however, who already are apostates

[271] Hippolytus a S. Familia, "art. cit."—*Analecta O. C. D.*, IV (1930), 161.

[272] Toso, *loc. cit.*

[273] Tabera, *ibid.*, p. 417.

[274] ". . . nonnulli auctores solummodo sub determinatis condicionibus fugam admittunt (quae sententia non tamen est certa) ; deficientibus tamen his condicionibus certo in hoc casu non habetur fuga religiosi cum muliere ad normam c. 646, § 1, n. 2."—Ledwolorz, " Recensiones librorum "—*Apollinaris*, X (1937), 478.

[275] Cf. *supra*, p. 127.

[276] Schaefer, *De Religiosis*, n. 576; Smith, *op. cit.*, p. 49, note 48; Riesner, *ibid.*, p. 79; cf. *infra*, p. 185.

or fugitives from their religious institute, and who only later associate with a person of the other sex in their flight, cannot be regarded as having invoked against them the sanction enacted in canon 646, § 1, 2°; for, having once begun their flight from the religious institute, they are juridically apostates or fugitives. Their subsequent association with a person of the other sex does not change the pristine character of their "*fuga*" to that of a "*fuga . . . cum muliere, aut . . . cum viro.*"[277]

Article 3. Marriage and the Civil Bond

> Canon 646, § 1. *Ipso facto habendi sunt tanquam legitime dimissi religiosi:*
> 3°. *Attentantes aut contrahentes matrimonium aut etiam vinculum, ut aiunt, civile.*

This section of the canon is a restatement of the pre-Code law. While retaining all the elements of the former law, the Code rearranges the items enumerated there, and omits an explanatory phrase.[278] The object of this delict centers in the contract of marriage.[279]

Marriage, considered as a contract, is an agreement by which a man and a woman who are not incapacitated by any law freely give to each other the right, perpetual and exclusive, to those acts by which in the normal course children are procreated.[280] The consent of the parties creates the marriage contract,[281] and this consent consists in an act of the will.[282] Even knowledge of the invalidity of the marriage does not necessarily exclude this matrimonial consent.[283]

However, for the baptized this contract has been raised to the

[277] Cf. *supra*, pp. 86–87, 124.

[278] Cf. *supra*, p. 61, note 11.

[279] Hippolytus a S. Familia, "De Dimissione Religiosorum"—*Analecta O. C. D.*, IV (1930), 161.

[280] Canon 1081. Cf. Lydon, *Ready Answers in Canon Law*, pp. 342–343; Sabetti-Barrett, *Compendium Theologiae Moralis* (8. ed. post Codicem, New York: Pustet, 1939), p. 843.

[281] Canon 1081, § 1.

[282] Canon 1081, § 2.

[283] Canon 1085.

dignity of a sacrament,[284] and thus the contract and the sacrament have been made to exist as inseparable from each other.[285] Christian marriage is governed not only by divine law, but also by canon law.[286] Accordingly only the supreme ecclesiastical authority has the right to judge whether divine law prohibits or invalidates a marriage,[287] and to establish ecclesiastical impediments [288] which no inferior authority may abrogate, derogate, or dispense from unless it has been authorized to do so.[289] In virtue of this power the Church has laid down rules requiring specific formalities for the valid making of the contract,[290] and has established both prohibitive and diriment impediments.[291]

The Church accords religious vows the status of *public* vows.[292] Moreover, she distinguishes between simple and solemn vows.[293] The former, whether temporary or perpetual, render acts contrary to the vow illicit but not invalid, unless other provision be made; the latter render such acts invalid.[294] In this manner the Church has excluded religious from the married state as a state incompatible with their profession.[295] This exclusion is a diriment in the case of religious bound by solemn vows or by vows which have been given this special force; [296] it is a prohibitive impediment in relation to the vows of all other religious.[297]

In canon 646, § 1, 3°, then, the law considers religious who are so unmindful of their vow of chastity [298] as to enter or to attempt to enter a state incompatible with their profession. The delict thus envisioned may be threefold; namely, the religious may in-

284 Canon 1012, § 1.
285 Canon 1012, § 2.
286 Canon 1016.
287 Canon 1038, § 1.
288 Canon 1038, § 2.
289 Canon 1040.
290 Canons 1094–1098.
291 Canons 1035–1080.
292 Cf. canons 488, 1°, and 1308, § 1.
293 Canon 1308, § 2.
294 Canon 579.
295 Wernz-Vidal, *Ius Canonicum,* III, n. 438.
296 Canon 1073.
297 Canon 1058, § 2.
298 Brandys, *Kirchliches Rechtsbuch,* p. 104.

tend a true canonical marriage, but may fail in the contracting of it by reason of a diriment impediment; or they may intend and actually succeed in validly contracting a marriage; or, finally, they may resort to the contracting of a union which is designated as a civil bond of marriage.[299] It is immediately evident that the canon is not concerned with the validity or the invalidity of the act,[300] but rather looks to the mutual giving of consent [301] under some external semblance of marriage.[302] The purpose of the law in canon 646 is not that of punishing the act of marriage, whether valid, or attempted, or merely civil. The purpose is simply that of invoking a constituted canonical sanction against any religious who has committed a flagrant breach of contract against the religious institute of which he was a member.[303]

A. *Attentantes . . . matrimonium . . .*

First of all, those are said to attempt marriage who cannot juridically contract a valid marriage.[304] This classification embraces all who are bound by diriment impediments. For the sake of easier recognition in this matter, as it applies to the sanction enacted in canon 646, it is convenient to list them as follows: (a) religious bound either by solemn vows, or by simple vows to which the Holy See has attached this special effect, and, conversely, other religious who attempt marriage with the religious here mentioned; [305] (b) religious in sacred Orders,[306] no matter whether their vows are temporary or perpetual, and other re-

[299] Tabera, "De Dimissione Religiosorum"—*CpR,* XI (1930), 418.

[300] Smith, *The Penal Law for Religious,* p. 119; Leitner, *Das Ordensrecht,* p. 489; Schönsteiner, *Grundriss des Ordensrechtes,* p. 626.

[301] Creusen-Garesché-Ellis, *Religious Men and Women in the Code,* n. 345; Bouscaren-Ellis, *Canon Law,* p. 310.

[302] Smith, *ibid.,* p. 112; Coronata, *Manuale Practicum,* n. 237.

[303] Cf. *supra,* p. 73, note 62.

[304] Fanfani, *De Iure Religiosorum,* n. 496; Bastien, *Directoire Canonique,* p. 128; Gerster a Zeil, *Ius Religiosorum,* p. 147; Blat, *Ius de Religiosis,* n. 658; Schönsteiner, *loc. cit.;* Berutti, *De Religiosis,* n. 158; Oesterle, *Praelectiones Iuris Canonici,* I, 370; Hippolytus a S. Familia, *loc. cit.;* Regatillo, *Institutiones Iuris Canonici,* I, n. 759; Geser, *The Canon Law Governing Communities of Sisters,* n. 1158.

[305] Canon 1073.

[306] Canon 1072.

ligious who attempt marriage with the afore-mentioned; and (c) religious bound by any other diriment impediment (e.g., nonage, disparity of cult, existing bond, etc., on the side of the proposed partner in the attempted marriage) without regard to the type of vows by which they are bound.[307]

A few authors in defining this delict require that at least one of the parties place the act knowingly,[308] in bad faith,[309] with deceit,[310] or with presumption.[311] It is in this sense that Alford defines "*matrimonium attentatum.*"[312] The authors, no doubt, mention this element in reference to the present canon from an association of it with canon 2388, § 1, where they treat *ex professo* of attempted marriage. Ordinarily the element of presumption will be present in the religious, but the question may be raised whether this element is absolutely necessary here.

The decree *Quum singulae* used the simple term "*attentatio,*"[313] and it is certain that the word "*attentantes*" in the present law does not imply any more than it did in that decree. Moreover, if this term of itself presupposed presumptuous conduct, there would be no need anywhere else of adding words which indicate the accompaniment of presumption, e.g., the words "*ausi sunt,*" as used with the verb "*attentare*" in canon 985, 3°. Furthermore, the circumstances present in the introduction of the present law indicate that regarding the delict here contemplated it was to have a wider extension than that implied in the law which enacted an excommunication for a very similar delict.[314] Finally, no penalty is directly involved in canon 646, § 1, 3°. Accordingly, since it appears very evident that the purpose of the law is not the invoking of a punishment for the religious, but the protec-

---

307 Tabera, *loc. cit.;* Coronata, *Institutiones,* I, n. 646; Schönsteiner, *loc. cit.;* Mayer, *Benediktinisches Ordensrecht,* III, 362.

308 Palombo, *De Dimissione Religiosorum,* n. 197; Toso, *Commentaria Minora,* Lib. II, pars II, p. 248.

309 Tabera, *loc. cit.;* Goyeneche, *De Religiosis,* n. 106.

310 Coronata, *Manuale Practicum,* n. 237.

311 Schaefer, *De Religiosis,* n. 576.

312 Alford, *Jus Matrimoniale Comparatum* (Romae: Anonima Libraria Cattolica Italiana, 1938), n. 31.

313 Cf. *supra,* p. 61, note 11.

314 Cf. *supra,* pp. 71–72.

tion of the institute and the proper regulating of the profession-contract, there seems given in rare cases the possibility in which an invalid but reciprocally putative marriage could be accompanied with factors which suffice to verify the condition inherent in the phrase "*attentantes matrimonium.*"

Thus far the element of "attempt" has been considered only in its relation to diriment impediments; the observance of the proper form has been presumed as a matter of course. It is within these limits that the authors in general speak of this attempt. Coronata [315] and Blat [316] require explicitly that the proposed contracting of the marriage be undertaken in the form prescribed by law, i.e., by means of a matrimonial ceremony performed in accord with the acceptance of the Church; [317] while the other authors at least imply this by their manner of treatment. With reference to the form of marriage, then, a marriage may still be only an attempted marriage even with the observance of the canonical form as prescribed in canons 1094 and 1098. It is necessary to note that an attempted common law marriage, if the conditions set by canon 1098 are verified, also comes under the canonical sanction invoked by canon 646, § 1, 3°, against an attempted marriage.[318] This attempted common law marriage opens the way for the application of this sanction even in those states which do not recognize such a marriage, since baptized persons remain unaffected by the civil laws which regulate the form for entrance into marriage.[319]

However, it remains now to investigate whether a marriage which is null for lack of the requisite canonical form can also meet the terms which according to canon 646 would brand it as an attempted marriage. In this, then, reference is made, not to a marital union contracted outside the Church, which will be con-

---

315 *Manuale Practicum*, n. 237.

316 *Loc. cit.*

317 ". . . in facie Ecclesiae . . ."—Coronata, *loc. cit.;* Blat, *loc. cit.;* cf. *supra*, p. 72.

318 Dillon, *Common Law Marriage*, The Catholic University of America Canon Law Studies, n. 153 (Washington, D. C.: The Catholic University of America Press, 1942), p. 129; Blat, *loc. cit.*

319 Dillon, *op. cit.*, pp. 127–128; McDevitt, *The Renunciation of an Ecclesiastical Office*, p. 142.

sidered later, but to a substantial defect in the proper form as affecting a marriage undertaken in the Church, such as results from an insufficient number of witnesses, or from the lack of requisite authorization on the part of the official witness. Since in such a case the prescribed form is not entirely neglected, the contracted union retains the aspect of a marriage,[320] and the act whereby the union was contracted adequately meets the notion of the attempted marriage which calls for the application of the sanction enacted in canon 646.

B. . . . *contrahentes matrimonium* . . .

In § 1 of canon 646 the noun on which the word "*contrahentes*" as well as the word "*attentantes*" depends is "*religiosi.*" The subject, then, of the delict involved in the contracting of the marriage against which canon 646 invokes its enacted sanction is a religious who can validly contract marriage. As has been noted above,[321] simple vows, whether temporary or perpetual, render contrary acts illicit but not invalid, and as such constitute simply a prohibitive impediment to marriage.[322] It is religious who are bound by these vows who are primarily contemplated as the potential subjects of the delict involved in their *contracting* of marriage. As is evident, the marriage must be performed according to the canonical form as prescribed in canons 1094 and 1098; otherwise there could be no question of a *valid* marriage.[323] However, though religious in simple vows can contract marriage validly, they do so illicitly. In this manner they commit a sin and a sacrilege by assuming a state not in keeping with their religious profession.[324] It is this breach of contract in relation to which the law invokes its canonical sanction.

Furthermore, under the heading "*contrahentes*" must be in-

---

[320] Payen, *De Matrimonio in Missionibus et Potissimum in Sinis Tractatus Practicus et Casus* (2. ed., 3 vols., Zi-ka-weí: In typographia T'ou-sè-wè, 1935–1936), I, n. 137; cf. canon 1139, § 1.

[321] Cf. *supra*, p. 145.

[322] Canon 1058, § 2; cf. canon 1036, § 1.

[323] Bastien, *Directoire Canonique*, p. 129; Blat, *loc. cit.;* Coronata, *Manuale Practicum*, n. 237.

[324] Wernz-Vidal, *Ius Canonicum*, III, n. 438; Frey, *The Act of Religious Profession*, p. 127; Eichmann, *Lehrbuch des Kirchenrechts*, p. 257.

cluded any religious who, though bound by a diriment impediment, has been dispensed in accordance with the norms of canons 1043–1045. It is to be noted, with special reference to solemn vows and the vows that have the same force in law, that these canons authorize the possible granting of a dispensation only from the *impediment,* and not also from the *vows,*[325] for the dispensation of public vows is reserved to the Holy See.[326] The force of a dispensation granted in accordance with these canons is that the impediment does not bind for a particular marriage; but the vow still binds outside of the lawful use of marriage, and both vow and impediment bind in regard to all future marriages, until such time as the vow is dispensed.[327] Though a religious in this manner could contract licitly and validly as concerns the impediment, he would nevertheless act illicitly in his placing of an act that militates against the vow which still remains binding on him.[328]

Though the words of the decree *Quum singulae, "celebratio matrimonii, etiam validi,"* with their explanatory phrase, *"seu quando vota non sint solemnia vel non habeant solemnium effectum,"* [329] have been omitted in the process of the revision of the Church's law on this point, their meaning is preserved and conveyed in the words *"contrahentes matrimonium"* of the present law.

C. . . . *aut etiam* [*attentantes aut contrahentes*] *vinculum, ut aiunt, civile.*

Inasmuch as at least one of the parties must certainly be assumed to be a subject of the Church by reason of baptism,[330] the lawgiver in canon 646, § 1, 3°, first considers marriage as at-

---

[325] O'Keeffe, *Matrimonial Dispensations, Powers of Bishops, Priests and Confessors,* The Catholic University of America Canon Law Studies, n. 45 (Washington, D. C.: The Catholic University of America, 1927), p. 76; Fang, *Dispensatio Matrimonialis Urgente Mortis Periculo et Instante Nuptiarum Contractu ad normam can. 1043–1045* (Romae: Officium Libri Catholici, 1946), pp. 103, 110.

[326] Canon 1308, § 3.

[327] O'Keeffe, *ibid.*, p. 77.

[328] Cf. canon 579.

[329] Cf. *supra,* p. 61, note 11.

[330] Cf. canon 538.

attempted or contracted before the Church's forum. Yet, realizing that the religious may spurn or through a self-imposed necessity ignore the sacramental bond,[331] the Church has seen fit to include also the *civil bond* within the scope of the delict against which canon 646 invokes its enacted canonical sanction. In fact, the special signification of the word "*etiam*" seems to be almost that of an equivalent for "*a fortiori,*" for in a preparatory copy of the decree *Quum singulae* the phrase *civil marriage* alone occurred,[332] and in the decree itself the expression *civil contract* was initially employed in the law.[333]

It is noteworthy that both in the decree and in the Code the Church does not dignify the contraction of such a union with the term "marriage," but simply applies to it the name superficially adopted by usage—"*ut aiunt*"—for the civil act involved. The law does not take up at this point the question of the State's competence over the marriage of Catholics,[334] but rather shows its reprobation of the presumption that would give any status to a purely civil bond, and implicitly asserts the Church's exclusive right over the marriages of the baptized.[335]

The authors in various ways state what constitutes this civil bond. Thus, some[336] require specifically that it take place before a civil official or magistrate, while others[337] understand it in a wider sense as that union which, in the eyes of the civil law, is reckoned as marriage. Dillon observes that most of the authors

---

[331] Toso, *Commentaria Minora,* Lib. II, pars II, p. 248.

[332] Cf. *supra,* p. 65, note 22.

[333] Cf. *supra,* p. 61, note 11.

[334] Cf. canon 1016; Goldsmith, *The Competence of Church and State over Marriage—Disputed Points,* The Catholic University of America Canon Law Studies, n. 197 (Washington, D. C.: The Catholic University of America Press, 1944), pp. 37-54.

[335] Roberti, "Respectus sociales in Codice iuris Canonici"—*Apollinaris,* X (1937), 388.

[336] Palombo, *De Dimissione Religiosorum,* n. 197; Gerster a Zeil, *Ius Religiosorum,* p. 147; Schönsteiner, *Grundriss des Ordensrechtes,* p. 626; Mayer, *Benediktinisches Ordensrecht,* III, 362; Geser, *The Canon Law Governing Communities of Sisters,* n. 1157.

[337] Berutti, *De Religiosis,* n. 158; Tabera, "De Dimissione Religiosorum"—*CpR,* XI (1930), 419; Schaefer, *De Religiosis,* n. 576.

hold to the latter view.[338] Berutti[339] defines the civil bond as "any form of marriage ceremony established by the laws of the land in consequence of which its citizens may acquire the rights of legitimate spouses." Hence, in states where common law marriages are recognized, such unions constitute a civil bond,[340] and as such come under the sanction invoked by canon 646, § 1, 3°, against them.[341] In short, common law marriage, as attempted or contracted according to canon 1098, comes under the first part of canon 646, § 1, 3°; as attempted or contracted according to the civil law, it comes under the present section.

Moreover, the words "*attentantes*" and "*contrahentes*" employed in canon 646 apply also to the civil bond. The very wording of the canon—"*attentantes aut contrahentes*" and "*matrimonium aut etiam vinculum, ut aiunt, civile*"—requires this. These terms, however, are used only in the sense that such a bond *de facto* exists either as recognized or as unrecognized according to the norms of said civil power. Thus, a civil bond is contracted when the requirements of the law are met;[342] it is to be considered as only attempted if in fact it lacked all legal effect,[343] namely, inasmuch as the act for the contracting of the union militated against the requirements for a valid contract. Hence, whether a religious actually contracts a civil bond or positively attempts to do so, he is subject to the sanction of automatic dismissal invoked in the law of canon 646.

Through its included mention of the civil bond in canon 646, § 1, 3°, the Church does not grant these unions any shred of legality. Since one of the parties at least is certainly subject to the observance of the form of marriage as prescribed by the Church's law, the so-called civil marriage begets simply a status of public concubinage which is given the cloak of respectability

---

[338] Dillon, *Common Law Marriage*, p. 127.

[339] *Loc. cit.*

[340] Dillon, *loc. cit.*

[341] Dillon, *op. cit.*, p. 129.

[342] Berutti, *loc. cit.;* Blat, *loc. cit.;* Michalicka, *Judicial Procedure in Dismissal of Clerical Exempt Religious*, p. 13; Bastien, *loc. cit.;* Palombo, *loc. cit.;* Dillon, *op. cit.*, p. 127.

[343] Tabera, *ibid.*, p. 419, nota 29; Blat, *loc. cit.;* Hippolytus a S. Familia, "*art. cit.*"—*Analecta O. C. D.*, IV (1930), 161.

by the law.[344] The Church nevertheless recognizes that even in such cases there is an exchange of matrimonial consent regarded as legally effective and valid by the civil authority,[345] and hence invokes the sanction of an automatic dismissal for such evident unmindfulness on the part of the religious with reference to his vows, to the duties of his state in life, and to the profession-contract which bound him to the religious institute as a member.

Though civil marriage for subjects of the Church reflects but a form of concubinage, it does not follow that all concubinage simply reflects a form of civil marriage. Hence, mere concubinage, even though it be public, if practiced without any previous exchange of matrimonial consent upon which the State could predicate a valid marriage, is not contemplated in canon 646.[346] Lacking recognition either by the Church or the State, as based on matrimonial consent, it cannot be said to have the semblance of a marriage.[347] In fact, it is quite definite that the law does not intend to include concubinage as such within the enumeration contained in canon 646. For, in a preparatory copy of the decree *Quum singulae* concubinage was considered as one of the delicts that might be included as calling for the application of the sanction of dismissal,[348] but it was not incorporated in that decree,[349] and its mention likewise does not occur in the present law as enacted in canon 646.

After this brief survey of the three forms of the present delict, there remain to be discussed a few points which are common to all three forms.

To constitute the delict of canon 646 the desire or the intention of the parties to marry,[350] the civil or ecclesiastical publica-

---

[344] Bastien, *loc. cit.;* Fanfani, *loc. cit.;* Blat, *loc. cit.;* Toso, *loc. cit.*

[345] Smith, *op. cit.*, p. 112.

[346] Schönsteiner, *loc. cit.;* Prümmer, *Manuale Iuris Canonici*, p. 346; Hippolytus a S. Familia, *loc. cit.;* Claeys Bouuaert-Simenon, *Manuale Juris Canonici*, p. 385; Tabera, "art. cit."—*CpR*, XI (1930), 419; Palombo, *loc. cit.;* Goyeneche, *De Religiosis*, n. 106; Coronata, *Institutiones*, I, n. 646; Schaefer, *loc. cit.;* Gerster a Zeil, *loc. cit.;* Bastien, *loc. cit.;* Fanfani, *loc. cit.*

[347] Smith, *op. cit.*, p. 119.

[348] Cf. *supra*, p. 65, note 22.

[349] Cf. *supra*, p. 61, note 11.

[350] Hippolytus a S. Familia, *loc. cit.*

tion of the banns,[351] or the procurement of the license for marriage would not be sufficient. There must be an act which constitutes an attempt at or a contract of marriage. When this is present no other condition is required.[352] Moreover, since marriage is of its very nature a public matter,[353] the fact that the actual commission of the delicts in question is occult or even remains occult does not free the religious from the application of the sanction enacted in canon 646. The dismissal takes effect immediately upon the commission of the act, with all the effects of law accompanying the fact of the dismissal.[354]

Under the assumption that consent has been given, the present article focused its attention mainly on impediments and on the form or the lack of form in relation to the matter under consideration. However, what if *de facto* there is no consent? Most of the authors state that if consent is lacking, the delict postulated in canon 646 is not verified. Force and fear, error, and simulation are enumerated as the causes which preclude matrimonial consent.[355] The authors generally treat this point *ex professo* in connection with canon 2388, § 1.[356] In the present analysis, however, only those authors will be consulted who have made application of these principles to the canon here in question.

---

[351] Creusen-Garesché-Ellis, *Religious Men and Women in the Code*, n. 345.

[352] Tabera, *loc. cit.*

[353] ". . . quoad attentationem matrimonii ejusque celebrationem ac matrimonium civile dicendum quod et ipsa sunt et constituunt factum de se publicum."—Aleixo, "De Religiosis Ipso Iure Dimissis"—*Rev. Ecl. Bras.*. VI (1946), 391.

[354] Toso, *loc. cit.*

[355] "Die meisten Autoren nehmen mit Recht an, dass dieser Fall des can. 646, § 1, n. 3, nicht gegeben ist, wenn bei dem Religiosen der eheliche Wille fehlt (infolge Irrtum, Verstellung, Gewalt und Furcht); freilich dürfte dieser Fall selten vorkommen."—Mayer, *Benediktinisches Ordensrecht*, III, 363.

[356] Cf. Sole, *De Delictis et Poenis* (Romae: Pustet, 1920), n. 448; Vermeersch-Creusen, *Epitome*, III, n. 592; Ayrinhac-Lydon, *Penal Legislation in the New Code of Canon Law* (revised edition, New York: Benziger, 1936), n. 362; and others. Cerato (*Censurae Vigentes Ipso Facto a Codice Iuris Canonici Excerptae* [2. ed., Patavii: Typis Seminarii, 1921], pp. 131, 132) opposes the general opinion.

Thus, the authors [357] generally exclude from the applied sanction enacted in canon 646, § 1, 3°, any form of marriage entered upon through grave force or fear. Leitner [358] and Schaefer [359] cite canons 2205, §§ 1 and 2, 2218, and 103 as the basis for this exception, but it seems properly indicated to refer also to canon 1087, for the force and fear in question must be the cause of the external compliance and of the internal lack of consent.[360] Mayer [361] and Smith [362] make mention also of error, but it is hard to see how this would have application to the presently considered delict. The only admissible case seems to be that in which the act of the religious, in accordance with the norms of canon 2202, §§ 1 and 3, lacks all delictual imputability.[363]

It was approximately in this sense that Villien spoke of error in reference to the law of the decree.[364] Moreover, inculpable ignorance of the fact that marriage is forbidden to or illicit for religious would take away all delictual imputability for the act,[365] but, as Villien noted in commenting on the source of the present law,[366] such ignorance is not at all likely. Certainly, since marriage is interdicted for religious by canons 1058, § 2, and 1073, and not by canon 646, § 1, 3°, ignorance of the latter canon alone would not excuse from the application of the canonical sanction there enacted as entailed by the committed delict.

---

[357] Leitner, *Das Ordensrecht,* p. 489; Chelodi, *Ius de Personis,* p. 457, nota 5; Schönsteiner, *loc. cit.;* Palombo, *De Dimissione Religiosorum,* p. 238, nota 3; Schaefer, *loc. cit.;* Tabera, "art. cit."—*CpR,* XI (1930), 418–419; Hippolytus a S. Familia, *loc. cit.;* Sipos, *Enchiridion,* p. 409; Geser, *The Canon Law Governing Communities of Sisters,* n. 1158; Mayer, *loc. cit.*

[358] *Loc. cit.*

[359] *Loc. cit.*

[360] Canon 1087, § 2. Cf. Sangmeister, *Force and Fear as Precluding Matrimonial Consent,* The Catholic University of America Canon Law Studies, n. 80 (Washington, D. C.: The Catholic University of America, 1932).

[361] *Loc. cit.*

[362] *The Penal Law for Religious,* pp. 119–120.

[363] Cf. *supra,* p. 107.

[364] Cf. *supra,* p. 73, note 60.

[365] Cf. canon 2202, § 1.

[366] Cf. *supra,* p. 73, note 61.

The element of simulation is considered by Hippolytus a S. Familia,[367] Tabera,[368] Mayer,[369] Smith,[370] and others. Hippolytus a S. Familia sums up the matter as follows:

> "What of him who feigns to contract marriage? He does not incur dismissal, for in order that one be said to attempt a crime it is required that he seriously, knowingly and willingly, place the act ordained to the execution of it; and when it is required that the attempt be carried to the extent of acts sufficient to complete the crime, then, if the attempt does not produce its effect, the negative result must depend on some other cause outside the will of the agent. Hence, for the attempt at contracting marriage it is necessary that the agent place the necessary act with the true intention of contracting marriage as far as possible, and that, if the marriage proves null, the resultant effect of nullity arise from some cause outside his own mind." [371]

He continues:

> "Nevertheless the internal consent of the mind is always presumed to conform to the words or signs used in the celebration of the marriage (canon 1086, § 1). Therefore a religious who simulates the contracting of marriage is to be considered as legitimately dismissed, and is also to be declared as dismissed by the Superior as long as he (the religious) has not legitimately proved in the external forum the fact of his simulation." [372]

---

[367] "Art. cit."—*Analecta O. C. D.*, IV (1930), 161-162.

[368] *Loc. cit.*

[369] *Loc. cit.*

[370] *Loc. cit.*

[371] "Quid vero dicendum de eo qui *simuletur* contrahere matrimonium? Nec ipse incurret in dimissionem. Ratio est quia ad hoc ut quis dicatur delictum attentare, conari requiritur ut *serio* sciens volens ponat actus ad illius executionem ordinatos; et quando requiritur ut conatus deducatur usque ad actus per se sufficientes ad delictum perficiendum, tunc, si conatus non sortitur suum effectum, id pendere debet ex alia causa praeter voluntatem agentis. Itaque ad hoc ut quis attentet matrimonium necesse est ut vera intentione illud, in quantum possibile, contrahendi ponat actus necessarios et, si nullum evadit, id ab alia causa dependeat praeter voluntatem agentis."—Hippolytus a S. Familia, *loc. cit.*, cf. Smith, *ibid.*, p. 113.

[372] "Internus tamen animi consensus semper praesumitur conformis verbis

Though Tabera [373] and Hippolytus a S. Familia [374] speak of simulation only in connection with attempted marriage, it must be noted that this concept and principle applies also to all three section of the present article.[375]

Coronata [376] notes that some authors make an exception for the case of defective or deficient consent in the present matter, but he deems this of little practical moment, since the religious in question would certainly then become chargeable with the crime which is designated as the "*fuga cum muliere.*" This assumption, however, loses force when it is viewed in relation to the elements that have already been shown as postulated for this latter delict.[377]

Furthermore, it seems that in its nature of precluding the delict against which canon 646 invokes its canonical sanction the lack of consent as resulting from force, fear, error, ignorance, simulation, etc., must attach to the person of the religious without any respect to the dispositions of the other party,[378] for the crime is considered only inasfar as it is verified in the religious.[379] Though a religious may escape the enacted sanction of the present law by proving his act of simulation or by demonstrating the status of a simple concubinage in his case, he can still be dismissed according to the norms of canons 653 and 668, for it is almost certain that his action will occasion grave scandal outside the community and very grave harm to the community itself.[380]

Moreover, since canon 646 treats also of such religious who are

---

vel signis in celebrando matrimonio adhibitis (c. 1086, § 1); quapropter religiosus simulans matrimonium haberi debet uti legitime dimissus et a Superiore ut talis declarari usquedum ipse simulationem legitime in foro externo probaverit."—Hippolytus a S. Familia, *ibid.*, p. 162.

[373] *Loc. cit.*

[374] *Loc. cit.*

[375] Smith, *ibid.*, p. 120; Mayer, *loc. cit.*

[376] *Institutiones*, I, n. 646.

[377] Cf. *supra*, Chapter VIII, Article 2, pp. 121–144.

[378] Smith, *op. cit.*, p. 116; McDevitt, *The Renunciation of an Ecclesiastical Office*, p. 144.

[379] Cf. *supra*, pp. 131, 132.

[380] Hippolytus a S. Familia, *loc. cit.;* Schaefer, *loc. cit.;* Fanfani, *loc. cit.;* Gerster a Zeil, *loc. cit.;* Schönsteiner, *loc. cit.*

professed with merely temporary vows,[381] its scope is much wider in extent than is the scope of canon 2388 in both its parts together, since this latter canon affects only religious who are in perpetual vows.[382] Accordingly, a religious in temporary vows is subject to the application of the sanction enacted in canon 646, but is free from the penalties established in canon 2388.[383] The same would be true of religious in perpetual vows if the element of presumption were lacking in their delictual deed, for then they would not incur the penalties, but would still be liable for the sanction which canon 646 invokes as a direct consequence of their criminal act.

Finally, to remove all doubt, it is useful to state again that canon 646 is applicable even to religious who are not living the community life, i.e., to apostates, to fugitives, and to dismissed religious who have not yet been released from their vows.[384] Moreover, the religious who commits this delict would usually, though not necessarily, incur also the penalties enacted in canons 2385 and 2386.[385]

---

[381] Cf. *supra,* p. 89.

[382] Smith, *ibid.,* p. 119.

[383] Cf. *infra,* p. 186.

[384] Smith, *ibid.,* p. 120; cf. *supra,* pp. 90–91.

[385] Cf. Riesner, *Apostates and Fugitives from Religious Institutes,* p. 79.

CHAPTER IX

THE DECLARATION OF FACT

Canon 646, § 2. *In his casibus sufficit ut Superior maior cum suo Capitulo vel Consilio ad normam constitutionum emittat declarationem facti; curet autem probationes facti collectas in domus regestis asservare.*

The law introduced by means of the decree *Quum singulae* [1] has undergone many changes in the text of the law as now contained in canon 646, § 2. The most notable of these, namely, the change from "*sententiam declaratoriam facti*" to "*declarationem facti,*" has already been noted.[2] This and other changes will be given due attention in the course of the present chapter.

For the sake of a clearer presentation the chapter is divided into two articles. The first considers the declaration of fact in its relation to dismissal and consequently also to the religious, while the second explores the rôle of superior and the institute in the making of the declaration.

Article 1. Regarding the Necessity and Force of this Declaration

The prescription of the canon to the effect that the declaration of fact is to be made by the competent superior and that this suffices [3] became the subject of controversy soon after the promulgation of the Code. It was disputed whether the dismissal was already incurred before the declaration of fact was given, or whether a previous declaration of fact was required as an essential condition for the dismissal.[4] Some authors [5] interpreted the canon

[1] Cf. *supra,* p. 61, note 11.

[2] Cf. *supra,* pp. 99–100.

[3] Canon 646, § 2.

[4] Maroto, "Annotationes."—*CpR,* XV (1934), 352; Goyeneche, "Annotationes"—*Apollinaris,* VIII (1935), 552.

[5] Bastien, *Directoire Canonique,* p. 129; Fanfani, *De Iure Religiosorum,*

to mean that the commission of the offense unaccompanied with any subsequent declaration did not suffice for effecting the dismissal, and that the declaration was required as a condition for the validity of the dismissal. Other authors opposed this view.[6]

On July 30, 1934, a response[7] of the Pontifical Commission for the Authentic Interpretation of the Code removed all doubt, and at the same time ended the dispute.[8] This response states that the declaration of fact is not necessary in order that a religious may be considered as *ipso facto* legitimately dismissed.[9] That this always was the sense of the canon seemed clear and is now indisputable.[10] Hence the interpretation is declaratory. The reasons that support this view are substantially the same as those advanced by Tabera in 1930.[11]

First of all, there is nothing in the canon from which it can be deduced that the declaration of fact is required for validity.[12] Such was once thought to be the force of the word "*sufficit*," but obviously it was never meant in that sense. The peculiar function of the word "*sufficit*" is to contrast this dismissal with the other forms of dismissal in the Code.[13] Thus, in the cases enumerated in canon 646, superiors are not required to institute a

---

n. 497; Pejška, *Ius Canonicum,* p. 189; Oesterle, *Praelectiones Iuris Canonici,* p. 370.

[6] Cf. Tabera, "De Dimissione Religiosorum"—*CpR,* XI (1930), 419, and also nota 31.

[7] "D. I. An declaratio facti, de qua in canone 646, § 2, requiritur ad hoc ut Religiosus ipso facto habendus sit tanquam legitime dimissus.

R. ad I. Negative."—P. C. I., 30 iul. 1934, ad III—*AAS,* XXVI (1934), 494.

[8] Alvarez Melcón, "Boletin Canónico"—*Religión y Cultura* (34 vols., Madrid, Monasterio de el Escorial, 1928–1936), XXX (1935), 277.

[9] "The Code Commission was asked:

I. Is it necessary that the fact which is referred to in c. 646, § 2, shall have been declared, in order that the religious be considered *ipso facto* as legitimately dismissed?

Reply. In the negative."—Bouscaren, *The Canon Law Digest* (2 vols., Milwaukee: Bruce, 1934, 1943), II, 175.

[10] Smith, *The Penal Law for Religious,* p. 48.

[11] Cf. Tabera, *ibid.,* p. 419.

[12] Tabera, *loc. cit.;* Coronata, *Institutiones,* I, 867, nota 7.

[13] Oesterle, *loc. cit.*

process or pass a sentence properly so called;[14] it is enough that they issue a declaration of the fact.[15]

This flows naturally from what is said in the first paragraph of the canon[16] in reference to the manner of operation. For in the present case the dismissal is effected *ipso facto,* i.e., by the very fact that the religious commits one of the delicts enumerated in § 1 of the canon.[17] Hence, the dismissal is immediate and complete at that moment, and thus the religious must be considered as dismissed even before the declaration of the fact takes place.[18] Even though the superior through neglect or excessive indulgence should fail to issue the declaration of the fact, or defer its issuance, the dismissal nevertheless always obtains its effect from the very moment of the committing of the delict,[19] for the law itself inflicts the sanction.[20]

Mention has been made of the fact that the decree "*Quum singulae*" required a "declaratory sentence of the fact," but that this requirement has undergone a revision.[21] The word "sentence" was already omitted in the preparatory Schemata of the Code, and the word "declaration" was deemed sufficient. The latter terminology is preserved in the text of the Code.[22] This is altogether fitting, for the word "sentence" has a proper sense in the Code and connotes a judicial process along with its formalities.[23] Since no procedural formality is required in canon 646, and since the dismissal is effected by the law, it would be incor-

---

[14] Creusen-Garesché-Ellis, *Religious Men and Women in the Code,* n. 345; Eichmann, *Lehrbuch des Kirchenrechts,* p. 107; cf. *supra,* p. 86.

[15] Maroto, *ibid.,* p. 355; Smith, *loc. cit.*

[16] Coronata, *loc. cit.*

[17] Cf. *supra,* p. 87.

[18] Tabera, *loc. cit.;* Maroto, "art. cit."—*CpR,* XV (1934), 352 and 355; Goyeneche, "Annotationes"—*Apollinaris,* VIII (1935), 552.

[19] [Anonymous], "Annotationes"—*Periodica,* XXIII (1934), 147; Berutti, *De Religiosis,* n. 158; Jombart, "De religiosis dimissis"—*Nouvelle Revue Théologique* (Paris, 1869—), LXI (1934), 1080–1081; Sartori, *Enchiridion Canonicum* (7. ed., Romae: ex Typographia Augustiniana, 1944), p. 182; cf. *supra,* pp. 86–87.

[20] Sartori, *loc. cit.;* Schaefer, *loc. cit.;* cf. *supra,* p. 86.

[21] Cf. *supra,* pp. 99–100 and 159.

[22] Goyeneche, "Studia Canonica"—*CpR,* XIII (1932), 103.

[23] Goyeneche, *loc. cit.;* cf. canons 1868, § 1; 2223, § 4; 2232.

rect to speak of a sentence. Hence the legislator designedly and wisely makes mention only of a declaration.[24] In like manner this declaration cannot be termed a " decree " in the strict canonical sense,[25] for as such the latter term has a technical meaning with reference to judicial acts.[26]

Although the authors readily agree that the declaration of the fact is an entity distinct from a declaratory sentence, they nevertheless are divided on a further problem, namely, the applicability of canon 2232, § 1, to the present canon. Many authors consider canon 646 as enacting a *latae sententiae* penalty,[27] and consequently some [28] deem that the norms of canon 2232, § 1, are pertinent in this matter.

Maroto (1875–1937) [29] and O'Leary [30] are the chief proponents of this application of doctrine in full. They state that all the canonical effects of dismissal bind the guilty party from the moment of the perpetration of the crime, both in the internal and in the external forums, if he is conscious of his offense. However, before the declaration of the fact is made according to canon 646, § 2, they excuse the dismissed religious from the observance of the external canonical effects, whenever he cannot observe them without the loss of his reputation. No one can demand that he observe the canonical effects in the external forum unless the offense is notorious.[31]

Blat,[32] on the other hand, makes careful distinctions in presenting his view. He judges that, since the Code is lacking in an ex-

---

[24] Goyeneche, *loc. cit.;* Goyeneche, " Annotationes "—*Apollinaris,* VIII (1935), 553; Hippolytus a S. Familia, " De Dimissione Religiosorum "—*Analecta O. C. D.,* IV (1930), 162.

[25] Cf. canon 1868, § 2.

[26] Goyeneche, " Studia Canonica "—*CpR,* XIII (1932), 104; Goyeneche, " Annotationes "—*Apollinaris,* VIII (1935), 553.

[27] Cf. *supra,* Chapter VII, Article 4, pp. 93–106.

[28] Maroto, *art. cit.*—*CpR,* XV (1934), 355; Smith, *op. cit.,* p. 47; O'Leary, *Religious Dismissed after Perpetual Profession,* p. 46; Coronata, *Institutiones,* I, n. 646; Schaefer, *De Religiosis,* p. 988, nota 25.

[29] *Loc. cit.*

[30] *Loc. cit.*

[31] O'Leary, *loc. cit.;* Maroto, *ibid.,* p. 354.

[32] *Ius de Religiosis,* n. 659.

planation of "the declaration of fact," its effects can be determined by way of analogy with canon 2232, § 1. First of all, he states that the *ipso facto* effected dismissal binds the religious immediately in both the internal and the external forums. He observes, especially, that that portion of canon 2232, § 1, which in certain instances excuses the delinquent from the observance of effects, does not apply in the present case, for in the case of an automatic dismissal no declaration is required. Lastly he notes that prior to the declaration of the fact the religious cannot be forced to observe the effects of this dismissal in the external forum, but that with the executed declaration even this exception is taken away.[33] But Goyeneche denies that the authors have any justification for applying canon 2232 to this declaration of fact.[34]

The crux of the solution centers in the problem whether the same force can be attributed to the declaration of fact as to the declaratory sentence. In § 1 canon 2232 indicates that there are instances in which a declaratory sentence is necessary for the execution of the effects of a penalty, and this is confirmed by § 2 of the same canon. The declaration of fact, however, is never necessary for the effecting of the dismissal treated in canon 646.[35] Moreover, it is generally accepted that the declaration of fact in accordance with the norm of canon 646, § 2, is one thing, and that

[33] "Effectus declarationis facti per analogiam can. 2232.—Revera can. 2232 loquitur de sententia proprie dicta declaratoria, quae datur ad definiendum iudicium criminale. Talis ergo non est haec declaratio facti §i 2ae canonis 646. Sed cum desit in Codice explicatio huius declarationis facti, possumus tales effectus per analogiam determinare. 'Poena latae sententiae . . . sive vindicativa (ut est haec dimissio a iure) delinquentem, qui delicti sibi sit conscius, (ut in casu), ipso facto in utroque foro tenet'; ante (declarationem autem facti) a poena observanda, etc. non habet locum in tali dimisso, quia dimissio (non requiritur aliquem ipsius actum, sed) 'in foro externo ab eo eiusdem poenae observantiam exigere nemo potest (et in casu nostro dimissionis effectus), nisi delictum sit notorium.' Ista ergo exemptio in foro externo ab eo aufertur vi declarationis facti dimissionis ipso facto."—Blat, *loc. cit.*

[34] ". . . Shaefer (*op. cit.*[2], n. 576, p. 756) et alii applicabant immerito huic declarationi can. 2232 . . ."—Goyeneche, "Annotationes"—*Apollinaris,* VIII (1935), 552, nota 10.

[35] P. C. I., 30 iul. 1934, ad III—*AAS,* XXVI (1934), 494.

the declaratory sentence of a penalty in accordance with the norm of canon 2232, § 1, is quite another.[36] Consequently, one should not attribute to this simple declaration all those effects which in law are proper to a true declaratory sentence.[37] This seems to be the logical conclusion to be drawn from the express change made in the present law, in its substitution of the word " declaration " for the very words " declaratory sentence " of the former law.[38]

Though Blat, in common with the other authors just mentioned, views this matter on the assumption that the dismissal is a penalty, and hence that canons 2232, § 1, and 646 have in common the element of a *latae sententiae* penalty, his opinion is all the more to be urged when dismissal is treated as a canonical sanction only. As he himself surmises,[39] his explanation is in conformity with the letter of the canon as manifested in the authentic interpretation. Thus, all the effects of this dismissal are present immediately upon the commission of one of the specified delicts, and these bind in the internal and in the external forum even before the declaration of the fact.[40] Accordingly the religious in so far as regards his activities as a religious, must conduct himself as one legitimately dismissed, even though the matter be as yet occult.[41] This is a matter involving justice toward the institute.[42]

While it is true that the religious cannot be juridically *forced*

---

[36] Goyeneche, "Studia Canonica"—*CpR,* XIII (1932), 104, nota 18; Schaefer, *De Religiosis,* p. 989, nota 27; Blat, *loc. cit.*

[37] Goyeneche, *loc. cit.;* Goyeneche, "Annotationes"—*Apollinaris,* VIII (1935), 552–553.

[38] Cf. *supra,* pp. 99–100, 159, 161.

[39] Blat, *loc. cit.*

[40] Goyeneche, "Annotationes"—*Apollinaris,* VIII (1935), 553; Jombart, "De religiosis dimissis"—*Nouvelle Revue Théologique,* LXI (1934), 1080; Mayer, *Benediktinisches Ordensrecht,* III, 363; Berutti, *De Religiosis,* n. 158; Blat, *loc. cit.*

[41] "Mais déjà avant cette declaration, le religieux est renvoyé conformément ã la loi canonique. Il doit se considerer comme renvoyé et, si sa faute est notoire, tout le monde doit le traiter comme tel."—Jombart, *loc. cit.*; ". . . der Religiose ist daher verpflichtet, die Entlassung sofort zu beobachten, wenn er eines der Delikte des can. 646, § 1, begangen hat, es sei denn, dass das Delikt geheim ist und nicht bewiesen werden kann."—Mayer, *loc. cit.*

[42] Cf. *supra,* p. 7.

to observe these effects before a declaration of the fact has been issued, this does not excuse him from the obligation of observing the effectively invoked sanction. Hence, the absence of the declaration of the fact does not offer a cause for the non-observance of the effects of the dismissal, but the declaration must be made before the observance can juridically be demanded. Finally, since all the effects are present immediately, there can be no room for any retroactive force for this declaration.[43]

Nevertheless, though this dismissal is complete at the moment of the commission of a specified delict, the Code still desires that the declaration of the fact, at least as a complement,[44] should be forthcoming. There are many advantages that recommend the fulfillment of this wise provision.[45] First of all, not all the cases envisioned will be notorious, and so there will be room for doubt. A careful investigation of the facts with a subsequent declaration will dispel doubt as to the existence and commission of the delict,[46] and consequently of the juridic condition of the delinquent in the external forum,[47] and thus will beget juridic certitude.[48]

Jombart states that such a declaration will clear the atmosphere of doubt and suspicion, and will inform good religious how to view the matter.[49] Moreover, what is evident today may not be so tomorrow, and hence it prudently serves the good of the institute to gather the proofs while they are available. Otherwise the religious may later deny the fact or the delict, and may perhaps succeed in calling the earlier certitude into question.[50] Through the declaration the community is protected against future claims of the guilty party in this or in other matters.[51] Finally, the

---

[43] Cf. canon 2232 § 2; Beste, *Introductio in Codicem,* p. 439; Hippolytus a S. Familia, *loc. cit.;* Blat, *loc. cit.*

[44] Tabera, "art. cit."—*CpR,* XI (1930), 413.

[45] Cf. Aleixo, "De Religiosis Ipso Iure Dimissis"—*Rev. Ecl. Bras.,* VI (1946), 393.

[46] Maroto, "art. cit."—*CpR,* XV (1934), 355; Berutti, *loc. cit.*

[47] Beste, *loc. cit.;* Palombo, *De Dimissione Religiosorum,* n. 198.

[48] ". . . iuridica e contra certitudo facti gignitur ex facti declaratione . . ." —Maroto, *ibid.,* p. 356; Aleixo, *loc. cit.*

[49] Jombart, *ibid.,* p. 1081.

[50] Maroto, *ibid.,* pp. 355–356; Aleixo, *loc. cit.*

[51] Creusen-Garesché-Ellis, *loc. cit.;* Goyeneche, "Annotationes"—*Apollinaris,* VIII (1935), 553.

declaration will serve as evidence in the event that the religious should have recourse to the Holy See.[52]

This declaration of fact, then, though it is something that is to be executed at the behest of the law, is not a condition on which the dismissal itself depends.[53] Its rôle is primarily that of declaring authentically for the external forum [54] the juridic certitude of the fact and its existence,[55] and in this it furnishes a full juridical basis for enforcing the observance of the applied sanction.

Article 2. The Duty of Superior and Institute

In the interest of establishing juridic certainty with regard to the perpetration of any of the delictual acts mentioned in § 1 of canon 646, the legislator in § 2 commits to the major superior and the institute the task of gathering proofs and of declaring the existence of the facts as established in the case.[56]

In order to facilitate the commentary on this portion of the canon, the present writer deems it advisable to proceed according to particular word groups, without however adhering invariably to the order of the canon.[57]

A. . . . *ad normam constitutionum* . . .

This phrase is an addition inserted by the present law. At first

[52] Brandys, *Kirchliches Rechtsbuch,* p. 104; Berutti, *loc. cit.;* Hippolytus a S. Familia, *ibid.,* p. 163; Geser, *The Canon Law Governing Communities of Sisters,* n. 1162.

[53] Goyeneche, " Annotationes "—*Apollinaris,* VIII (1935), 551–552; " Nil ergo illa declaratio dimissioni addit."—Sartori, *Enchiridion Canonicum,* p. 182.

[54] " Dimissio in casu ab ipso iure infligitur et proinde religiosus aliquod delictum huiusmodi patrans revera iam est dimissus ante declarationem; vis huius est effectus legis ad forum externum authentice declarare."—Hippolytus a S. Familia, *loc. cit.;* Palombo, *loc. cit.;* Regatillo, *Institutiones Iuris Canonici,* I, n. 759; Wernz-Vidal, *Ius Canonicum,* III, n. 438; Beste, *loc. cit.,* and others.

[55] Maroto, *ibid.,* p. 356; Mayer, *loc. cit.*

[56] Mayer, *Benediktinisches Ordensrecht,* III, 363.

[57] Since reference has already been made to the first words in § 2, namely, *" in his casibus "* (cf. *supra,* p. 92) and *" sufficit "* (*supra,* p. 160), these will not again be considered here.

glance it seems to apply to the phrase "*cum suo Capitulo vel Consilio,*" where the Code itself allows for variations. In this sense it is accepted without question by a number of authors.[58] Nevertheless, some authors [59] judge that the constitutions are permitted to determine not only what body is to participate, but also whether it enjoys a deliberative or only a consultative vote. Other authors [60] deem that the constitutions are permitted to determine: (1) which superior is to act; (2) with what body; and (3) with what kind of vote. This latter view includes the previously noted two, and seems to indicate that the entire declaration of the fact is to be made according to the norms of the constitutions.[61]

Toso,[62] Woywod [63] and O'Leary [64] state simply that the declaration of the fact is to be made according to the prescriptions of the constitutions. Palombo, in stating that the constitutions can prescribe other requirements beyond those enacted in the common law,[65] concurs in this view. Thus it seems certain that the phrase "*ad normam constitutionum,*" except with reference to the question regarding the type of the vote,[66] has reference to the entire declaration of fact.

---

[58] Jansen, *Ordensrecht* (3. ed., Paderborn: Schöningh, 1931), p. 285; Leitner, *Das Ordensrecht,* p. 488; Prümmer, *Manuale Iuris Canonici,* p. 346; Regatillo, *Institutiones Iuris Canonici,* I, n. 759; Bastien, *Directoire Canonique,* p. 129.

[59] Schönsteiner, *Grundriss des Ordensrechtes,* p. 627; Fanfani, *De Iure Religiosorum,* n. 497; Cocchi, *Commentarium,* IV, n. 145; Sipos, *Enchiridion,* p. 409; Blat, *Ius de Religiosis,* n. 658; Schaefer, *De Religiosis,* n. 576; Coronata, *Institutiones,* I, p. 867, nota 8; Beste, *Introductio in Codicem,* p. 439.

[60] Tabera, "De Dimissione Religiosorum"—*CpR,* XI (1930), 419; Hippolytus a S. Familia, "De Dimissione Religiosorum"—*Analecta O.C.D.,* IV (1930), 162; Augustine, *A Commentary,* III, 386; Berutti, *De Religiosis,* n. 158; Palombo, *De Dimissione Religiosorum,* n. 198.

[61] ". . . ad normam constitutionum emittat declarationem facti; . . ."—Canon 646, § 2.

[62] *Commentaria Minora,* Lib. II, pars II, pp. 248–249.

[63] *A Practical Commentary on the Code of Canon Law,* I, 289.

[64] *Religious Dismissed after Perpetual Profession,* p. 45.

[65] Palombo, *loc. cit.*

[66] Cf. *infra,* pp. 173–174.

B. . . . *Superior maior* . . .

The alternative form "*Superior Generalis vel Provincialis*" of the former law [67] has given way to the form "*Superior maior*" in the present law. While a few authors [68] accept the words "major superior" without any comment as clear in themselves, Brandys [69] and Prümmer [70] understand them as designating the provincial, the general, or the abbot. Though the latter interpretation is certainly in conformity with the pre-Code law, it does not account for the definite change in the present terminology. In its revision of the former law the Code has employed a word that has a wider application. Moreover, since the term "major superior" is defined in canon 488, 8°, and since there are no limitations attached here, it is to be understood according to the definition of canon 488.[71]

Canon 488, 8°, first points to those who are constituted as major superiors among monastic groups, namely, the abbot primate, the abbots who are superiors of monastic congregations, and the abbots of independent and autonomous monasteries which usually belong to some monastic congregation.[72] According to canon 501, § 3, the abbot primate and the abbot president of a monastic congregation do not have the same power and jurisdiction as other major superiors, but only as much as they receive from their own constitutions and from the special decrees of the Holy See.[73]

Hence, Blat rightly notes that these two may be excluded from the term "major superior" in canon 646, § 2.[74] Ordinarily, in monastic groups, the abbot of an independent and autonomous monastery is the major superior spoken of in the present canon.[75]

---

[67] Cf. *supra*, p. 61, note 11.

[68] Cocchi, *loc. cit.;* Sipos, *loc. cit.;* Regatillo, *loc. cit.;* Coronata, *Institutiones*, I, n. 646; Geser, *The Canon Law Governing Communities of Sisters*, n. 1159.

[69] *Kirchliches Rechtsbuch*, p. 104.

[70] *Loc. cit.*

[71] Leitner, *loc. cit.;* Schönsteiner, *loc. cit.;* Fanfani, *loc. cit.;* Blat, *loc. cit.;* Palombo, *loc. cit.;* Beste, *loc. cit.*

[72] Cf. Augustine, *A Commentary*, III, 49, 59–60.

[73] Augustine, *ibid.*, p. 111.

[74] Blat, *loc. cit.*

[75] "In Congregationibus monasticis spectabit ius in casu ad abbatem

According to a private response of the Pontifical Commission for the Authentic Interpretation of the Code, conventual priors in monastic congregations as also the superiors of independent houses in centralized monastic congregations are to be included among the major superiors,[76] and hence they are to be regarded as major superiors who are competent in the matter treated in canon 646, § 2.

In other religious institutes the term "major superior" designates not only the supreme moderators, but also provincials, their vicars, and others who have the power of provincials.[77] The major superior mentioned in canon 646, § 2, could be any one of these;[78] hence it is readily evident that the constitutions should determine which major superior, immediate or supreme, is competent in this matter. However, if the constitutions are silent or do not make any express determination, then the immediate major superior is competent,[79] without any need of intervention by the supreme moderator.[80]

Moreover, since the norms of canon 488, 8°, apply also to women religious in consequence of the norm indicated in canon 490, they too must have major superiors. It cannot be advanced that their major superior is the local ordinary; for the latter's relation to the institute or the community is that of a member of an external hierarchy, whereas the major superior belongs to the internal hierarchy.[81] Though the Code often makes mention of the local ordinary in matters pertaining to women religious, it always refers to him as a local ordinary and never as a major superior.[82] Accordingly, commentators draw the conclusion that an abbess, the superioress general of an institute of women, and

---

monasterii sui iuris, nisi propriae constitutiones aliud expresse caveant."—Hippolytus a S. Familia, *loc. cit.*

[76] Larraona, "Commentarium Codicis—Canon 488, 8°"—*CpR,* IV (1923), 41; Schaefer, *De Religiosis,* n. 103.

[77] Canon 488, 8°.

[78] Fanfani, *loc. cit.*

[79] Berutti, *loc. cit.;* Hippolytus a S. Familia, *loc. cit.;* Palombo, *op. cit.,* p. 239, nota 2.

[80] Schaefer, *De Religiosis,* n. 576.

[81] Larraona, *ibid.,* pp. 42–44; Schaefer, *De Religiosis,* n. 103.

[82] Larraona, *loc. cit.;* Schaefer, *loc. cit.,* and n. 223.

other superioresses of independent houses are to be regarded as major superiors in the sense of canon law.[83] Likewise provincials, their vicars, and others who have the power of provincials in institutes of women are to be regarded as major superiors.[84]

According to canon 646, § 2, then, the authors [85] state that the major superiors in institutes of women are to issue the declaration of the fact. Palombo,[86] on the other hand, is of the opinion that, if the constitutions are silent, the local ordinary is competent in the case of institutes of diocesan approval and of monasteries of nuns. As Wernz-Vidal point out, though it may prove opportune to ask his intervention, this is not required by law,[87] and it is still the *major superior* who must issue the declaration of the fact. This is the more readily understandable in view of the fact that the declaration involves only the exercise of dominative power and not of jurisdiction.[88] Thus, Berutti,[89] Coronata [90] and Wernz-Vidal [91] state that, since no distinction is made in canon 646, § 2, and since its prescription is entirely general, it extends to all religious, not even excepting lay congregations and institutes of women.

Major superiors, as is evident, are to proceed to this declaration of fact only in reference to the acts of their own subjects.[92]

In commenting on the source of the present law Villien stated that the obligation regarding the declaration rested equally on the superior and his council, but that the law appointed the superior to collect the votes and to execute the decision of the

---

[83] Geser, *The Canon Law Governing Communities of Sisters,* n. 169; Schaefer, *De Religiosis,* n. 103; Larraona, *loc. cit.*

[84] Geser, *ibid.*, n. 170.

[85] "Ipsa Antistita vel Superiorissa generalis aut provincialis cum suo Consilio hanc declarationem facti emittere valet."—Schaefer, *De Religiosis,* n. 576; Cappello, *Summa Iuris Canonici,* II, n. 70; Tabera, "art. cit."—*CpR,* XI (1930), 419.

[86] *Op. cit.*, p. 239, nota 2.

[87] Wernz-Vidal, *Ius Canonicum,* III, 475, nota 13.

[88] Mayer, *op. cit.*, III, 364; cf. *supra,* 121; *infra,* p. 176.

[89] *Loc. cit.*

[90] *Institutiones,* I, 867, nota 7.

[91] *Loc. cit.*

[92] Berutti, *loc. cit.*

majority.[93] While it seems that this may still be the sense of the present law,[94] it is certain that the initiative in this matter will rest primarily upon the superior.

Finally, local superiors have little more to do in these cases than to inform the major superior of the fact, if this be necessary. Any further action is reserved to the major superior.[95]

C. . . . *probationes facti collectas* . . .

Natural reason itself indicates that the superior should institute an investigation before proceeding to the declaration of the fact.[96] This concept embodied in the words of the present law is taken from n. 13 of the decree *Quum singulae.*[97]

The first duty of the superior, then, is diligently to gather proofs from which it will certainly and undoubtedly appear that the religious really committed one of the crimes listed in canon 646, § 1.[98] The religious, by force of his profession, enjoys a vested right which excludes arbitrary action regarding the disposition of that right.[99] Hence the superior must investigate all the circumstances that have a direct bearing on establishing the nature of the act,[100] in order to arrive at a summary proof of the fact. A superior is not excused from this diligence, even if it is asserted that the fact is notorious. For then he must gather proofs from which the notoriety itself will appear demonstrated. This is all

---

93 Cf. *supra,* p. 73, note 64.

94 Cf. *infra,* p. 174.

95 Clancy, *The Local Religious Superior,* The Catholic University of America Canon Law Studies, n. 175 (Washington, D. C.: The Catholic University of America Press, 1943), p. 125.

96 Hippolytus a S. Familia, *loc. cit.*

97 S. C. de rel., decr. *Quum singulae,* 16 maii 1911, n. 13: "Superior Provincialis vel quasi-Provincialis Religiosi delinquentis . . . omnia acta et documenta, quae de huius Religiosi reitate extant diligenter colliget . . ."—*AAS,* III (1911), 236.

98 Hippolytus a S. Familia, *loc. cit.;* Palombo, *op. cit.,* n. 198; Coronata, *Manuale Practicum,* n. 238; Blat, *loc. cit.*

99 "Superior debet certus esse de existentia causae, vi enim professionis, religiosus *iure quaesito* gaudet, quod excludit arbitrariam dimissionem."—Cocchi, *Commentarium,* IV, n. 144.

100 Toso, *Commentaria Minora,* Lib. II, pars II, p. 248.

the more to be urged, since many things are termed notorious which are not such.[101]

Strictly judicial proofs are not required, for this is not a judicial process;[102] any proof, even extrajudicial, is sufficient.[103] The usual proofs are: authentic documents,[104] the testimony of trustworthy witnesses,[105] an official declaration of civil status,[106] and a sworn statement of the delinquent which is equivalent to an extrajudicial confession.[107]

In listing the last mentioned form of proof, Michalicka describes it as follows:

> Extrajudicial confession is a personal acknowledgment of the author by word of mouth or in writing of the fact of a violation made to another person outside of a trial. It may be made to a Superior as such, when not acting in the capacity of a judge in a tribunal. Various circumstances are to be taken into account with the confession, i.e., if it is repeated and the facts agree, if the cause of a violation is known and is certain.[108]

Although any extrajudicial proof suffices, it seems indicated for the superior to put the proofs into a somewhat judicial form, so that they will really serve as proof.[109] In their nature of evidence the proofs should be sufficient to convince any prudent man.[110]

The superior may himself assume the task of gathering the proofs, or he may entrust it to another.[111] The constitutions,

---

[101] Hippolytus a S. Familia, *ibid.*, p. 163.

[102] Cf. *supra*, p. 86.

[103] Coronata, *loc. cit.*

[104] Berutti, *loc. cit.*

[105] Coronata, *loc. cit.;* Berutti, *loc. cit.;* Hippolytus a S. Famalia, *loc. cit.;* Michalicka, *Judicial Procedure in Dismissal of Clerical Exempt Religious*, p. 39.

[106] Coronata, *loc. cit.*

[107] Michalicka, *loc. cit.*

[108] Michalicka, *ibid.*, p. 51.

[109] Coronata, *loc. cit.*

[110] Blat, *loc. cit.*

[111] Palombo, *loc. cit.;* Coronata, *loc. cit.*

moreover, may prescribe some directives as to the manner in which the proofs are to be gathered.[112]

Hippolytus a S. Familia observes that the crimes listed in canon 646, § 1, 3°, will be easy to prove, since an authentic document is sufficient. Similarly the crime mentioned in canon 646, § 1, 1°, can fairly easily be established through witnesses, since the law postulates that it be a public crime if it is to effect dismissal. He notes, however, that the crime adverted to in canon 646, § 1, 2°, will be harder to prove in view of the number of elements postulated for its occurrence, but he deems that the superiors must act on legitimate presumptions of law, and that the burden of proof to the contrary rests on the religious.[113]

D. . . . *cum suo Capitulo vel Consilio* . . .

In these words the Code retains the exact word-order of the former law, but adds a new element by offering an alternative. Thus, where the decree *Quum singulae* made mention only of "*cum suo . . . Consilio*"[114] the present law gives a choice of the chapter or the council.

After gathering the evidence the major superior is directed to confer with his chapter or council.[115] The "chapter" is to be understood in accordance with canon 501, § 1, and the "council" in accordance with canon 516, § 1. At times the Code requires the intervention of the one, and at times of the other, but here it allows the intervention of either.[116] Hence the constitutions must decide which of the two is to concur with the superior.[117] The constitutions may decide this explicitly or implicitly;[118] but if they are silent, it suffices that the superior act with his council.[119]

Many authors[120] state further that the constitutions are to de-

---

[112] Palombo, *loc. cit.*

[113] Hippolytus a S. Familia, *loc. cit.*

[114] Cf. *supra*, p. 61, note 11.

[115] Brandys, *Kirchliches Rechtsbuch*, p. 104.

[116] Larraona, "Commentarium Codicis—Canon 501"—*CpR*, VI (1925), 428.

[117] Coronata, *Institutiones*, I, 867, nota 8; Palombo, *loc. cit.;* Hippolytus a S. Familia, "art. cit."—*Analecta O. C. D.*, IV (1930), 162.

[118] Blat, *loc. cit.*

[119] Coronata, *loc. cit.;* Hippolytus a S. Familia, *loc. cit.*

[120] Cf. *supra*, p. 167.

termine whether the respective body that participates in issuing the declaration of the fact is to enjoy a deliberative or only a consultative vote. If the constitutions should be silent on this matter, Hippolytus a S. Familia [121] is of the opinion that the kind of vote required must be determined from procedure in similar cases, while Coronata [122] deems that it will be sufficient if the superior consults his council.

Villien, however, noted that the wording of the law in the decree *Quum singulae* explicitly required the superior to proceed with the *consent* of his council in every instance, for the obligation of declaring the fact was not entrusted to the superior alone, but to the superior and his council.[123] The word-order "*Superior . . . cum . . . Consilio*" incorporates an ablative of accompaniment which makes the phrase equivalent in meaning to "*Superior et Consilium.*" Since there is no essential change in the text of the present law, the present writer deems that the explanation of Villien is still in full force.[124] Consequently, the constitutions are only to determine which body—chapter or council—is to participate in the matter of declaration, and in all cases the designated body must participate with a deliberative vote.

With his chapter or council, then, the major superior is required carefully to consider and examine the evidence,[125] weighing the circumstances [126] and discussing their bearing on the deed.[127] Afterwards, when on the basis of the evidence at hand the fact of the commission of the delict has been established in a session

---

[121] *Loc. cit.*

[122] *Loc. cit.*

[123] "La seule condition de procédure imposée est que le Supérieur Général ou le Provincial obtiennent le consentement de leur conseil. Qu'il s'agisse d'assentiment et non d'avis à demander, c'est ce qui résulte du texte lui-même où la sentence déclaratoire est attribuée, non au seul Supérieur ou au seul Provincial, mais à l'un ou à l'autre avec leur conseil respectif. C'est Supérieur et Conseil qui émettent la déclaration par la voix du seul Supérieur."—Villien, "La Procédure Canonique pour L'Expulsion des Religieux"—*Le Canoniste Contemporain,* XXXVI (1913), 214.

[124] Canon 6, 3o.

[125] Palombo, *loc. cit.;* Geser, *op. cit.,* n. 1160.

[126] Toso, *op. cit.,* pp. 248–249.

[127] Palombo, *loc. cit.*

of the chapter or council, the major superior has the obligation to issue the declaration of the fact.[128]

E. . . . *emittat declarationem facti;* . . .

Frequent reference has already been made to the change in the text of the law from "*sententiam declaratoriam facti*" to "*declarationem facti.*" [129] Hence it will not be necessary to consider that matter anew.

In declaring that by the law of canon 646, § 2, the declaration of the fact is not necessary for the effecting of the dismissal, the Pontifical Commission for the Authentic Interpretation of the Code certainly did not intend to exempt superiors and communities from the task and duty of proceeding to a declaration of fact; for that would have been to abolish the prescript set up in the canon itself.[130] The Response indeed stated that the dismissal is not conditioned on the declaration of fact, but is effected immediately upon the commission of the specified delict; but it did not suppress the superior's subsequent duty of declaring the fact as ordered in § 2 of the canon. Hence the duty of declaring the fact still remains incumbent on the superior.[131]

The rôle of the superior in this matter was very aptly described by Villien in commenting on the law of the decree *Quum singulae.*[132] Thus, the superior is the agent of the religious institute and the authorized voice of the law who declares that the act as committed fulfills all the conditions postulated by the law, and that from the union of these two elements—the law and the fact—there results an automatic effect—the dismissal.[133] In this capacity the superior is not free to do his own bidding, but must proceed according to the directions of the law.[134]

---

[128] Brandys, *loc. cit.;* cf. *supra,* p. 165.

[129] Cf. *supra,* pp. 99–100, 159, 161, 164.

[130] Maroto, "art. cit."—*CpR,* XV (1934), 355; Jombart, "art. cit."—*Nouvelle Revue Théologique,* LXI (1934), 1081; Smith, *op. cit.,* p. 48.

[131] Maroto, *loc. cit.;* [Anonymous], "Annotationes"—*Periodica,* XXIII (1934), 147; Sartori, *Enchiridion Canonicum,* p. 182.

[132] Villien, *ibid.,* p. 137.

[133] Cf. *supra,* p. 66.

[134] Cf. *supra,* pp. 65–66.

In this manner the actual declaration of the fact pertains exclusively to the major superior and cannot be committed to another. It is determined in the law that this matter is entrusted to a specified person, and it is so indicated that the commission constitutes not a mere power of the superior but a true duty. Hence the superior must complete the matter himself and cannot delegate another to do so in his place.[135] He may commission another to draw up the formula, but he himself must issue the declaration. Since in the present case there is need only of dominative power,[136] canon 199, § 1, cannot be invoked. Moreover, the latter canon is understood of mere power, and not of an office or of a duty already determined in the law and assigned to superiors.[137]

The major superior and his chapter or council, then, must decide with evidence at hand whether the religious is guilty of one of the crimes mentioned in çanon 646, § 1, and is therefore to be considered as legitimately dismissed from the institute.[138] This is the entire scope of the declaration, which is one of *fact* and not of law.[139] The force of this declaration, then, is not that of dismissing the religious, but one of declaring authentically that the dismissal has been incurred.[140]

In harmony with the character of this dismissal there is no determined method or form of procedure prescribed for the manner in which this declaration is to be made.[141] Consequently, a formal decree is not required, but a simple declaration suffices.[142]

---

[135] Goyeneche, "Consultationes"—*CpR,* XII (1931), 131.

[136] Mayer, *Benediktinisches Ordensrecht,* III, 364.

[137] Goyeneche, *loc. cit.*

[138] Brandys, *loc. cit.;* Blat, *loc. cit.;* Berutti, *loc. cit.;* Geser, *loc. cit.*

[139] Toso, *op. cit.,* p. 249.

[140] Hippolytus a S. Familia, "art. cit."—*Analecta O. C. D.,* IV (1930), 163.

[141] Coronata, *Institutiones,* I, n. 646; Mayer, *ibid.,* p. 363; Beste, *loc. cit.:* "N.B. Ad emittendam declarationem facti nulla determinata methodus seu forma procedendi praescribitur."—Aleixo, "De Religiosis Ipso Iure Dimissis"—*Rev. Ecl. Bras.,* VI (1946), 393; cf. *supra,* pp. 86–87.

[142] Cappello, *Summa Iuris Canonici,* II, n. 70; Bastien, *Directoire Canonique,* p. 129; Creusen-Garesché-Ellis, *Religious Men and Women in the Code,* n. 345; Goyeneche, "Studia Canonica"—*CpR,* XIII (1932), 103–104.

Goyeneche states that, since nothing is prescribed in the canon, it would seem arbitrary to assert that this declaration requires any special juridic formalities.[143] This view, moreover, is supported by the practice of the Sacred Congregation of Religious in approving constitutions in which the simple declaration of the fact is deemed sufficient.[144]

Nevertheless, in this declaration of the fact some judicial form should be imitated. Thus, the declaration is to be in writing,[145] and it is advisable that it contain mention of the following elements: the date, the place, the statement regarding competence (i.e., with reference to the major superior and his chapter or council), the purpose of the meeting, the name and identification of the religious, a summary of the proof,[146] the decision of the majority,[147] the declaration that the professed member N. N. was guilty of one of the delicts mentioned in canon 646, § 1, and is therefore to be regarded as dismissed from the community,[148] the signature affixed by the superior and his chapter or council, the seal of the superior. The documents and testimony of the witnesses should be attached to the declaration.[149]

Coronata notes that if the delict in question was that which is mentioned in canon 646, § 1, 1°, the matter is to be referred to the Holy Office, and it issues the declaration of dismissal.[150] This, no doubt, is a matter of practice, since such matters will ordinarily have been brought to the attention of the Holy Office before they reach the publicity postulated in the canon for the perpetration of the specified delict. However, if there arise a case which has

---

143 Goyeneche, *ibid.*, p. 103; cf. *supra*, pp. 161–162.

144 "Quae omnia abunde confirmantur et praxi S. Congr. in approbandis Constitutionibus in quibus simplex facti declaratio, . . . quin ei maiorem vim vel specialem formam sententiae vel decreti tribuat, vel iniungat—ad omnes effectus dimissionis sufficiens reputatur."—Goyeneche, *ibid.*, p. 104.

145 Berutti, *loc. cit.;* Jansen, *op. cit.*, p. 285; O'Leary, *op. cit.*, 45.

146 Cf. Coronata, *Manuale Practicum*, p. 111, nota 1.

147 Villien, *loc. cit.;* cf. supra, pp. 170–171.

148 Schönsteiner, *Grundriss des Ordensrecht,* p. 627; Geser, *loc. cit.*

149 Coronata, *Manuale Practicum,* n. 238.

150 "Si agatur de religioso a fide apostata, cum agatur de re ad Sanctum Officium spectante, quaestio ad ipsum deferenda est et ipsum declarationem dimissionis emittit."—Coronata, *loc. cit.*

not been submitted to Holy Office, then from the wording of the canon it seems that the superior would still be competent to issue the declaration of the fact.[151]

Should this declaration be made known to the religious himself? The law makes no comment on this matter, and only two authors refer to it in passing. Pejška states that ecclesiastical law does not prescribe that in this case the sentence [*sic*] be presented to the one dismissed.[152] Alvarez Melcón, on the other hand, deems it equitable that the declaration of the fact be made known to the dismissed religious.[153] Natural justice appears to suggest this course, if no evil results are anticipated, for despite appearances and facts the religious may be able to disprove the matter. In the latter event the religious could avail himself of recourse to a superior of a higher order.[154] This superior authority in the case appears to be the Holy See, the author of the law, as whose representative the major superior has acted in the case.[155] However, if there would arise a case wherein it could be conclusively shown that the facts alleged in the declaration actually never occurred, and the superior and his chapter or council would recognize and acknowledge their error, it seems that a simple declaration to the effect that the prior declaration had no juridic value, since *de facto* the dismissal was never incurred, would be sufficient.

Some authors,[156] moreover, state that, if the religious is in sacred orders, the superior must make known the fact of the dismissal to the ordinary of the dismissed cleric's place of origin, and to

---

[151] Hippolytus a S. Familia, *loc. cit.;* cf. *supra,* pp. 120–121.

[152] Pejška, *Ius Canonicum Religiosorum,* p. 189.

[153] Alvarez Melcón, "Boletin Canónico"—*Religión y Cultura,* XXX (1935), 277.

[154] "Contra talem declarationem datur religioso inculpato ius recursus ad Superiorem altioris ordinis. Id non dicitur expresse in canone, sed pro certo habendum est cum ius naturae sit cuilibet iustam defensionem concedere."—Hippolytus a S. Familia, *loc. cit.*

[155] Cf. *supra,* p. 175.

[156] Jansen, *op. cit.,* p. 286; Gerster a Zeil, *Ius Religiosorum,* pp. 147–148; Pejška, *loc. cit.;* Prümmer, *Manuale Iuris Canonici,* p. 346; Cappello, *Summa Iuris Canonici,* II, n. 70; Coronata, *Institutiones,* I, n. 646; Schaefer, *De Religiosis,* n. 576.

the ordinary of the place where the dismissed cleric will live, or to the ordinary of the place where it is assumed that he will live. This was a norm (n. 19) of the decree *Quum singulae,*[157] but was not incorporated into the present law. Hence there is no obligation imposed by law to follow this procedure.[158] Blat notes that it may be followed as a directive norm,[159] and so it may be required by the constitutions.[160]

Finally, there is no obligation in law to inform the Holy See immediately,[161] but the matter must certainly be included in the quinquennial report under questions 32 and 33.[162]

F. . . . *curet autem . . . asservare.*

This prescription of the law is dictated by natural reason and prudence for the sake of insuring the attainment of the declaration's purpose.[163] The words used in the expression of this concept in the present canon seem to be an adaptation of n. 11 of the decree *Quum singulae.*[164]

Having gathered the evidence and issued the declaration of the fact, the superior is directed to preserve the proofs.[165] These are mainly documents (letters, official notices, etc.) and the sworn

---

[157] Cf. *supra,* p. 77, note 83.

[158] Blat, *Ius de Religiosis,* n. 659; Tabera, "art. cit."—*CpR,* XI (1930), 420; Mayer, *Benediktinisches Ordensrecht,* III, 364, nota 3; O'Leary, *op. cit.,* pp. 46–47; Aleixo, *ibid.,* p. 394.

[159] Blat, *loc. cit.*

[160] O'Leary, *op. cit.,* p. 47.

[161] "Pro dimissis *ipso facto* non adest praescriptum in iure, ut Sanctae Sedi dimissio communicetur."—*Larraona,* "Quaestio Canonica"—*CpR,* III (1922), 326, nota 24.

[162] Cf. S. C. de Rel., "Instructio," 25 martii, 1922—*AAS,* XIV (1922), 280; Bouscaren, *Canon Law Digest,* I, 286–287.

[163] Hippolytus a S. Familia, "art. cit."—*Analecta O. C. D.,* IV (1930), 162.

[164] S. C. de Rel., decr. *Quum singulae,* 16 maii 1911, n. 11: "Ut constet de facto . . . regulariter de hoc afferri debet authenticum documentum. Proinde oportet:

(b) ut documentum redigatur . . . et in Regestis vel Tabulario, servandum: vel ut exemplar conficiatur . . . et in Regestis vel Tabulario pariter asservandum."—*AAS,* III (1911), 236.

[165] Canon 646, § 2.

testimony of witnesses which the superior has gathered as a preliminary measure in proceeding to the declaration.[166] It is these proofs that the superior must preserve in the archives of the religious house.

Though some authors,[167] in keeping with the wording of the Code, mention only the preservation of the proofs, it seems that the declaration of the fact should also be preserved. The latter is but the culmination of a series of proofs, and a juridic notification of the fact that the dismissal has been incurred. Hence, authors quite generally state that the declaration of the fact is to be accorded the same treatment as the proofs.[168] This, no doubt, is the intent of the law, for in ordering the declaration of fact, it would naturally wish to have it preserved as an official record.

It is important that the proofs be preserved, for in case of recourse on the part of the religious it is these primarily that will be reconsidered and will be employed for the determining of the outcome.[169] Moreover, only those proofs which serve to establish the case in question should be preserved.[170]

Finally, as Brandys states,[171] these proofs are to be kept until the death of the religious. This is in keeping with the principle that cases regarding the status of a person are never closed.[172] But, in view of the analogy of the case with the one considered in canon 379, § 1, it appears that such proofs should be destroyed upon the death of the religious.

G. . . . *in domus regestis* . . .

Authors are not in agreement as to the meaning of the word

---

[166] Cf. *supra*, pp. 171–173.

[167] Blat, *Ius de Religiosis*, n. 658; Jansen, *loc. cit.;* Leitner, *Das Ordensrecht*, p. 488; Augustine, *A Commentary,* III, 386; Eichmann, *Lehrbuch des Kirchenrechts*, p. 257; Mayer, *op. cit.*, 363.

[168] Brandys, *Kirchliches Rechtsbuch,* p. 104; Berutti, *loc. cit.;* Coronata, *Manuale Practicum,* n. 238; Toso, *Commentaria Minora,* Lib. II, pars II, p. 249; Palombo, *op. cit.*, n. 198; O'Leary, *op. cit.*, p. 45; and others.

[169] Hippolytus a S. Familia, *ibid.*, p. 163; Geser, *op. cit.*, n. 1162.

[170] Brandys, *loc. cit.*

[171] Brandys, *loc. cit.*

[172] Cf. canon 1903.

"*regestis.*" Aside from the authors who are content to repeat the words of the Code,[173] Blat [174] and Geser [175] understand the term as designating a "register" or "the records," and it is in these that the proofs are to be entered. Blat explains further that, if the proofs are documents, they are to be guarded in the archives, with an indication to that effect in the register.[176] The majority of the authors,[177] however, interprets the word as designating "archives." This signification of the word is in conformity with the usage of the former law.[178] Köstler [179] lists two meanings in the Code for the word "*regestum*": thus, in canons 646, § 2, and 374, § 1, 3°, it signifies archives, while in canons 1988 and 1813, § 1, 4°, it denotes a register or entry-book. Hence it appears practically certain that the proofs in question are to be kept in the archives.

Augustine,[180] in commenting on canon 576, § 2, states that the law implies that every order, or congregation, or convent, or monastery has its own archives. Coronata [181] and Michalicka,[182] moreover, in referring to the preservation of the admonitions required by canon 656, make mention of secret archives. In the present matter, then, it may be urged that the proofs, due to the character of the delicts involved, should be kept in the secret archives. Notification of this custody should be made in the common archives, either in the form of the declaration of fact itself, or by means of a separate entry in the files or register.[183]

---

173 Prümmer, *Manuale Iuris Canonici,* p. 346; Toso, *loc. cit.;* Tabera, "art. cit."—*CpR,* XI (1930), 420; and others.

174 *Loc. cit.*

175 *Ibid.*, n. 1159.

176 Blat, *loc. cit.*

177 Brandys, *loc. cit.;* Schönsteiner, *Grundriss des Ordensrechts,* p. 627; Leitner, *loc. cit.;* Jansen, *Ordensrecht,* p. 285; Augustine, *loc. cit.;* Berutti, *loc. cit.;* Coronata, *Manuale Practicum,* n. 238; O'Leary, *loc. cit.;* and others.

178 Cf. *supra,* p. 179, note 164.

179 *Wörterbuch zum Codex Iuris Canonici* (München: Kösel & Pustet, 1927–1929), p. 302.

180 *A Commentary,* III, 266.

181 *Institutiones,* I, 881.

182 *Op. cit.,* pp. 53, 54.

183 Cf. Blat, *loc. cit.*

Finally, the location where the archives are situated is designated by the canon as a "*domus.*" Palombo[184] states that this is the religious house where the dismissed religious had his dwelling place, but he immediately observes that the religious house of the major superior may lend itself by way of preference. The majority of the authors maintains that the archives where the proof is to be kept are the archives of the religious house of the major superior.[185] Since the canon places upon the major superior the obligation of preserving and guarding the proofs, and since he must produce the proofs in the event of an instituted recourse,[186] the logical conclusion is that the archives in the present canon are the archives of the religious house of the major superior.

---

[184] *Op. cit.*, n. 198.

[185] Brandys, *loc. cit.;* Augustine, *ibid.*, 386; Berutti, *loc. cit.;* O'Leary, *loc. cit.;* and others.

[186] Berutti, *loc. cit.*

CHAPTER X

EFFECTS AND RETURN

ARTICLE 1. THE EFFECTS OF THIS DISMISSAL

The effects of automatic dismissal, as has been noted in the explanation of the words "*tanquam legitime*" of canon 646, § 1,[1] are listed in canons 648 and 669–672. These canons have already been the subject of a thorough study by O'Neill[2] and O'Leary.[3] Hence, a summary indication of the chief effects, with a brief consideration of a few special points, is deemed sufficient for the purposes of the present work.

A. Common to All Religious.

In commenting on n. 20 of the decree *Quum singulae*,[4] Villien observed that the earlier law had employed dismissal only as a provisory measure, and that it had always provided for the return of the delinquent.[5] With the decree, however, a new discipline entered in; the dismissed person was no longer considered a religious.[6] This discipline remained in force from 1911 to 1918, and was even incorporated into the schemata of the Code. For, in the schemata, as Larraona points out,[7] it was proposed that dismissal bring about the dissolution of the vows for the temporary and perpetually professed alike.

In the enactment of the Code, however, the contrary principle—namely, that perpetual vows retain their effect after dismissal[8]—

---

[1] Cf. *supra*, pp. 87–89.

[2] *The Dismissal of Religious in Temporary Vows*, pp. 126, 146–161.

[3] *Religious Dismissed after Perpetual Profession*, pp. 55–95, 115–126; 138–149, 169–182.

[4] Cf. *supra*, p. 75, note 77.

[5] Villien, "La Procédure Canonique pour L'Expulsion des Religieux"—*Le Canoniste Contemporain*, XXXVI (1913), 220–221; cf. *supra*, pp. 74–75.

[6] Cf. *supra*, pp. 75–76.

[7] Larraona, "Quaestio Canonica"—*CpR*, III (1922), 322.

[8] Cf. canon 669, § 1.

appeared for those in perpetual vows.[9] The adoption of this principle seems to imply a return to the practice of the earlier discipline. Larraona advances three reasons for this reversal: (1) lest dismissal serve as a favor to the erstwhile religious; (2) that an opportunity be offered for repentance whenever a well-founded hope existed; [10] and (3) especially that the continued anomaly of acephalous clerics be forestalled.[11]

In the present law, then, the juridic condition of the dismissed religious varies according as the bond with the institute remains or is dissolved. Thus, the religious who has professed perpetual vows, whether solemn or simple, is bound by these vows after the dismissal from the religious organization. The exceptions to this general principle occur when the religious is dispensed from the vows by virtue of the constitutions of the institute or by virtue of an apostolic indult.[12]

Religious in temporary vows, on the other hand, are freed from the vows by the very fact of dismissal.[13] Since canon 646 as a general canon applies to all religious,[14] the legislator wisely inserted the words "*tanquam legitime*" into the canon to allow for the variations of effects introduced by the Code. Exception has already been taken to the view of Sweeney and McGrath,[15] and hence it suffices here to reassert that the effects of automatic dismissal for religious in temporary vows are to be sought in canon 648. This contention rests on the words "*tanquam legitime,*" of canon 646. The juridic condition, then, of religious dismissed by force of the law contained in canon 646 is the same as it would have been had an ordinary form of dismissal been employed.[16]

---

[9] Larraona, *ibid.*, p. 322, nota 19.

[10] Larraona, *loc. cit.*

[11] Larraona, *ibid.*, p. 322. O'Leary (*op. cit.*, pp. 173–176) notes that this purpose is somewhat defeated by the provision of the latter part of canon 669, § 1.

[12] Canon 669, § 1.

[13] Canon 648.

[14] Cf. *supra*, pp. 91, 127, 157–158.

[15] Cf. *supra*, pp. 88–89.

[16] Hippolytus a S. Familia, "De Dimissione Religiosorum"—*Analecta O. C. D.*, IV (1930), 163; Aleixo, "De Religiosis Ipso Iure Dimissis"—*Rev. Ecl. Bras.*, VI (1946), 393.

Dismissal is defined as " the compulsory or unwilled separation of a religious from the religious institute or from communal life, imposed by legitimate authority according to the norms of law." [17] It is in this separation that the canonical sanction as entailed by the violation of the profession-contract primarily consists.[18]

The separation is complete—from the religious institute—for religious in temporary vows and for some religious in perpetual vows.[19] In this case the sanction is chiefly a remedy favoring the religious institute, and is marked with the cessation of the vows and of the obligations flowing from membership in that institute. On the other hand, the separation is only partial for most of the religious in perpetual vows, since the vows, the profession-contract, and the obligations remain. The violation of the profession-contract by these religious draws upon itself the sanction of a separation from the communal life with the concomitant forfeiture of the rights thus acquired, entailing the obligation to put aside the religious habit and involving the loss of the suffrages and privileges formerly shared by the religious.[20]

Moreover, in addition to the sanction invoked by the law of canon 646, the religious usually incurs the specific penalties enacted for the crimes there listed, namely, the penalties enacted in canons 2314, 2385, 2386, and 2388.[21] The preceding statement is advisedly qualified, for there may be cases in which the religious will escape some or all of the penalties and still be subject to the canonical sanction which canon 646 has in store for them. The relation between canons 2385 and 2386, on the one hand, and canon 646, § 1, 2°, on the other, offers the clearest exemplification of this point. In reference to the former, Riesner

---

[17] Cf. *supra,* p. 12.

[18] Cf. *supra,* p. 102.

[19] Cf. O'Neill, *op. cit.,* pp. 146–147; O'Leary, *op. cit.,* pp. 169–182.

[20] Cf. O'Leary, *op. cit.,* pp. 55–95, 141–142; McGrath, *The Privilege of the Canon,* p. 76; Kealy, *Dowry of Women Religious,* The Catholic University of America Canon Law Studies, n. 134 (Washington, D. C.: The Catholic University of America Press, 1941), p. 110.

[21] Cance, *Le Code de Droit Canonique,* II, 149; Beste, *Introductio in Codicem,* p. 439; Riesner, *Apostates and Fugitives from Religious Institutes,* p. 79; O'Leary, *op. cit.,* pp. 121–123; Aleixo, *loc. cit.;* cf. *supra,* pp. 120, 143, 158.

concludes that religious with temporary vows, as also the members of societies whose members live in common without vows, if they desert their institute or society with the intention of not returning to it, are not apostates in the strict sense, nor are they fugitives, and hence do not incur the penalties enacted for apostates and fugitives.[22]

Thus, if these religious, in the act of their desertion, would also commit the delict of flight with a person of the other sex, they could be free of the penalties since they lacked the precise intention postulated for the existence of the punishable delict, but they still would be subject to the enacted sanction of dismissal, for which the intention to return or not to return is not a constitutive element of the delict against which the sanction is invoked.[23] In like manner religious in temporary vows, by their inclusion under the law of canon 646, are liable for the sanction of dismissal in the event of an attempted or contracted marriage, though they do not incur the penalty which canon 2388 enacts for religious in perpetual vows. Hence, though these or other causes may excuse the religious from incurring a particular penalty, this fact does not necessarily and concomitantly rule out the application of the sanction invoked for the breach of the profession-contract. Penalty and canonical sanction are two separate and distinct juridical realities. In order to establish the non-application of the canonical sanction it is not enough to prove that a certain penalty was not incurred, but it must be shown that the act was not delictual in character or not the kind of delict which by the operative norm of canon 646 entails the sanction there threatened.[24] In this connection Blat specifically mentions that the members of societies without vows are subject to the application of this sanction even if they be free from the penalties.[25]

The religious, moreover, is subject to any other penalty (e.g.,

---

[22] Riesner, *op. cit.*, pp. 54–57.

[23] Cf. *supra*, pp. 124, 127.

[24] Cf. *supra*, pp. 107–109.

[25] "Applicatio Societatibus sine votis—Canoni 646 plene aptatur absque difficultate. Quoad poenas autem, canones non urgent sic dimissos, nisi proprie comprehendantur in verbis illorum."—Blat, *Ius de Religiosis,* n. 661.

the ones enacted in canons 2342, 3°, 2353, etc.) that may have been established in punishment of his act.

B. Proper to Minor Clerics.

A minor cleric religious, whether bound by temporary or by perpetual vows, who has been dismissed from his religious institute is by that very fact reduced to lay state.[26]

Sweeney [27] and McGrath [28] hold that this general principle does not include minor cleric religious in temporary vows who are dismissed in accordance with the rule of canon 646. They question the application of canon 648 to canon 646, and consequently maintain that these minor clerics are neither released from their vows nor reduced to the lay state. However, this application seems certain by force of the words "*tanquam legitime*" of canon 646,[29] and so the reduction to the lay state applies to all cleric religious dismissed while in minor orders.[30]

The law thus indicates that such clerics are no longer deemed worthy of or fit for the clerical state.[31] In accordance with canons 123 and 213, § 1, all offices and benefices, as also the clerical rights and privileges are lost, so that the ones thus dismissed are forbidden to wear the ecclesiastical habit and tonsure.[32]

C. Proper to Major Clerics.

In canon 646 the law invokes the sanction of an automatic dismissal for the specific violations of the profession-contract by any member—lay or clerical—of a religious institute. In this manner the welfare of the religious state is provided for. The grave faults, however, that occasion the dismissal of a cleric religious from the religious family have a repercussion on his status in the clerical society as well. Accordingly, as a complementary measure,

---

[26] Canons 648, 669, § 2; cf. Sweeney, *Reduction to the Lay State*, pp. 70–83, 85–88; O'Neill, *op. cit.*, pp. 147–150; O'Leary, *op. cit.*, pp. 115–117.

[27] *Ibid.*, pp. 74–75.

[28] *Op. cit.*, pp. 76–77.

[29] Cf. *supra*, pp. 87–89, 184.

[30] O'Leary, *op. cit.*, p. 115.

[31] Cf. *supra*, p. 78.

[32] Cf. Smith, *The Penal Law for Religious*, p. 88.

the law adds provisions to safeguard the clerical state.[33]

If a major cleric with perpetual vows has committed any of the crimes listed in canon 646, he is perpetually forbidden to wear the ecclesiastical garb.[34] Since the prohibition to wear the ecclesiastical garb is entailed by the delict, as is evident from the text of canon 670, it is incurred simultaneously with the dismissal; and, though it does not result from the dismissal, it can be incurred only when the dismissal becomes operative, as is clear from the context.[35] Most of the canonists state that the perpetual prohibition to wear the ecclesiastical garb as mentioned in canon 670 is a vindicative penalty, namely, the particular penalty mentioned in canons 2298, 11°, and 2304, § 1.[36] The deprivation of the clerical privileges is a result of this penalty.[37]

The authors, moreover, are unanimous in stating that clerics dismissed in consequence of the applied norm of canon 646 are suspended, even though the Code states nothing expressly about the matter.[38] Some authors merely state that such clerics incur a suspension without referring to its source.[39] Some trace it to the individual crimes committed by the delinquent,[40] or derive it *a fortiori* from the argument inherent in canon 671, 1°.[41] Others trace the suspension to the penalty of the perpetual prohibition to wear the ecclesiastical garb.[42]

Palombo has considered the variant opinions of the authors and has concluded that the best explanation is that a suspension is incurred in view of the penalty of the perpetual prohibition to

---

[33] Cf. *supra*, p. 76.

[34] "Clericus in sacris qui aliquod delictum commisit de quo in can. 646, . . . , perpetuo prohibetur deferre habitum ecclesiasticum."—canon 670; cf. O'Leary, *op. cit.*, pp. 118–126.

[35] O'Leary, *op. cit.*, p. 118; Palombo, *De Dimissione Religiosorum*, n. 202; Smith, *op. cit.*, p. 91; Larraona, "art. cit."—*CpR*, III (1922), 328.

[36] Cf. O'Leary, *op. cit.*, p. 119.

[37] Canon 2304, § 2.

[38] Cf. O'Leary, *op. cit.*, p. 121.

[39] Vermeersch-Creusen, *Epitome*, I, n. 822; De Meester, *Juris Canonici et Juris Canonico-Civilis Compendium*, II, n. 1064, 2°; *supra*, p. 77.

[40] Goyeneche, *De Religiosis*, n. 128.

[41] Prümmer, *Manuale Iuris Canonici*, p. 353; Jansen, *Ordensrecht*, p. 306; Beste, *Introductio in Codicem*, p. 453; cf. canon 2219, § 3.

[42] Coronata, *Institutiones*, I, n. 660; Schaefer, *De Religiosis*, n. 597.

wear the ecclesiastical garb. Although this penalty is distinct from the penalty of suspension, it is a greater and more stringent penalty, and accordingly comprehends the effects of suspension in it.[43]

Article 2. Return to the Religious Institute

The general rule for dismissed religious still bound by vows is that they are required to return to their institute, and that the institute is bound to receive them back after three years of amendment.[44] O'Leary [45] treats at length the problems involved in the return of a dismissed religious to full participation in the life of his religious institute. In the present article, then, only a recapitulation of the relation between this juridical factor and the invoked sanction of automatic dismissal will be given.

Soon after the promulgation of the Code the norms of canon 672, § 1, became the subject of controversy. While the greater number of the authors applied the norms of this canon to all dismissed religious, whether lay or clerical, a few restricted its use to those in sacred orders.[46] The argument of the latter group rested mainly on the fact that after canon 669 the law makes no further mention of lay or laicized members, but legislates exclusively for those who have been raised to a higher station in Christian society—major clerics.[47] Larraona then proposed the opinion that canon 672 applied only to the minor delicts treated in canon 671, and not to the graver crimes summarily dealt with in canon 670, amongst which crimes are those whose commission effects an automatic dismissal in virtue of canon 646.[48]

---

[43] Palombo, *loc. cit.*

[44] Canon 672, § 1: "Dimissus, votis in religione emissis non solutus, tenetur ad claustra redire; et si argumenta plenae emendationis per triennium dederit, religio tenetur eum recipere; . . ."

[45] *Religious Dismissed after Perpetual Profession,* pp. 95–114, 152–161, 183–186; cf. O'Neill, *The Dismissal of Religious in Temporary Vows,* pp. 154–155.

[46] Cf. O'Leary, *op. cit.,* pp. 96–108; Goyeneche, "Annotationes"—*Apollinaris,* VIII (1935), 353–354; Alvarez Melcón, "Boletin Canónico"—*Religión y Cultura,* XXX (1935), 277–278.

[47] Goyeneche, *loc. cit.;* cf. *supra,* pp. 76–78.

[48] Larraona, "Quaestio Canonica"—*CpR,* III (1922), 318–329; cf. Smith, *op. cit.,* pp. 48–50; O'Leary, *op. cit.,* pp. 98–108.

In answer to a proposed doubt,[49] the Pontifical Commission for the Authentic Interpretation of the Code stated that the provisions of canon 672, § 1, do not apply to those religious who have been dismissed for the crimes mentioned in canon 646. On the basis of this decision, then, many authors conclude that the religious institute is entirely free from all obligation of ever receiving back the members who have been dismissed in consequence of the commission of any of the crimes mentioned in canon 646, and that the religious thus dismissed are likewise liberated from the obligation of returning, not as a favor to them, but as a favor to the institute, since it is obviously impossible for them to return if the institute employs its option not to receive them.[50] O'Leary, on the other hand, deems that this general opinion is too extensive an interpretation of the response, and that the most that one can deduce from it is that there is no longer an obligation which arises from positive law.[51]

In this manner all authors assume that the words *"praescriptum canonis 672, § 1"* of the proposed doubt refer primarily[52] to the obligation of the institute to receive back a dismissed religious. However, without touching upon the obligations of either the institute or the member in the matter of return, there are intrinsic reasons why the norms of canon 672, § 1, do not extend to those who have been dismissed in consequence of the applied

---

[49] "II. An praescriptum canonis 672, § 1, extendatur etiam ad Religiosis ipso facto dimisso ad normam canonis 646.

"Ad II. Negative."—P.C.I., 30 iul. 1934, ad III—*AAS,* XXVI (1934), 494; cf. Bouscaren, *Canon Law Digest,* II, 175.

[50] Maroto, "Annotationes"—*CpR,* XV (1934), 356; [Anonymous], "Annotationes"—*Periodica,* XXIII (1934), 147; Goyeneche, *ibid.,* p. 354; Smith, *op. cit.,* p. 50; Alvarez Melcon, *ibid.,* p. 278; Goyeneche, "Consultationes"—*CpRM,* XXIII (1942), 28; Aleixo, "art. cit."—*Rev. Ecl. Bras.,* VI (1946), 394; Sartori, *Enchiridion Canonicum,* p. 185; cf. Jombart, "De religiosis dimissis"—*Nouvelle Revue Théologique,* LXI (1934), 1081–1082.

[51] O'Leary, *op. cit.,* pp. 108–112; 155–158.

[52] The "dubium" speaks only of a "praescriptum," whereas canon 672, § 1, treats of three distinct elements: (1) the obligation of dismissed religious to return; (2) the obligation of the institute to receive the religious after three years of full amendment; and (3) the submission of difficulties to the decision of the Holy See.

norm of canon 646. Thus, while canon 672, § 1, provides for the readmission of a dismissed religious by the institute after three years of amendment, canon 646 contains in itself a general reason which excludes the application of this norm in behalf of members thus dismissed. For the latter are dismissed by the law, and not by superiors, and the law considers them absolutely and perpetually dismissed.[53]

Dismissal in canon 646 exists as a sanction imposed by the common law [54]—an *appositio manus* of the Holy See [55]—and the effects remain until one who has power over the common law lifts the applied sanction. This faculty is not given to superiors by the Code and, unless they have special faculties, they cannot annul this effect which has been engendered by the law.[56] Accordingly, in stating that the norm of canon 672, § 1, does not apply to canon 646, the response simply recognizes what is already intrinsically present.

In virtue of this exclusive competence, then, recourse must be made to the Holy See when the occasion arises, and its decision then remains to be followed.[57] In effect, it seems that the return to his religious institute on the part of a religious who has been dismissed according to the norm of canon 646 can be implemented solely through the grant of an apostolic indult.[58]

---

[53] Goyeneche, "Consultationes"—*CpRM,* XXIII (1942), 29.

[54] Cf. *supra,* p. 86.

[55] Palombo, *De Dimissione Religiosorum,* p. 255, nota 1; cf. *supra,* pp. 66; 78, note 92.

[56] Goyeneche, *loc. cit.*

[57] Larraona, *ibid.,* p. 327, nota 31; O'Leary, *op. cit.,* p. 110; cf. *supra,* p. 78, note 94.

[58] Goyeneche, *loc. cit.;* Sartori, *Enchiridion Canonicum,* p. 185.

CONCLUSIONS

1. The administrative discipline—expulsion for persistent incorrigibility—remained within the power of religious superiors almost exclusively for many centuries (pp. 19–25). When, in the period of the Decretals, the expulsion became the object of general legislation, the norms enacted were quite consonant with the general monastic practice (pp. 27, 28–36). This period was followed by that in which papal indults were granted to certain Orders, extending to provincials with their council the power of expulsion previously possessed by the general superiors. These privileges were intercommunicated with other institutes, so that quite a common practice arose in this regard (pp. 36–39).

2. Urban VIII in 1624 reorganized the various norms that had grown out of particular constitutions and privileges, and decreed that for the future a religious could be expelled only if the conditions of the general law were observed (pp. 41–43). With the exception of minor changes granted by Innocent XII in 1694 (pp. 48–49), these norms prevailed substantially until 1911, when they were reorganized and rendered more adaptable to contemporary circumstances (pp. 52, 58).

3. Before 1911, *ipso facto* effected expulsion or dismissal was unheard of as a *juridical* institute. In that year it appeared as the legal sanction against religious guilty of four specified crimes (pp. 61, 64–80).

4. Canon 646 retains many of the elements of the former law (pp. 94, 96–97, 100, 110, 121, 144), but has likewise introduced opportune changes (pp. 89, 92, 100, 159, 183–184).

5. This sanction of dismissal is imposed by the common law and is effected by the very fact that a religious commits one of the delicts enumerated in canon 646 (pp. 85–87, 161.) It is not a canonical penalty, but is a sanction of law for a breach of the profession-contract and a remedy for the religious institute (pp. 93–106.) The sanction consists primarily in the separation of

the religious from the religious institute or from the communal life (pp. 12, 185), and as such it is perpetual and remains until it is lifted by one who has power over the common law (p. 191.)

6. The words "*apostatae a fide Catholica*" have their own proper signification; they are not to be interpreted in line with the concepts delineated in canon 1325, § 2 (p. 119).

7. The word "*fugam*" in canon 646 points to a departure from the religious house, or from the place assigned by obedience, for the purpose of withdrawing oneself from religious obedience or the regular observance (pp. 126–127). The flight contemplated in canon 646, § 1, 2°, then, must be this kind of flight as further qualified through the association of a person of the other sex in the flight with complicity and a libidinous intent (pp. 128–133). All these elements must be present at the beginning of the flight p. 143). Publicity is not postulated for the existence of this delict (pp. 137–139).

8. The favor of the presumption rests with the religious when the other party of the flight is a near relative or a person below the age of puberty (pp. 136–137).

9. The declaration of the fact of the crime and its consequences does not have the force of a declaratory sentence or of a decree (pp. 161–162), but is intended only to offer juridic certitude of what has already been effected by law (pp. 165–166). As regards his activities as a religious, the dismissed person is bound in both forums to observe the sanction even before the executed declaration; but until the declaration has been issued he cannot be forced to do so (pp. 162–164).

10. The words "*tanquam legitime*" in canon 646 denote that the juridic condition of the dismissed religious is the same as it would have been had an ordinary form of dismissal been employed. These effects vary according as the bond with the institute remains or is dissolved (pp. 87–89, 184).

BIBLIOGRAPHY

SOURCES

Acta Apostolicae Sedis, Commentarium Officiale, Romae, 1909–1929; Civitate Vaticana, 1929–

Acta Sanctae Sedis, 41 vols., Romae, 1865–1908.

Bouscaren, T. Lincoln, *The Canon Law Digest,* 2 vols., Milwaukee: Bruce, 1934, 1943.

Bullarum Diplomatum et Privilegiorum Sanctorum Romanorum Pontificum Taurinensis Editio, 24 tomes in 25 vols., Augustae Taurinorum, 1857–1872.

Canonical Legislation Concerning Religious, Authorized English Translation, Rome: Vatican Printing Office, 1918.

Codex Iuris Canonici Pii X Pontificis Maximi iussu digestus Benedicti Papae XV auctoritate promulgatus, Romae: Typis Polyglottis Vaticanis, 1917. Reimpressio, 1934.

Codicis Iuris Canonici Fontes, cura Emi Petri Card. Gasparri editi, 9 vols., Romae (postea Civitate Vaticana): Typis Polyglottis Vaticanis, 1923–1939 (Vols. VII, VIII, IX ed. cura et studio Emi Iustiniani Card. Serédi).

Collectanea in Usum Secretariae Sacrae Congregationis Episcoporum et Regularium, ed. noviss. A. Bizzarri, Romae, 1885.

Confettio, J. B., *Privilegiorum Sacrorum Ordinum Fratrum Mendicantium et Non-Mendicantium Collectio,* Postrema Editio, Venetiis, 1616.

Constitutiones Fratrum S. Ordinis Praedicatorum, ed. nova, Parisiis, 1886.

Corpus Iuris Canonici, ed. Lipsiensis secunda, post Aemilii Richteri curas . . . instruxit Aemilius Friedberg, 2 vols., Lipsiae, 1879–1881.

Corpus Iuris Civilis, Institutiones, quas recognovit P. Krueger, *Digesta,* quae recognovit T. Mommsen et retractavit P. Kreuger, *Codex Iustinianus,* quem recognovit et retractavit P. Kreuger, *Novellae,* quas recognovit R. Schoell et absolvit G. Kroll, 3 vols., Berolini, 1928–1929.

Decretales D. Gregorii Papae IX, una cum Glossis Restitutae, Romae, 1582.

Decretum Gratiani Emendatum et Notationibus Illustratum una cum glossis, 2 vols., Romae, 1582.

Jaffé, P., *Regesta Pontificum Romanorum, ab condita ecclesia ad annum post Christum natum 1198,* 2. ed., correctam et auctam auspiciis Gulielmi Wattenbach curaverunt S. Loewenfeld, F. Kaltenbrunner, P. Ewald, 2 vols. in 1, Lipsiae, 1885–1888.

Jordanus de Saxonia, *Liber Vitasfratrum,* ad fidem codicum recensuerunt, prolegomenis, apparatu critico, notis instruxerunt Rudolphus Arbesmann et Winfridus Hümpfner, New York: Cosmopolitan Science and Art Service Co., Inc., 1943—*Appendix C, Regula Sancti Augustini Secunda,* pp. 494–504.

Mansi, J. D., *Sacrorum Conciliorum Nova et Amplissima Collectio,* 53 vols., in 60, Florentiae, Parisiis, Arnhem et Leipzig, 1901-1927.

Monumenta Germaniae Historica, Epistolae, Tom. I, II, III, ed. P. Ewald, et L. Hartmann, Berolini, 1867-1899.

———, *Legum Sectio II, Capitularia Regum Francorum,* 2 tomes in 5 vols., ed. A. Boretius et V. Krause, Hannoverae, 1883-1897.

Normae Secundum Quas S. Cong. Episcoporum et Regularium Procedere Solet in Approbandis Novis Institutis Votorum Simplicium, Romae, 1901.

Pallottini, S., *Collectio Omnium Conclusionum et Resolutionem Quae in Causis Propositis apud Sacram Congregationem Cardinalium S. Concilii Tridentini Interpretum Prodierunt ab eius institutione anno MDLXIV ad annum MDCCCLX, distinctis titulis alphabetico ordine per materias digesta,* 18 vols., Romae, 1868–1895.

Potthast, A., *Regesta Pontificum Romanorum inde ab A. post Christum natum 1198 ad A. 1804,* 2 vols., Berolini, 1874–1875.

Sancti Benedicti Regula Monasteriorum, ed. critico-practica, Cuthbert Butler, Friburgi Brisgoviae, 1912.

Seebass, O., "Regula Coenobialis S. Columbani Abbatis"—*Zeitschrift für Kirchengeschichte* (Gotha: F. A. Perthes, 1876–) XVII (1897), 215 sq.

REFERENCE WORKS

Acta Congressus Iuridici Internationalis . . . Romae, 1934, 5 vols., Romae: Libraria Pont. Instituti Utriusque Iuris, 1935–1937.

Alford, C. B., *Ius Matrimoniale Comparatum,* Romae: Anonima Libraria Cattolica Italiana, 1938.

Alzog, J., B., *Manual of Universal Church History,* 3 vols., Cincinnati, 1903.

Andreae, Ioannes, *In Quinque Decretalium Libros Novella Commentaria,* 4 vols., Venetiis, 1581.

Augustine, C., *A Commentary on the New Code of Canon Law,* 8 vols., Vol. III (Religious and laymen), 5. ed., St. Louis: Herder, 1938.

Ayrinhac, H. A.-Lydon, P. J., *Penal Legislation in the New Code of Canon Law,* revised edition, New York: Benziger, 1936.

Bachofen, A., *Compendium Juris Regularium,* New York, 1903.

Barbosa, A., *Collectanea Doctorum tam Veterum quam Recentiorum in Ius Pontificium Universum,* 6 vols., Lugduni, 1669.

Bastien, P., *Directoire Canonique a L'usage des Congregations a voeux simplex* 3. ed., Bruges: Beyaert, 1923.

Benedictus XIV, *De Synodo Dioecesana,* 2. ed., 2 vols., Parmae, 1764.

Berutti, C., *Institutiones Iuris Canonici,* 6 vols., Vol. III (De Religiosis), Taurini, Romae: Marietti, 1936.

Beste, U., *Introductio in Codicem,* editio altera, Collegeville, Minn.: St. John's Abbey Press, 1944.

Biederlack, J.-Führich, M., *De Religiosis,* Oeniponte: Typis Feliciani Rauch, 1919.

Billuart, C. R., *Summa Sancti Thomae,* 9 vols. in 8, ed. nova, Parisiis: Letouzey et Ané, n. d.

Blat, A., *Commentarium Textus Codicis Iuris Canonici,* 5 vols. in 6, lib. II, Pars II–III (*Ius de Religiosis et Laicis Iuxta Codicis Ordinem*), 3. ed., Romae: Apud "Angelicum," 1938.

Bouix, D., *Tractatus de Jure Regularium,* 2 vols., ed. 3., Parisiis, 1882–1883.

Bouscaren, T. L.-Ellis, A., *Canon Law,* Milwaukee: Bruce, 1946.

Brandys, M., *Kirchliches Rechtsbuch für die religiösen Laiengenossenschaften der Brüder und Schwestern nach dem neuen Gesetzbuch der hl. Kirche* 2. ed., Paderborn: Schöningh, 1920.

Butler, E. C., *Benedictine Monachism,* 2. ed. with supplementary notes, New York: Longmans, Green & Co., 1924.

Cance, A., *Le Code de Droit Canonique,* 6. ed., 3 vols., Paris: Librairie Lecoffre, J. Gabalda et fils, 1930.

Cappello, F., *Summa Iuris Canonici,* 3 vols., Vol. II, 4. ed., Romae: Apud Aedes Pontificiae Universitatis Gregorianae, 1945.

Castropalao, F., *Opus Morale,* 7 vols. in 3, noviss. ed., Lugduni, 1682.

Cerato, P., *Censurae Vigentes Ipso Facto a Codice Iuris Canonici Excerptae,* 2. ed., Patavii: Typis Seminarii, 1921.

Cervia, E. P., *De Professione Religiosa,* Dissertatio ad Lauream in Iuris Canonici Facultate Pontificiae Universitatis Gregorianae: Bologna, 1938.

Chapman, J., *St. Benedict and the Sixth Century,* London: Sheed and Ward, 1929.

Chelodi, I., *Ius Canonicum de Personis,* 3. ed., curavit Pius Ciprotti, Trento: Libreria Moderna Editrice, 1942.

———, *Ius Canonicum de Delictis et Poenis,* 5. ed., recognita et aucta a Pio Ciprotti, Trento: Libreria Moderna Editrice, 1943.

Claeys Bouuaert, F.-Simenon, G., *Manuale Juris Canonici,* Gandae et Leodii: prostat apud Auctores, 1924.

Clancy, P., *The Local Religious Superior,* The Catholic University of America Canon Law Studies, n. 175, Washington, D. C.: The Catholic University of America Press, 1943.

Cocchi, G., *Commentarium in Codicem Iuris Canonici,* 8 vols. in 5, Lib. II, Pars II–III (*De Religiosis et Laicis—Vol.* IV), Taurinorum Augustae: Marietti, 1922.

Coronata, M. Conte a, *Institutiones Iuris Canonici,* 5 vols., Vols. I, 2. ed., 1939, Taurini-Romae: Marietti.

———, *Manuale Practicum Iuris Disciplinaris et Criminalis Religarium,* Taurini: Marietti, 1938.

Corpus Scriptorum Ecclesiasticorum Latinorum, editum consilio et impensis Academiae Litterarum Caesareae Vindobonensis, Vindobonae, 1866–

Coussa, A., *Epitome Praelectionum de Iure Ecclesiastico Orientali*, 2 vols., Vol. II, Venetiis: Typis Polyglottis Insulae S. Lazari, 1941.

Craisson, D., *Elementa Juris Canonici ad usum Galliae seminariorum*, 7. ed., Parisiis, 1887.

Crane, J. A., *Handbook of the Law of Partnership*, St. Paul, Minn.: West Publishing Co., 1938.

Creusen, J.-Garesché, E.-Ellis, A., *Religious Men and Women in the Code*, 4. English ed., Milwaukee: Bruce, 1942.

Creusen, I.-Vermeersch, A., *Summa Novi Iuris Canonici Commentarium Aucta*, ed. 4., Mechlinae: Dessain, 1921.

De Ameno, L., *Opera Omnia*, 3 tomes, Romae, 1753–1754.

Delatte, P., *Commentary on the Rule of St. Benedict*, New York: Benziger, 1921.

Deutsch, A., *Manual for Oblates of St. Benedict*, Collegeville, Minnesota: St. John's Abbey Press, 1937.

De Meester, A., *Juris Canonici et Juris Canonico-Civilis Compendium*, nova ed., 3 vols. in 4, Brugis, Desclée, 1921–1928.

Dillon, R., *Common Law Marriage*, The Catholic University of America Canon Law Studies, n. 153, Washington, D. C.: The Catholic University of America Press, 1942.

Eichmann, E., *Lehrbuch des Kirchenrechts*, 2. ed., Paderborn: Schöningh, 1926.

Eltz, L., *Cooperation in Crime*, The Catholic University of America Canon Law Studies, n. 156, Washington, D. C.: The Catholic University of America Press, 1942.

Engel, L., *Collegium Universi Iuris Canonici*, ed. nona; post omnes alias recognita et locupletata: cui nunc primum adjectae sunt annotationes Caspari Barthel: Beneventi: 1760.

Fagnanus, P., *Commentaria in Quinque Libros Decretalium*, 4 vols., Venetiis, 1709.

Falco, M., *Corso di Diritto Ecclesiastico*, Padova: Casa Editrice Dott. A. Milani Cedam, 1930.

Fanfani, L., *De Iure Religiosorum ad Normam Codicis Iuris Canonici*, 2. ed., Taurini-Romae: Marietti, 1925.

Fang, F., *Dispensatio Matrimonialis Urgente Mortis Periculo et Instante Nuptiarum Contractu ad normam can. 1043–1045*, Romae: Officium Libri Catholici, 1946.

Ferraris, L., *Prompta Bibliotheca Canonica, Juridica, Moralis, Theologica, necnon Ascetica, Polemica, Rubricistica, Historica*, 8 vols., ed. noviss., mendis expurgata, Parisiis, 1852–1857.

Frey, W., *The Act of Religious Profession*, The Catholic University of America Canon Law Studies, n. 63, Washington, D. C.: The Catholic University of America, 1931.

Funk, F. X., *A Manual of Church History, Authorized Translation of 5th German Edition,* 2 vols., Luigi Cappadelta, St. Louis, 1910.

Gerster a Zeil, T., *Ius Religiosorum in Compendium Redactum pro Iuvenibus Religiosis,* Taurini: Marietti, 1935.

Geser, F., *The Canon Law Governing Communities of Sisters,* St. Louis: Herder, 1939.

Goldsmith, J. W., *The Competence of Church and State over Marriage—Disputed Points,* The Catholic University of America Canon Law Studies, n. 197, Washington, D. C.: The Catholic University of America Press, 1944.

Gonzalez-Tellez, E., *Commentaria Perpetua in Singulos Textus Quinque Librorum Decretalium,* 5 tomes in 4 vols., Venetiis, 1699.

Goyeneche, S., *Iuris Canonici Summa Principia, De Religiosis,* Romae: Commentarium Pro Religiosis, 1938.

Heneghan, J., *The Marriage of Unworthy Catholics: Canons 1065 and 1066,* The Catholic University of America Canon Law Studies, n. 188, Washington, D. C.: The Catholic University of America Press, 1944.

Hickey, J., *Irregularities and Simple Impediments in the New Code of Canon Law,* The Catholic University of America Canon Law Studies, n. 7, Washington, D. C.: The Catholic University of America, 1920.

Horoy, C. A., *Bibliotheca Patristica Medii Aevii—ab anno MCCXVI usque ad Conc. Trident.* (Series Prima, Paris, 1880), Tomus Sextus, *S. Francisci Assiss. Opuscula.*

Hostiensis (Henricus de Segusio), *Commentaria in Quinque Libros Decretalium,* 5 vols. in 3, Venetiis, 1581.

Jansen, J., *Ordensrecht,* 3. ed., Paderborn: Schöningh, 1931.

Kealy, T., *Dowry of Women Religious,* The Catholic University of America Canon Law Studies, n. 134, Washington, D. C.: The Catholic University of America Press, 1941.

Köstler, R., *Wörterbuch zum Codex Iuris Canonici,* München: Kösel & Pustet, 1927–1929.

Laver, A., *Index Verborum Codicis Iuris Canonici,* Civitate Vaticana: Typis Polyglottis Vaticanis, 1941.

Leitner, M., *Handbuch des katholischen Kirchenrechts auf Grund des neuen Kodex,* 5 vols., Vol. III (*Das Ordensrecht*), 2 ed., Regensburg: Pustet, 1922.

Lydon, P. J., *Ready Answers in Canon Law,* 2. ed., New York: Benziger, 1937.

MacKenzie, E., *The Delict of Heresy in its Commission, Penalization, Absolution,* The Catholic University of America Canon Law Studies, n. 77, Washington, D. C.: The Catholic University of America, 1932.

Maroto, P., *Institutiones Iuris Canonici ad Normam Novi Codicis,* 2 vols., Romae, 1918–1919.

Matulenas, R., *Communication—A Source of Privileges,* The Catholic University of America Canon Law Studies, n. 183, Washington, D. C.: The Catholic University of America Press, 1943.

Mayer, H. S., *Benediktinisches Ordensrecht in der Beuroner Kongregation,* 4 vols., Beuron: Kunstverlag, 1929–1936.

McDevitt, G., *The Renunciation of an Ecclesiastical Office,* The Catholic University of America Canon Law Studies, n. 218, Washington, D. C.: The Catholic University of America Press, 1946.

McGrath, J., *The Privilege of the Canon,* The Catholic University of America Canon Law Studies, n. 242, Washington, D. C.: The Catholic University of America Press, 1946.

Michalicka, W., *Judicial Procedure in Dismissal of Clerical Exempt Religious,* The Catholic University of America Canon Law Studies, n. 19, Washington, D. C.: The Catholic University of America, 1923.

Michiels, G., *De Delictis et Poenis,* Vol. I, Lublin: Universitas Catholica, 1934.

Migne, J. P., *Patrologiae Cursus Completus, Series Graeca,* 161 vols., Paris, 1856–1866.

———, *Patrologiae Cursus Completus, Series Latina,* 221 vols., Paris, 1844–1864.

Molitor, R., *Religiosi Juris Capita Selecta,* Ratisbonae, 1909.

Neuberger, N., *Canon 6 or the Relation of the Codex Juris Canonici to Preceding Legislation,* The Catholic University of America Canon Law Studies, n. 44, Washington, D. C.: The Catholic University of America, 1927.

Oesterle, G., *Praelectiones Iuris Canonici,* Vol. I, Romae: in Collegio S. Anselmi, 1931.

O'Brien, J., *The Exemption of Religious in Church Law,* Milwaukee: Bruce, 1943.

O'Keeffe, G., *Matrimonial Dispensations, Powers of Bishops, Priests, and Confessors,* The Catholic University of America Canon Law Studies, n. 45, Washington, D. C.: The Catholic University of America, 1927.

O'Leary, G., *Religious Dismissed after Perpetual Profession,* The Catholic University of America Canon Law Studies, n. 184, Washington, D. C.: The Catholic University of America Press, 1943.

O'Neill, F., *The Dismissal of Religious in Temporary Vows,* The Catholic University of America Canon Law Studies, n. 166, Washington, D. C.: The Catholic University of America Press, 1942.

Palombo, J., *De Dimissione Religiosorum,* Taurini-Romae: Marietti, 1931.

Panormitanus (Nicolaus de Tudeschis), *Commentaria in Quinque Libros Decretalium,* 5 vols. in 7, Venetiis, 1588.

Papi, H., *Religious Profession,* New York: Kenedy, 1918.

Payen, G., *De Matrimonio in Missionibus et Potissimum in Sinis Tractatus Practicus et Casus,* 2. ed., 3 vols., Zi-ka-wei: in typographia T'ou-sè-wè, 1935–1936.

Pejška, J., *Ius Canonicum Religiosorum,* 3. ed., Friburgi Brisgoviae: Herder, 1927.

Piontek, C., *De Indulto Exclaustrationis necnon Saecularizationis,* The Catholic University of America Canon Law Studies, n. 29, Washington, D. C.: The Catholic University of America, 1925.

Prümmer, D., *Manuale Iuris Canonici,* 6. ed., Friburgi Brisgoviae: Herder, 1933.

Regatillo, E., *Institutiones Iuris Canonici,* 2 vols., Santander: Sal Terrae, 1941–1942.

Reiffenstuel, A., *Jus Canonicum Universum,* 5 vols. in 7, Parisiis, 1864–1870.

Reinmann, G., *The Third Order Secular of Saint Francis,* The Catholic University of America Canon Law Studies, n. 50, Washington, D. C.: The Catholic University of America, 1928.

Ried-Brig, T. P. a, *Manuale Practicum Juris Disciplinaris et Criminalis Regularium ad usum Ff. Minorum Capuccinorum exaratum,* Romae, 1902.

Riesner, A., *Apostates and Fugitives from Religious Institutes,* The Catholic University of America Canon Law Studies, n. 168, Washington, D. C.: The Catholic University of America Press, 1942.

Roberti, F., *De Delictis et Poenis,* Vol. I, Partes I & II, ed. altera, Romae: Apud Custodiam Librariam Pontificii Instituti Utriusque Iuris, 1944.

Roderico, E., *Quaestiones Regulares seu Resolutiones Quaestionum Regularium,* Lugduni, 1634.

Sabetti, A.-Barrett, T., *Compendium Theologiae Moralis,* 8. ed., post Codicem, New York: Pustet, 1939.

Sanchez, T., *Opus Morale in Praecepta Decalogi,* 2 vols., Antverpiae, 1631–1637.

Sangmeister, J., *Force and Fear as Precluding Matrimonial Consent,* The Catholic University of America Canon Law Studies, n. 80, Washington, D. C.: The Catholic University of America, 1932.

Sartori, C., *Enchiridion Canonicum,* 7. ed., Romae: ex Typographia Augustiniana, 1944.

Schaefer, T., *De Religiosis,* 3. ed., Roma: S. A. L. E. R., 1940.

Schmalzgrueber, F., *Ius Ecclesiasticum Universum,* 5 vols. in 12, Romae, 1843–1845.

Schönsteiner, F., *Grundriss des Ordensrechtes,* Wien: Ludwig Auer, 1930.

Sipos, S., *Enchiridion Iuris Canonici,* 3. ed., Pecs: Ex Typographia "Haladas R. T.," 1936.

Smith, M., *The Penal Law for Religious,* The Catholic University of America Canon Law Studies, n. 98, Washington, D. C.: The Catholic University of America, 1935.

Sole, I., *De Delictis et Poenis,* Romae: Pustet, 1920.

Suarez, F., *Opera Omnia,* ed. C. Berton, 26 vols., Parisiis, 1856–1866.

Sweeney, F., *The Reduction of Clerics to the Lay State,* The Catholic University of America Canon Law Studies, n. 223, Washington, D. C.: The Catholic University of America Press, 1945.

Tamayo, S., *Procedimientos de Derecho Penal Canónico,* Manila: Tip. del Colegio de Sto. Tomás, 1913.

Thomassinus, L., *Vetus et Nova Ecclesiae Disciplina circa Beneficia et Beneficiarios,* Editio postrema, cum Parisiensi accuratissime collata, 10 vols., Magontiaci, 1787.

Toso, A., *Ad Codicem Iuris Canonici Commentaria Minora,* Lib. II, pars II, Romae: Jus Pontificium, 1927.

Tummulo, R.-Iorio, T., *Compendium Theologiae Moralis,* 2 vols. in 4, Vol. II, *Supplementum,* 5. ed., Neapoli: M. D. 'Auria, 1936.

Van Espen, Z. B., *Jus Ecclesiasticum Universum,* 4 vols., Lugduni, 1778.

Vermeersch, A., *De Religiosis Institutis et Personis,* 2 vols., Vol. I, Brugis, 1902; Vol. II, 3. ed., Brugis, 1904.

Vermeersch, A.-Creusen, J., *Epitome Iuris Canonici,* 3 vols., 6. ed., Mechliniae-Romae: Dessain, 1937–1946.

Wernz, F. X., *Ius Decretalium,* 2. ed., 6 vols., Romae et Prati, 1905–1914.

Wernz, F. X.-Vidal, P., *Ius Canonicum,* 7 tomes in 8 vols., Tom. III (*De Religiosis*), Romae: Apud Aedes Universitatis Gregorianae, 1933.

Woywod, S., *A Practical Commentary on the Code of Canon Law,* 8. ed., revised by Callistus Smith, 2 vols., New York: Wagner, 1944.

ARTICLES

Aleixo, Frei, "De Religiosis Ipso Iure Dimissis"—*Rev. Ecl. Bras.,* VI (1946), 387–394.

Alvarez Melcón, B., "Boletin Canónico"—*Religión y Cultura,* XXX (1935), 272–281.

[Anonymous], "Annotationes"—*Periodica,* XXIII (1934), 144–147.

Bastien, P., "Conspectus Historico-Juridicus de Regimine Monasterii in Ordine Sancti Benedicti"—*Jus Pontificium,* IX (1929), 295–305; X (1930), 44–55.

——, "De Evolutione Historico-Juridica Processus Dimissionis"—*Jus pontificium,* XI (1931), 20–29.

Diaz, M., "Studia Varia—Congressus Iuridicus Internationalis"—*CpR,* XV (1934), 419–432.

Fuchs, V., "Von der gerichtlichen oder gerichtsähnlichen Gewalt der Ordensoberinnen und ihrer Assistentinnen"—*Theologisch-praktische Quartalschrift,* LXXXVII (1934), 808–813.

Goyeneche, S., "Annotationes"—*Apollinaris,* VIII (1935), 552–554.

——, "Consultationes"—*CpR,* IX (1928), 428–429.

——, "Consultationes"—*CpR,* XII (1931), 131–133.

——, "Consultationes"—*CpRM,* XVII (1936), 343–345.

——, "Consultationes"—*CpRM,* XXIII (1942), 27–29.

——, "Studia Canonica"—*CpR,* XIII (1932), 103–105.

Hippolytus a S. Familia, "De Dimissione Religiosorum"—*Analecta O. C. D.,* IV (1929–1930), 98–107, 156–163.

Jeličić, V., "De Mente Gregorii IX in adornanda Collectione Decretalium"—*Acta Congressus Iuridici Internationalis,* III (1936), 1–20.

Jombart, E., "De religiosis dimissis"—*Nouvelle Revue Theologique,* LXI (1934), 1080–1082.

Larraona, A., "Commentarium Codicis in partem secundam libri II codicis quae est: De Religiosis"—*CpR,* I (1920), 16–21; II (1921), 134–139; "Canon 488, 8°"—*CpR,* IV (1923), 39–46.

———, "Consultationes"—*CpR,* III (1922), 13–16.

———, "Quaestio Canonica"—*CpR,* III (1922), 318–329.

———, "Quaestio Canonica"—*CpR,* IV (1923), 174–178.

La Puma, V., "Statuta a Sororibus Externis Servanda"—*CpR,* XII (1931), 409–425; XV (1934), 13–16.

Ledwolorz, A., "Recensiones librorum"—*Apollinaris,* X (1937), 477–478.

Maroto, P., "Annotationes"—*CpR,* II (1921), 129–133.

———, "Annotationes"—*CpR,* XV (1934), 352–356.

Roberti, F., "Respectus sociales in Codice iuris canonici"—*Apollinaris,* X (1937), 342–394.

Schaefer, T., "Iustinianus I et Vita Monachica"—*Acta Congressus Iuridici Internationalis,* I (1935), 173–188.

Serédi, I., "De Relatione inter Decretales Gregorii Papae IX et Codicem iuris canonici"—*Acta Congressus Iuridici Internationalis,* IV (1937), 11–26.

Tabera, A., "De Dimissione Religiosorum"—*CpR,* XI (1930), 277–285, 411–420.

———, "De Ordinatione Status Monachalis in Fontibus Iustinianeis"—*CpR,* XIV (1933), 87–95; 199–206.

Vermeersch, A., "Annotationes"—*Periodica,* X (1922), 326–327.

———, "De fuga cum persona alterius sexus, in casu can. 646, § 1, n. 2"—*Periodica,* XIX (1923), 121–122.

———, "Forma Expellendi vel Dimittendi Religiosos et Moniales"—*Periodica,* VI (1912), 44–53.

Villien, A., "La Procédure Canonique pour L'Expulsion des Religieux"—*Le Canoniste Contemporain,* XXV (1912), 713–718; XXXVI (1913), 129–142; 211–221.

Zeiger, I., "Professio in manus"—*Actus Congressus Iuridici Internationalis,* III (1936), 187–202.

PERIODICALS

American Ecclesiastical Review, Vols. I-XXXII, Philadelphia, 1880–1905; from 1905: *The Ecclesiastical Review,* Vols. XXXIII-CIX, Philadelphia, 1905–1943; from 1944: *The American Ecclesiastical Review,* Washington, D. C., Vol. CX, 1944–.

Analecta Ordinis Carmelitarum Discalceatorum, Romae, 1926–.

Apollinaris, Romae, 1928–.

Canoniste Contemporain, Le, 45 vols., Paris, 1878–1922 (later, *Le Canoniste,* Paris, 1924–1926).

Commentarium pro Religiosis (later [1935] *Commentarium pro Religiosis et Missionariis*), Romae, 1920–.

Jus Pontificium, Romae, 1921–.

Nouvelle Revue Théologique, Paris, 1869–.

Periodica de Religiosis et Missionariis, 8 vols., Brugis, 1905–1919; from 1920: *Periodica de Re Canonica et Morali utili praesertim Religiosis et Missionariis*, 7 vols., Brugis, 1920–1927; from 1927: *Periodica de Re Morali, Canonica, Liturgica*, Brugis (1927–1936), et Romae (1937–).

Religión y Cultura, 34 vols., Madrid, Monasterio de el Escorial, 1928–1936.

Revista Eclesiastica Brasileira, Petrópolis, Estado do Rio: Editora Vozes Ltda., 1941–.

Theologisch-praktische Quartalschrift, Linz, 1832–.

Zeitschrift für Kirchengeschichte, Gotha: F. A. Perthes, 1876–.

ABBREVIATIONS

AAS—Acta Apostolicae Sedis.

Analecta O. C. D.—Analecta Ordinis Carmelitarum Discalceatorum.

ASS—Acta Sanctae Sedis.

BRT—Bullarium Romanum, ed. Tauriensis.

CpR—Commentarium pro Religiosis (1920–1934).

CpRM—Commentarium pro Religiosis et Missionariis (1935–).

Fontes—Codicis Iuris Canonici Fontes cura . . . Gasparri editi.

JE, JK, JL—Jaffé, *Regesta Pontificum Romanorum* (Ewald, Kalterbrunner, Loewenfeld).

Mansi—*Sacrorum Conciliorum Nova et Amplissima Collectio.*

MGH—Monumenta Germaniae Historica.

MPG—Migne, *Patrologia, Series Graeca.*

MPL—Migne, *Patrologia, Series Latina.*

Pallottini—Pallottini, *Collectio . . . S. C. C.*

P. C. I.—Pontificia Commissio ad Codicis Canones authentice Interpretandos.

Periodica—Periodica de Re Canonica, Morali, etc.

Potthast—Potthast, *Regesta Pontificium Romanorum. . . .*

Rev. Ecl. Bras.—Revista Eclesiastica Brasileira.

S. C. C.—Sacra Congregatio Concilii.

S. C. de Rel.—Sacra Congregatio de Religiosis.

S. C. Ep. et Reg.—Sacra Congregatio Episcoporum et Regularium.

S. C. S. Off.—Suprema Congregatio Sancti Officii.

S. C. super Disciplina Regularium—Sacrae Congregatio super Disciplina Regularium

S. C. super statu Regularium—Sacra Congregatio super statu Regularium.

ALPHABETICAL INDEX

BIOGRAPHICAL NOTE

Benedict Anthony Pfaller was born on January 16, 1918, at Herreid, South Dakota. He received his early education in the Herreid Public School. In 1934 he entered Assumption Abbey School, Richardton, North Dakota, and after two years of college training in the same institution he entered the novitiate of the Order of St. Benedict, at Assumption Abbey. Here he made his temporary religious profession, July 11, 1939, which was followed by his solemn profession in 1942. His seminary course was likewise made at Assumption Abbey, where he was ordained to the priesthood on May 29, 1944. In the autumn of that year he entered the School of Canon Law at The Catholic University of America, where he received the degree of the Baccalaureate in Canon Law, May, 1945; and the degree of the Licentiate in Canon Law, June, 1946.

Canon Law Studies *

1. **Freriks, Rev. Celestine A., C.PP.S., J.C.D., Religious Congregations** in Their External Relations, 121 pp., 1916.
2. Galliher, Rev. Daniel M., O.P., J.C.D., Canonical Elections, 117 pp., 1917.
3. Borkowski, Rev. Aurelius L., O.F.M., J.C.D., De Confraternitatibus Ecclesiasticis, 136 pp., 1918.
4. Castillo, Rev. Cayo, J.C.D., Disertacion Historico-Canonica sobre la Potestad del Cabildo en Sede Vacante o Impedida del Vicario Capitular, 99 pp., 1919 (1918).
5. Kubelbeck, Rev. William J., S.T.B., J.C.D., The Sacred Penitentiaria and Its Relation to Faculties of Ordinaries and Priests, 129 pp., 1918.
6. **Petrovits, Rev. Joseph J. C., S.T.D., J.C.D., The New Church Law on** Matrimony, X-461 pp., 1919.
7. Hickey, Rev. John J., S.T.B., J.C.D., Irregularities and Simple Impediments in the New Code of Canon Law, 100 pp., 1920.
8. Klekotka, Rev. Peter J., S.T.B., J.C.D., Diocesan Consultors, 179 pp., 1920.
9. Wanenmacher, Rev. Francis, J.C.D., The Evidence in Ecclesiastical Procedure Affecting the Marriage Bond, 1920 (Printed 1935).
10. Golden, Rev. Henry Francis, J.C.D., Parochial Benefices in the New Code, IV-119 pp., 1921 (Printed 1925).
11. Koudelka, Rev. Charles J., J.C.D., Pastors, Their Rights and Duties According to the New Code of Canon Law, 211 pp., 1921.
12. Melo, Rev. Antonius, O.F.M., J.C.D., De Exemptione Regularium, X-188 pp., 1921.
13. Schaaf, Rev. Valentine Theodore, O.F.M., S.T.B., J.C.D., The Cloister, X-180 pp., 1921.
14. Burke, Rev. Thomas Joseph, S.T.D., J.C.D., Competence in Ecclesiastical Tribunals, IV-117 pp., 1922.
15. Leech, Rev. George Leo, J.C.D., A Comparative Study of the Constitution "Apostolicae Sedis" and the "Codex Juris Canonici," 179 pp., 1922.
16. Motry, Rev. Hubert Louis, S.T.D., J.C.D., Diocesan Faculties According to the Code of Canon Law, II-167 pp., 1922.
17. Murphy, Rev. George Lawrence, J.C.D., Delinquencies and Penalties in the Administration and the Reception of the Sacraments, IV-121 pp., 1923.

* From nn. 1–100 inclusive only n. 25 is still obtainable. From n. 101 onward all numbers are available except the following: 101–114, 116, 118, 120, 122, 123 and 162.

18. O'Reilly, Rev. John Anthony, S.T.B., J.C.D., Ecclesiastical Sepulture in the New Code of Canon Law, II-129 pp., 1923.
19. Michalicka, Rev. Wenceslas Cyrill, O.S.B., J.C.D., Judicial Procedure in Dismissal of Clerical Exempt Religious, 107 pp., 1923.
20. Dargin, Rev. Edward Vincent, S.T.B., J.C.D., Reserved Cases According to the Code of Canon Law, IV-103 pp., 1924.
21. Godfrey, Rev. John A., S.T.B., J.C.D., The Right of Patronage According to the Code of Canon Law, 153 pp., 1924.
22. Hagedorn, Rev. Francis Edward, J.C.D., General Legislation on Indulgences, II-154 pp., 1924.
23. King, Rev. James Ignatius, J.C.D., The Administration of the Sacraments to Dying Non-Catholics, V-141 pp., 1924.
24. Winslow, Rev. Francis Joseph, M.M., J.C.D., Vicars and Prefects Apostolic, IV-149 pp., 1924.
25. Correa, Rev. Jose Servelion, S.T.L., J.C.D., La Potestad Legislativa de la Iglesia Catolica, IV-127 pp., 1925.
26. Dugan, Rev. Henry Francis, A.M., J.C.D., The Judiciary Department of the Diocesan Curia, 87 pp., 1925.
27. Keller, Rev. Charles Frederick, S.T.B., J.C.D., Mass Stipends, 167 pp., 1925.
28. Paschang, Rev. John Linus, J.C.D., The Sacramentals According to the Code of Canon Law, 129 pp., 1925.
29. Piontek, Rev. Cyrillus, O.F.M., S.T.B., J.C.D., De Indulto Exclaustrationis necnon Saecularizationis, XIII-289 pp., 1925.
30. Kearney, Rev. Richard Joseph, S.T.B., J.C.D., Sponsors at Baptism According to the Code of Canon Law, IV-127 pp., 1925.
31. Bartlett, Rev. Chester Joseph, A.M., LL.B., J.C.D., The Tenure of Parochial Property in the United States of America, V-108 pp., 1926.
32. Kilker, Rev. Adrian Jerome, J.C.D., Extreme Unction, V-425 pp., 1926.
33. McCormick, Rev. Robert Emmett, J.C.D., Confessors of Religious, VIII-266 pp., 1926.
34. Miller, Rev. Newton Thomas, J.C.D., Founded Masses According to the Code of Canon Law, VII-93 pp., 1926.
35. Roelker, Rev. Edward G., S.T.D., J.C.D., Principles of Privilege According to the Code of Canon Law, XI-166 pp., 1926.
36. Bakalarczyk, Rev. Richardus, M.I.C., J.U.D., De Novitiatu, VIII-208 pp., 1927.
37. Pizzuti, Rev. Lawrence, O.F.M., J.U.L., De Parochis Religiosis, 1927. (Not Printed.)
38. Bliley, Rev. Nicholas Martin, O.S.B., J.C.D., Altars According to the Code of Canon Law, XIX-132 pp., 1927.
39. Brown, Mr. Brendan Francis, A.B., LL.M., J.U.D., The Canonical Juristic Personality with Special Reference to its Status in the United States of America, V-212 pp., 1927.

40. CAVANAUGH, REV. WILLIAM THOMAS, C.P., J.U.D., The Reservation of the Blessed Sacrament, VIII-101 pp., 1927.
41. DOHENY, REV. WILLIAM J., C.S.C., A.B., J.U.D., Church Property: Modes of Acquisition, X-118 pp., 1927.
42. FELDHAUS, REV. ALOYSIUS H., C.PP.S., J.C.D., Oratories, IX-141 pp., 1927.
43. KELLY, REV. JAMES PATRICK, A.B., J.C.D., The Jurisdiction of the Simple Confessor, X-208 pp., 1927.
44. NEUBERGER, REV. NICHOLAS J., J.C.D., Canon 6 or the Relation of the Codex Juris Canonici to the Preceding Legislation, V-95 pp., 1927.
45. O'KEEFE, REV. GERALD MICHAEL, J.C.D., Matrimonial Dispensations, Powers of Bishops, Priests, and Confessors, VIII-232 pp., 1927.
46. QUIGLEY, REV. JOSEPH A. M., A.B., J.C.D., Condemned Societies, 139 pp., 1927.
47. ZAPLOTNIK, REV. JOHANNES LEO, J.C.D., De Vicariis Foraneis, X-142 pp., 1927.
48. DUSKIE, REV. JOHN ALOYSIUS, A.B., J.C.D., The Canonical Status of the Orientals in the United States, VIII-196 pp., 1928.
49. HYLAND, REV. FRANCIS EDWARD, J.C.D., Excommunication, Its Nature, Historical Development and Effects, VIII-181 pp., 1928.
50. REINMANN, REV. GERALD JOSEPH, O.M.C., J.C.D., The Third Order Secular of Saint Francis, 201 pp., 1928.
51. SCHENK, REV. FRANCIS J., J.C.D., The Matrimonial Impediments of Mixed Religion and Disparity of Cult, XVI-318 pp., 1929.
52. COADY, REV. JOHN JOSEPH, S.T.D., J.U.D., A.M., The Appointment of Pastors, VIII-150 pp., 1929.
53. KAY, REV. THOMAS HENRY, J.C.D., Competence in Matrimonial Procedure, VIII-164 pp., 1929.
54. TURNER, REV. SIDNEY JOSEPH, C.P., J.U.D., The Vow of Poverty, XLIX-217 pp., 1929.
55. KEARNEY, REV. RAYMOND A., A.B., S.T.D., J.C.D., The Principles of Delegation, VII-149 pp., 1929.
56. CONRAN, REV. EDWARD JAMES, A.B., J.C.D., The Interdict, V-163 pp., 1930.
57. O'NEILL, REV. WILLIAM H., J.C.D., Papal Rescripts of Favor, VII-218 pp., 1930.
58. BASTNAGEL, REV. CLEMENT VINCENT, J.U.D., The Appointment of Parochial Adjutants and Assistants, XV-257 pp., 1930.
59. FERRY, REV. WILLIAM A., A.B., J.C.D., Stole Fees, V-136 pp., 1930.
60. COSTELLO, REV. JOHN MICHAEL, A.B., J.C.D., Domicile and Quasi-Domicile, VII-201 pp., 1930.
61. KREMER, REV. MICHAEL NICHOLAS, A.B., S.T.B., J.C.D., Church Support in the United States, VI-136 pp., 1930.
62. ANGULO, REV. LUIS, C.M., J.C.D., Legislation de la Iglesia sobre la intencion en la application de la Santa Misa, VII-104 pp., 1931.

63. FREY, REV. WOLFGANG NORBERT, O.S.B., A.B., J.C.D., The Act of Religious Profession, VIII-174 pp., 1931.
64. ROBERTS, REV. JAMES BRENDAN, A.B., J.C.D., The Banns of Marriage, XIV-140 pp., 1931.
65. RYDER, REV. RAYMOND ALOYSIUS, A.B., J.C.D., Simony, IX-151 pp., 1931.
66. CAMPAGNA, REV. ANGELO, PH.D., J.U.D., Il Vicario Generale del Vescovo, VII-205 pp., 1931.
67. COX, REV. JOSEPH GODFREY, A.B., J.C.D., The Administration of Seminaries, VI-124 pp., 1931.
68. GREGORY, REV. DONALD J., J.U.D., The Pauline Privilege, XV-165 pp., 1931.
69. DONOHUE, REV. JOHN F., J.C.D., The Impediment of Crime, VII-110 pp., 1931.
70. DOOLEY, REV. EUGENE A., O.M.I., J.C.D., Church Law on Sacred Relics, IX-143 pp., 1931.
71. ORTH, REV. CLEMENT RAYMOND, O.M.C., J.C.D., The Approbation of Religious Institutes, 171 pp., 1931.
72. PERNICONE, REV. JOSEPH M., A.B., J.C.D., The Ecclesiastical Prohibition of Books, XII-267 pp, 1932.
73. CLINTON, REV. CONNELL, A.B., J.C.D., The Paschal Precept, IX-108 pp., 1932.
74. DONNELLY, REV. FRANCIS B., A.M., S.T.L., J.C.D., The Diocesan Synod, VIII-125 pp., 1932.
75. TORRENTE, REV. CAMILO, C.M.F., J.C.D., Las Procesiones Sagradas, V-145 pp., 1932.
76. MURPHY, REV. EDWIN J., C.PP.S., J.C.D., Suspension Ex Informata Conscientia, XI-122 pp., 1932.
77. MACKENZIE, REV. ERIC F., A.M., S.T.L., J.C.D., The Delict of Heresy in its Commission, Penalization, Absolution, VII-124 pp., 1932.
78. LYONS, REV. AVITUS E., S.T.B., J.C.D., The Collegiate Tribunal of First Instance, XI-147 pp., 1932.
79. CONNOLLY, REV. THOMAS A., J.C.D., Appeals, XI-195 pp., 1932.
80. SANGMEISTER, REV. JOSEPH V., A.B., J.C.D., Force and Fear as Precluding Matrimonial Consent, V-211 pp., 1932.
81. JAEGER, REV. LEO A., A.B., J.C.D., The Administration of Vacant and Quasi-Vacant Episcopal Sees in the United States, IX-229 pp., 1932.
82. RIMLINGER, REV. HERBERT T., J.C.D., Error Invalidating Matrimonial Consent, VII-79 pp., 1932.
83. BARRETT, REV. JOHN D. M., S.S., J.C.D., A Comparative Study of the Third Plenary Council of Baltimore and the Code, IX-221 pp., 1932.
84. CARBERRY, REV. JOHN J., PH.D., S.T.D., J.C.D., The Juridical Form of Marriage, X-177 pp., 1934.
85. DOLAN, REV. JOHN L., A.B., J.C.D., The Defensor Vinculi, XII-157 pp., 1934.

86. HANNAN, REV. JEROME D., A.M., S.T.D., LL.B., J.C.D., The Canon Law of Wills, IX-517 pp., 1934.
87. LEMIEUX, REV. DELISE A., A.M., J.C.D., The Sentence in Ecclesiastical Procedure, IX-131 pp., 1934.
88. O'ROURKE, REV. JAMES J., A.B., J.C.D., Parish Registers, VII-109 pp., 1934.
89. TIMLIN, REV. BARTHOLOMEW, O.F.M., A.M., J.C.D., Conditional Matrimonial Consent, X-381 pp., 1934.
90. WAHL, REV. FRANCIS X., A.B., J.C.D., The Matrimonial Impediments of Consanguinity and Affinity, VI-125 pp., 1934.
91. WHITE, REV. ROBERT J., A.B., LL.B., S.T.B., J.C.D., Canonical Ante-Nuptial Promises and the Civil Law, VI-152 pp., 1934.
92. HERRERA, REV. ANTONIO PARRA, O.C.D., J.C.D., Legislacion Ecclesiastica sobra el Ayuno y la Abstinencia, XI-191 pp., 1935.
93. KENNEDY, REV. EDWIN J., J.C.D., The Special Matrimonial Process in Cases of Evident Nullity, X-165 pp., 1935.
94. MANNING, REV. JOHN J., A.B., J.C.D., Presumption of Law in Matrimonial Procedure, XI-111 pp., 1935.
95. MOEDER, REV. JOHN M., J.C.D., The Proper Bishop for Ordination and Dimissorial Letters, VII-135 pp., 1935.
96. O'MARA, REV. WILLIAM A., A.B., J.C.D., Canonical Causes for Matrimonial Dispensations, IX-155 pp., 1935.
97. REILLY, REV. PETER, J.C.D., Residence of Pastors, IX-81 pp., 1935.
98. SMITH, REV. MARINER T., O.P., S.T.Lr., J.C.D., The Penal Law for Religious, VII-169 pp., 1935.
99. WHALEN, REV. DONALD W., A.M., J.C.D., The Value of Testimonial Evidence in Matrimonial Procedure, XIII-297 pp., 1935.
100. CLEARY, REV. JOSEPH F., J.C.D., Canonical Limitations on the Alienation of Church Property, VIII-141 pp., 1936.
101. GLYNN, REV. JOHN C., J.C.D., The Promoter of Justice, XX-337 pp., 1936.
102. BRENNAN, REV. JAMES H., S.S., M.A., S.T.B., J.C.D., The Simple Convalidation of Marriage, VI-135 pp., 1937.
103. BRUNINI, REV. JOSEPH BERNARD, J.C.D., The Clerical Obligations of Canons 139 and 142, X-121 pp., 1937.
104. CONNOR, REV. MAURICE, A.B., J.C.D., The Administrative Removal of Pastors, VIII-159 pp., 1937.
105. GUILFOYLE, REV. MERLIN JOSEPH, J.C.D., Custom, XI-144 pp., 1937.
106. HUGHES, REV. JAMES AUSTIN, A.B., A.M., J.C.D., Witnesses in Criminal Trials of Clerics, IX-140 pp., 1937.
107. JANSEN, REV. RAYMOND J., A.B., S.T.L., J.C.D., Canonical Provisions for Catechetical Instruction, VII-153 pp., 1937.
108. KEALY, REV. JOHN JAMES, A.B., J.C.D., The Introductory Libellus in Church Court Procedure, XI-121 pp., 1937.

109. McManus, Rev. James Edward, C.SS.R., J.C.D., The Administration of Temporal Goods in Religious Institutes, XVI 196 pp., 1937.

110. Moriarty, Rev. Eugene James, J.C.D., Oaths in Ecclesiastical Courts, X-115 pp., 1937.

111. Rainer, Rev. Eligius George, C.SS.R., J.C.D., Suspension of Clerics, XVII-249 pp., 1937.

112. Reilly, Rev. Thomas F., C.SS.R., J.C.D., Visitation of Religious, VI-195 pp., 1938.

113. Moriarity, Rev. Francis E., C.SS.R., J.C.D., The Extraordinary Absolution from Censures, XV-334 pp., 1938.

114. Connolly, Rev. Nicholas P., J.C.D., The Canonical Erection of Parishes, X-132 pp., 1938.

115. Donovan, Rev. James Joseph, J.C.D., The Pastor's Obligation in Prenuptial Investigation, XII-322 pp., 1938.

116. Harrigan, Rev. Robert J., M.A., S.T.B., J.C.D., The Radical Sanation of Invalid Marriages, VIII-208 pp., 1938.

117. Boffa, Rev. Conrad Humbert, J.C.D., Canonical Provisions for Catholic Schools, VII-211 pp., 1939.

118. Parsons, Rev. Anscar John, O.M.Cap., J.C.D., Canonical Elections, XII-236 pp., 1939.

119. Reilly, Rev. Edward Michael, A.B., J.C.D., The General Norms of Dispensation, XII-156 pp., 1939.

120. Ryan, Rev. Gerald Aloysius, A.B., J.C.D., Principles of Episcopal Jurisdiction, XII-172 pp., 1939.

121. Burton, Rev. Francis James, C.S.C., A.B., J.C.D., A Commentary on Canon 1125, X-222 pp., 1940.

122. Miaskiewicz, Rev. Francis Sigismund, J.C.D., Supplied Jurisdiction According to Canon 209, XII-340 pp., 1940.

123. Rice, Rev. Patrick William, A.B., J.C.D., Proof of Death in Prenuptial Investigation, VIII-156 pp., 1940.

124. Anglin, Rev. Thomas Francis, M.S., J.C.D., The Eucharistic Fast, VIII-183 pp., 1941.

125. Coleman, Rev. John Jerome, J.C.D., The Minister of Confirmation, VI-153 pp., 1941.

126. Downs, Rev. John Emmanuel, A.B., J.C.D., The Concept of Clerical Immunity, XI-163 pp., 1941.

127. Esswein, Rev. Anthony Albert, J.C.D., Extrajudicial Penal Powers of Ecclesiastical Superiors, X-144 pp., 1941.

128. Farrell, Rev. Benjamin Francis, M.A., S.T.L., J.C.D., The Rights and Duties of the Local Ordinary Regarding Congregations of Women Religious of Pontifical Approval, V-195 pp., 1941.

129. Feeney, Rev. Thomas John, A.B., S.T.L., J.C.D., Restitutio in Integrum, VI-169 pp., 1941.

130. Findlay, Rev. Stephen William, O.S.B., A.B., J.C.D., Canonical

Norms Governing the Deposition and Degradation of Clerics, XVII-279 pp., 1941.

131. GOODWINE, REV. JOHN, A.B., S.T.L., J.C.D., The Right of the Church to Acquire Property, VIII-119 pp., 1941.
132. HESTON, REV. EDWARD LOUIS, C.S.C., Ph.D., S.T.D., J.C.D., The Alienation of Church Property in the United States, XII-222 pp., 1941.
133. HOGAN, REV. JAMES JOHN, A.B., S.T.L., J.C.D., Judicial Advocates and Procurators, XIII-200 pp., 1941.
134. KEALY, REV. THOMAS M., A.B., Litt.B., J.C.D., Dowry of Women Religious, IX-152 pp., 1941.
135. KEENE, REV. MICHAEL JAMES, O.S.B., J.C.D., Religious Ordinaries and Canon 198, V-164 pp., 1942.
136. KERIN, REV. CHARLES A., S.S., M.A., S.T.B., J.C.D., The Privation of Christian Burial, XVI-279 pp., 1941.
137. LOUIS, REV. WILLIAM FRANCIS, M.A., J.C.D., Diocesan Archives, X-101 pp., 1941.
138. McDEVITT, REV. GILBERT JOSEPH, A.B., J.C.D., Legitimacy and Legitimation, X-247 pp., 1941.
139. McDONOUGH, REV. THOMAS JOSEPH, A.B., J.C.D., Apostolic Administrators, X-217 pp., 1941.
140. **MEIER, REV. CARL ANTHONY, A.B., J.C.D., Penal Administrative Pro**cedure Against Negligent Pastors, XI-240 pp., 1941.
141. SCHMIDT, REV. JOHN ROGG, A.B., J.C.D., The Principles of Authentic Interpretation in Canon 17 of the Code of Canon Law, XII-331 pp., 1941.
142. SLAFKOSKY, REV. ANDREW LEONARD, A.B., J.C.D., The Canonical Episcopal Visitation of the Diocese, X-197 pp., 1941.
143. SWOBODA, REV. INNOCENT ROBERT, O.F.M., J.C.D., Ignorance in Relation to the Imputability of Delicts, IX-271 pp., 1941.
144. DUBÉ, REV. ARTHUR JOSEPH, A.B., J.C.D., The General Principles for the Reckoning of Time in Canon Law, VIII-299 pp., 1941.
145. McBRIDE, REV. JAMES T., A.B., J.C.D., Incardination and Excardination of Seculars, XX-585 pp., 1941.
146. KRÓL, REV. JOHN T., J.C.D., The Defendant in Contentious Trials, XII-207 pp., 1942.
147. COMYNS, REV. JOSEPH J., C.SS.R., A.B., J.C.D., Papal and Episcopal Administration of Church Property, XIV-155 pp., 1942.
148. BARRY, REV. GARRETT FRANCIS, O.M.I., J.C.D., Violation of the Cloister, XII-260 pp., 1942.
149. BOLDUC, REV. GATIEN, C.S.V., A.B., S.T.L., J.C.D., Les Études dans les Religions Cléricales, VIII-155 pp., 1942.
150. BOYLE, REV. DAVID JOHN, M.A., J.C.D., The Juridic Effects of Moral Certitude on Pre-Nuptial Guarantees, XII-188 pp., 1942.
151. **CANAVAN, REV. WALTER JOSEPH, M.A., Litt.D., J.C.D., The Profes**sion of Faith, XII-143 pp., 1942.

152. Desrochers, Rev. Bruno, A.B., Ph.L., S.T.B., J.C.D., Le Premier Concile Plénier de Québec et le Code de Droit Canonique, XIV-186 pp., 1942.
153. Dillon, Rev. Robert Edward, A.B., J.C.D., Common Law Marriage, X-148 pp., 1942.
154. Dodwell, Rev. Edward John, Ph.D., S.T.B., J.C.D., The Time and Place for the Celebration of Marriage, X-156 pp., 1942.
155. Donnellan, Rev. Thomas Andrew, A.B., J.C.D., The Obligation of the Missa pro Populo, VII-131 pp., 1942.
156. Eltz, Rev. Louis Anthony, A.B., J.C.D., Cooperation in Crime, XII-208 pp., 1942.
157. Gass, Rev. Sylvester Francis, M.A., J.C.D., Ecclesiastical Pensions, XI-206 pp., 1942.
158. Guiniven, Rev. John Joseph, C.SS.R., J.C.D., The Precept of Hearing Mass, XIV-188 pp., 1942.
159. Gulcynski, Rev. John Theophilus, J.C.D., The Desecration and Violation of Churches, X-126 pp., 1942.
160. Hammill, Rev. John Leo, M.A., J.C.D., The Obligations of the Traveler According to Canon 14, VIII-204 pp., 1942.
161. Haydt, Rev. John Joseph, A.B., J.C.D., Reserved Benefices, XI-148 pp., 1942.
162. Huser, Rev. Roger John, O.F.M., A.B., J.C.D., The Crime of Abortion in Canon Law, XII-187 pp., 1942.
163. Kearney, Rev. Francis Patrick, A.B., S.T.L., J.C.D., The Principles of Canon 1127, X-162 pp., 1942.
164. Linahen, Rev. Leo James, S.T.L., J.C.D., De Absolutione Complicis In Peccato Turpi, 114 pp., 1942.
165. McCloskey, Rev. Joseph Aloysius, A.B., J.C.D., The Subject of Ecclesiastical Law According to Canon 12, XVII-246 pp., 1942.
166. O'Neill, Rev. Francis Joseph, C.SS.R., J.C.D., The Dismissal of Religious in Temporary Vows, XIII-220 pp., 1942.
167. Prince, Rev. John Edward, A.B., S.T.B., J.C.D., The Diocesan Chancellor, X-136 pp., 1942.
168. Riesner, Rev. Albert Joseph, C.SS.R., J.C.D., Apostates and Fugitives from Religious Institutes, IX-168 pp., 1942.
169. Stenger, Rev. Joseph Bernard, J.C.D., The Mortgaging of Church Property, 186 pp., 1942.
170. Waldron, Rev. Joseph Francis, A.B., J.C.D., The Minister of Baptism, XII-197 pp., 1942.
171. Willett, Rev. Robert Albert, J.C.D., The Probative Value of Documents in Ecclesiastical Trials, X-124 pp., 1942.
172. Woeber, Rev. Edward Martin, M.A., J.C.D., The Interpellations, XII-161 pp., 1942.
173. Benko, Rev. Matthew Aloysius, O.S.B., M.A., J.C.D., The Abbot *Nullius*, XVI-148 pp., 1943.

174. Christ, Rev. Joseph James, M.A., S.T.L., J.C.D., Dispensation from Vindicative Penalties, XIV-285 pp., 1943.
175. Clancy, Rev. Patrick M. J., O.P., A.B., S.T.Lr., J.C.D., The Local Religious Superior, X-229 pp., 1943.
176. Clarke, Rev. Thomas James, J.C.D., Parish Societies, XII-147 pp., 1943.
177. Connolly, Rev. John Patrick, S.T.L., J.C.D., Synodal Examiners and Parish Priest Consultors, X-223 pp., 1943.
178. Drumm, Rev. William Martin, A.B., J.C.D., Hospital Chaplains, XII-175 pp., 1943.
179. Flanagan, Rev. Bernard Joseph, A.B., S.T.L., J.C.D., The Canonical Erection of Religious Houses, X-147 pp., 1943.
180. Kelleher, Rev. Stephen Joseph, A.B., S.T.B., J.C.D., Discussions with Non-Catholics: Canonical Legislation, X-93 pp., 1943.
181. Lewis, Rev. Gordian, C.P., J.C.D., Chapters in Religious Institutes, XII-169 pp., 1943.
182. Marx, Rev. Adolph, J.C.D., The Declaration of Nullity of Marriages Contracted Outside the Church, X-151 pp., 1943.
183. Matulenas, Rev. Raymond Anthony, O.S.B., A.B., J.C.D., Communication, a Source of Privileges, XII-225 pp., 1943.
184. O'Leary, Rev. Charles Gerard, C.SS.R., J.C.D., Religious Dismissed After Perpetual Profession, X-213 pp., 1943.
185. Power, Rev. Cornelius Michael, J.C.D., The Blessing of Cemeteries, XII-231 pp., 1943.
186. Shuhler, Rev. Ralph Vincent, O.S.A., J.C.D., Privileges of Regulars to Absolve and Dispense, XII-195 pp., 1943.
187. Ziolkowski, Rev. Thaddeus Stanislaus, A.B., J.C.D., The Consecration and Blessing of Churches, XII-151 pp., 1943.
188. Heneghan, Rev. John Joseph, S.T.D., J.C.D., The Marriages of Unworthy Catholics: Canons 1065 and 1066, XVI-213 pp., 1944.
189. Carroll, Rev. Coleman Francis, M.A., S.T.L., J.C.L., Charitable Institutions.
190. Ciesluk, Rev. Joseph Edward, Ph.B., S.T.L., J.C.D., National Parishes in the United States, VI-178 pp., 1944.
191. Coburn, Rev. Vincent Paul, A.B., J.C.D., Marriages of Conscience, XII-172 pp., 1944.
192. Connors, Rev. Charles Paul, C.S.Sp., A.B., J.C.D., Extra-Judicial Procurators in the Code of Canon Law, X-94 pp., 1944.
193. Coyle, Rev. Paul Raymond, A.B., J.C.D., Judicial Exceptions, X-142 pp., 1944.
194. Fair, Rev. Bartholomew Francis, A.B., S.T.L., J.C.D., The Impediment of Abduction, XII-122 pp., 1944.
195. Gallagher, Rev. Thomas Raphael, O.P., A.B., S.T.Lr., J.C.D., The Examination of the Qualities of the Ordinand, X-166 pp., 1944.
196. Gannon, Rev. John Mark, S.T.L., J.C.D., The Interstices Required for the Promotion to Orders, XII-100 pp., 1944.

197. **Goldsmith, Rev. J. William, B.C.S., S.T.L., J.C.D., The Competence** of Church and State over Marriage—Disputed Points, X-128 pp., 1944.
198. **Goodwine, Rev. Joseph Gerard, A.B., S.T.B., J.C.D., The Receptior** of Converts, XIV-326 pp., 1944.
199. Kowalski, Rev. Romuald Eugene, O.F.M., A.B., J.C.D., Sustenance of Religious Houses of Regulars, X-174 pp., 1944.
200. McCoy, Rev. Alan Edward, O.F.M., J.C.D., Force and Fear in Relation to Delictual Imputability and Penal Responsibility, XII-160 pp., 1944.
201. McDevitt, Rev. Vincent John, Ph.B., S.T.L., J.C.L., Perjury.
202. Martin, Rev. Thomas Owen, Ph.D., S.T.D., J.C.D., Adverse Possession, Prescription and Limitation of Actions: The Canonical "Praescriptio," XX-208 pp., 1944.
203. Miklosovic, Rev. Paul John, A.B., J.C.L., Attempted Marriages and Their Consequent Juridic Effects.
204. **Mundy, Rev. Thomas Maurice, A.B., S.T.L., J.C.D., The Union of** Parishes, X—164 pp., 1944.
205. O'Dea, Rev. John Coyle, A.B., J.C.D., The Matrimonial Impediment of Nonage, VIII-126 pp., 1944.
206. Olalia, Rev. Alexander Ayson, S.T.L., J.C.D., A Comparative Study of the Christian Constitution of States and the Constitution of the **Philippine Commonwealth, XII—136 pp., 1944.**
207. Poisson, Rev. Pierre-Marie, C.S.C., A.B., Ph.L., Th.L., J.C.L., Droits Patrimoniaux des Maisons et des Églises Religieuses.
208. Stadalnikas, Rev. Casimir Joseph, M.I.C., J.C.D., Reservation of Censures, X-141 pp., 1944.
209. **Sullivan, Rev. Eugene Henry, S.T.L., J.C.D., Proof of the Reception of the Sacraments, X—165 pp., 1944.**
210. Vaughan, Rev. William Edward, J.C.D., Constitutions for Diocesan Courts, X-210 pp., 1944.
211. **Paro, Rev. Gino, S.T.D., J.C.L., The Right of Apostolic Legation.**
212. Balzer, Rev. Ralph Francis, C.P., J.C.D., The Computation of Time in a Canonical Novitiate, X—227 pp., 1945.
213. Dougherty, Rev. John Whelan, A.B., S.T.L., J.C.D., De Inquisitione Speciali, XII—195 pp., 1945.
214. Dziob, Rev. Michael Walter, J.C.D., The Sacred Congregation for the Oriental Church, XII—181 pp., 1945.
215. Eidenschink, Rev. John Albert, O.S.B., B.A., J.C.D, The Election of Bishops in the Letters of Pope Gregory the Great, VII—200 pp., 1945.
216. Gill, Rev. Nicholas, C.P., J.C.D., The Spiritual Prefect in Clerical Religious Houses of Study, X—140 pp., 1945.
217. **Hynes, Rev. Harry Gerard, S.T.L., J.C.D., The Privileges of Cardinals, XII-183 pp., 1945.**
218. **McDevitt, Rev. Gerald Vincent, S.T.L., J.C.D., The Renunciation** of an Ecclesiastical Office, XIV—179 pp., 1945.

219. MANNING, REV. JOSEPH LEROY, J.C.D., The Free Conferral of Offices, VIII—116 pp., 1945.
220. MEYER, REV. LOUIS G., O.S.B., A.B., S.T.B., J.C.D., Alms-Gathering by Religious, XII—163 pp., 1945.
221. O'DONNELL, REV. CLETUS FRANCIS, M.A., J.C.D., The Marriage of Minors, XII—268 pp., 1945.
222. PRUNSKIS, REV. JOSEPH, J.C.D., Comparative Law, Ecclesiastical and Civil, in Lithuanian Concordat, X—161 pp., 1945.
223. SWEENEY, REV. FRANCIS PATRICK, C.SS.R., J.C.D., The Reduction of Clerics to the Lay State, X—199 pp., 1945.
224. VOGELPOHL, REV. HENRY JOHN, J.C.D., The Simple Impediments to Holy Orders, XVI—190 pp., 1945.
225. BROCKHAUS, REV. THOMAS AQUINAS, O.S.B., A.B., J.C.D., Religious who Are Known as *Conversi*, X—127 pp., 1945.
226. GRIESE, REV. N. ORVILLE, S.T.D., J.C.D., The Marriage Contract and the Procreation of Offspring, XVI-224 pp., 1946.
227. BOUDREAUX, REV. WARREN LOUIS, J.C.L., The "*ab acatholicis nati*" of Canon 1099, § 2.
228. BOWE, REV. THOMAS JOSEPH, A.B., J.C.D., Religious Superioresses, VIII-206 pp., 1946.
229. DIEDERICHS, REV. MICHAEL FERDINAND, S.C.J., J.C.D., The Jurisdiction of the Latin Ordinaries over their Oriental Subjects, XIV-153 pp., 1946.
230. DINGMAN, REV. MAURICE JOHN, A.B., S.T.L., J.C.L., The Plaintiff in Contentious Trials.
231. FRISON, REV. BASIL, C.M.F., M.MUS., J.C.D., The Retroactivity of Law, X-221 pp., 1946.
232. GALVIN, REV. WILLIAM ANTHONY, M.A., J.C.D., The Administrative Transfer of Pastors, XII-288 pp., 1946.
233. GORACY, REV. JOSEPH C., J.C.L., The Diriment Matrimonial Impediment of Major Orders.
234. HALE, REV. JOSEPH FRANCIS, M.A., S.T.L., J.C.L., The Pastor of Burial.
235. HENRY, REV. JOSEPH ARTHUR, A.B., J.C.D., The Mass and Holy Communion: Inter-Ritual Law, XII-138 pp., 1946.
236. LINENBERGER, REV. HERBERT, C.PP.S., J.C.L., The False Denunciation of an Innocent Confessor.
237. LOWRY, REV. JAMES MARTIN, A.B., J.C.D., Dispensation from Private Vows, XII-266 pp., 1946.
238. LYNCH, REV. GEORGE EDWARD, A.B., S.T.L., J.C.D., Coadjutors and Auxiliaries of Bishops, X-107 pp., 1947.
239. LYNCH, REV. TIMOTHY, M.S.SS.T., J.C.D., Contracts between Bishops and Religious Congregations, XIV-232 pp., 1946.
240. McCLUNN, REV. JUSTIN DAVID, A.B., S.T.L., J.C.D., Administrative Recourse, VII-142 pp., 1946.

241. LOHMULLER, REV. MARTIN NICHOLAS, A.B., J.C.D., The Promulgation of Law, XII-140 pp., 1947.
242. McGRATH, REV. JAMES, A.B., J.C.D., The Privilege of the Canon, XII-156 pp., 1946.
243. MARBACH, REV. JOSEPH FRANCIS, A.B., J.C.D., Marriage Legislation for the Catholics of the Oriental Rites in the United States and Canada, XIV-314 pp., 1946.
244. SHIMKUS, REV. BERNARD ALOYIUS, A.B., J.C.L., The Determination and Transfer of Rite.
245. SMITH, REV. VINCENT MICHAEL, A.B., S.T.L., J.C.L., Ignorance Affecting Matrimonial Consent.
246. WACHTRLE, REV. PAUL ANTHONY, A.B., J.C.L., The Baptism of the Children of Non-Catholics.
247. CROTTY, REV. MATTHEW MICHAEL, J.C.L., The Recipient of First Holy Communion.
248. EAGLETON, REV. GEORGE, J.C.L., The Quinquennial Faculties, Formula IV.
249. GIBBONS, REV. MARION LEO, C.M., J.C.L., Domicile of the Wife Unlawfully Separated from Her Husband.
250. KELLY, REV. BERNARD MATTHEW, S.T.L., J.C.D., The Functions Reserved to Pastors, IX-141 pp., 1947.
251. KILCULLEN, REV. THOMAS JOHN, LL.M., J.C.D., The Collegiate Moral Person as Party Litigant, X-150 pp., 1947.
252. LAFONTAINE, REV. GERMAIN JOSEPH, W.F., J.C.L., Relations Canoniques entre le Missionaire et Ses Superieurs.
253. LANE, REV. LORAS THOMAS, J.C.L., Matrimonial Procedure in Ordinary Court of Second Instance.
254. LOVER, REV. JAMES FRANCIS, C.Ss.R., J.C.L., The Master of Novices.
255. McNICHOLAS, REV. TIMOTHY JOSEPH, J.C.L., The *Septimae Manus* Witness.
256. MAROSITZ, REV. JOSEPH JOHN, M.S.C., J.C.L., Obligations and Privileges of Religious Promoted to the Episcopal or Cardinalitial Dignities.
257. MURPHY, REV. FRANCIS JOSEPH, J.C.L., Legislative Powers of the Provincial Council.
258. O'BRIEN, REV. ROMAEUS WILLIAM, O.Carm., J.C.L., The Provincial Superior in Religious Orders of Men.
259. PFALLER, REV. BENEDICT ANTHONY, O.S.B., J.C.L., *The ipso facto* Effected Dismissal of Religious.
260. POPEK, REV. ALPHONSE SYLVESTER, J.C.L., The Rights and Obligations of Metropolitans.
261. RISTUCCIA, REV. BERNARD JOSEPH, C.M., J.C.L., Quasi-Religious.
262. SONNTAG, REV. NATHANIEL LOUIS, O.F.M.Cap., J.C.L., Censorship of Special Classes of Books.
263. STADLER, REV. JOSEPH NICHOLAS, J.C.L., Frequent Holy Communion.

264. SZAL, REV. IGNATIUS JOSEPH, J.C.L., The Communication of Catholics with Schismatics.

265. WAGNER, REV. URBAN STANLEY, O.F.M.Conv., J.C.D., Parochial Substitute Vicars and Supplying Priests, IX-126 pp., 1947.

www.ingramcontent.com/pod-product-compliance
Lightning Source LLC
LaVergne TN
LVHW050246080826
844660LV00012B/604
* 9 7 8 0 8 1 3 2 2 4 3 7 4 *